Rethinking Disability and Human Rights

This book examines the role of disability in the right to political and social participation, an act of citizenship that many disabled people do not enjoy.

The disability rights movement does not accept the use of disability to create limits on citizenship, which poses challenges for contemporary societies that will become ever greater as the science and technology of enhancing human abilities evolves. Comprised of eight chapters, three interludes, and a postscript written by leading scholars and disability rights activists, the book explores citizenship for people with disabilities from an interdisciplinary perspective using the United Nations *Convention on the Rights of Persons with Disabilities* (CRPD) as a point of departure and the concept of universal design as a strategy for actualizing full citizenship for all. Situating disability in its historical and cultural contexts, the authors offer directions for rethinking citizenship, including implications for access to the built environment, information and communication systems, education, work, community life, and politics. This book will be of interest to all scholars and students working in disability studies, planning, architecture, public health, rehabilitation, social work, and education.

Inger Marie Lid is a Professor of Public Health and Rehabilitation at VID Specialized University. Her research interests include ethics, citizenship, universal design accessibility, and Human Rights. Lid has authored and edited many books, chapters and articles. Recent publications include "The significance of relations. Rethinking autonomy in a disability perspective" in *Lived Citizenship for Persons in Vulnerable Life Situations. Theories and Practices* (Scandinavian University Press). She is currently engaged in research on inclusion in higher education.

Edward Steinfeld, Arch.D., is a SUNY Distinguished Professor of Architecture and Director of the Center for Inclusive Design and Environmental Access at the School of Architecture, University at Buffalo, State University of New York. He is a co-author of *Universal Design: Creating Inclusive Environments*. His research interests include accessibility, universal design, and design for aging. He is currently engaged in research and public education on design for gender diversity.

Michael Rembis is the Director of the Center for Disability Studies and an Associate Professor in the Department of History at the University at Buffalo (SUNY). Rembis has authored or edited many books, articles, and book chapters. He is currently completing a book entitled, *Writing Mad Lives – in the Age of the Asylum*. He is the coeditor of *The Oxford Handbook of Disability History*.

Interdisciplinary Disability Studies
Series editor: Mark Sherry
The University of Toledo, USA

Disability studies has made great strides in exploring power and the body. This series extends the interdisciplinary dialogue between disability studies and other fields by asking how disability studies can influence a particular field. It will show how a deep engagement with disability studies changes our understanding of the following fields: sociology, literary studies, gender studies, bioethics, social work, law, education, or history. This ground-breaking series identifies both the practical and theoretical implications of such an interdisciplinary dialogue and challenges people in disability studies as well as other disciplinary fields to critically reflect on their professional praxis in terms of theory, practice, and methods.

Understanding Disability Throughout History
Interdisciplinary Perspectives in Iceland from Settlement to 1936
Edited by Hanna Björg Sigurjónsdóttir and James G. Rice

Disability and Art History from Antiquity to the Twenty-First Century
Edited by Ann Millett-Gallant and Elizabeth Howie

Dis/ability in Media, Law and History: Intersectional, Embodied AND Socially Constructed?
Edited by Micky Lee, Frank Rudy Cooper and Pat Reeve

Disability and Labour in the Twentieth Century
Historical and Comparative Perspectives
Edited by Radu Harald Dinu & Staffan Bengtsson

Rethinking Disability and Human Rights
Participation, Equality and Citizenship
Inger Marie Lid, Edward Steinfeld & Michael Rembis

Chronic Pain, BDSM and Crip Time
Emma Sheppard

For a full list of titles in this series, please visit: https://www.routledge.com/Interdisciplinary-Disability-Studies/book-series/ASHSER1401

Rethinking Disability and Human Rights

Participation, Equality and Citizenship

Edited by Inger Marie Lid, Edward Steinfeld, and Michael Rembis

Routledge
Taylor & Francis Group
LONDON AND NEW YORK

First published 2023
by Routledge
4 Park Square, Milton Park, Abingdon, Oxon OX14 4RN

and by Routledge
605 Third Avenue, New York, NY 10158

Routledge is an imprint of the Taylor & Francis Group, an informa business

British Library Cataloguing-in-Publication Data
A catalogue record for this book is available from the British Library

Library of Congress Cataloguing-in-Publication Data
Names: Lid, Inger Marie, editor. | Steinfeld, Edward, editor. | Rembis, Michael A., 1970- editor.
Title: Rethinking disability and human rights : participation, equality and citizenship / edited by Inger Marie Lid, Edvard Steinfeld, Michael Rembis.
Description: Abingdon, Oxon ; New York, NY : Routledge, 2023. | Series: Interdisciplinary disability studies | Includes bibliographical references and index. |
Identifiers: LCCN 2022061419 (print) | LCCN 2022061420 (ebook) | ISBN 9780367511746 (hardback) | ISBN 9780367511562 (paperback) | ISBN 9781003052708 (ebook)
Subjects: LCSH: People with disabilities--Civil rights--Developing countries. | Discrimination against people with disabilities--Developing countries. | Citizenship--Developing countries. | Barrier-free design--Developing countries.
Classification: LCC HV1559.D44 R4545 2023 (print) | LCC HV1559.D44 (ebook) | DDC 362.4/048091724--dc23/eng/20230407
LC record available at https://lccn.loc.gov/2022061419
LC ebook record available at https://lccn.loc.gov/2022061420

ISBN: 978-0-367-51174-6 (hbk)
ISBN: 978-0-367-51156-2 (pbk)
ISBN: 978-1-003-05270-8 (ebk)

DOI: 10.4324/9781003052708

Typeset in Goudy
by MPS Limited, Dehradun

Contents

Figures

Tables

Contributors

Anna Chalachanová is an Associate Professor and works at a master program of citizenship and collaboration at VID Specialized University. Currently, she is also a project leader for pilot project on higher education in human rights for students with intellectual disabilities. Her research interests include citizenship of people in vulnerable life situations, participatory action research, and participation of people with intellectual disabilities in society.

Gagan Chhabra is a Project Manager for Inclusion at the Atlas Alliance. His research interests include disability policies, labor market inclusion for persons with disabilities, discrimination and ableism, global North-South research, and youth studies. His recent publications include "Insider, Outsider or an In-betweener? Epistemological Reflections of a Legally Blind Researcher on Conducting Cross-National Disability Research."

Rosemarie Garland-Thomson is a bioethicist, author, educator, humanities scholar, and thought leader in disability justice and culture. She is professor emerita of Emory University. Garland-Thomson is the author and editor of numerous books and articles, among these are *Extraordinary Bodies*, *Staring: How We Look* and *About Us* edited by Peter Catapano.

Jan Grue is a Professor of Sociology at the University of Oslo. His research interests include disability, embodiment, normality, rhetoric, and discourse analysis. He is PI for the Norwegian Research Council project "The Politics of Disability Identity" (2021–2025) and the author of 15 books including academic works, fiction, and memoir. His latest book is *I Live a Life Like Yours* (Farrar, Straus & Giroux 2021).

Halvor Hanisch is professor of rehabilitation and disability research at VID Specialized University. Hanisch has a long-standing engagement in both disability studies and rehabilitation research. Hanisch' interests and publications primarily deal with representation of disability, the relation between disability and political theory, and finally the relation between disability, parenting, and care.

Stig Langvad is master in Political Science, former Chairperson of Disabled Peoples Organisations Denmark, Board Member of European Disability Forum, Member of the Committee under the Convention on the Rights of Persons with Disabilities, being employed in the Department of Social Affairs in the municipality of Aarhus, Denmark.

Inger Marie Lid is a Professor of Public Health and Rehabilitation at VID Specialized University. Her research interests include ethics, citizenship, universal design accessibility, and human rights. Her recent publication include "The significance of relations. Rethinking autonomy in a disability perspective" in *Lived Citizenship for Persons in Vulnerable Life Situations. Theories and Practices* (Scandinavian University Press). She is currently engaged in research on inclusion in higher education.

Dmitry Lukash is an Associate Professor of social education at VID Specialized University. His research interests include religion in the modern world, citizenship and rights of people with disabilities, methodologies of qualitative research. His recent publication is *Utviklingshemmedes rett til religionsutøvelse*. In: I. M. Lid & A. R. Solevåg (Red.), Religiøst medborgerskap. Oslo: Cappelen Damm Akademisk.

Ingunn Moser is the CEO of Diakonhjemmet Foundation and affiliated with VID specialized university. Her research interests focus upon subjectivity, dis/ability, and their embodied, material and technological relations. Her latest publications include *Ways of Home Making in Care for Later Life* (Palgrave Macmillan 2020), together with Bernike Pasveer and Oddgeir Synnes (eds.).

Michael Rembis is the Director of the Center for Disability Studies and an Associate Professor in the Department of History at the University at Buffalo (SUNY). Rembis has authored or edited many books, articles, and book chapters. He is currently completing a book entitled, *Writing Mad Lives – in the Age of the Asylum*. He is the coeditor of *The Oxford Handbook of Disability History*.

Natalia Pamula is an Assistant Professor at the American Studies Center at the University of Warsaw, Poland. She works on disability discourses and representations in Polish socialist and postsocialist culture. Her work has appeared, among others, in *Aspasia, East European Politics and Societies and Cultures*, and *Canadian Slavonic Papers*.

Korydon Smith, M.Arch., Ed.D., is a Professor of Architecture, Chair of the Department of Architecture, and Co-Director of the Community for Global Health Equity, University at Buffalo, SUNY. His research interests center on finding design solutions for people who have been traditionally marginalized from decisions about the design of their built environment.

Edward Steinfeld, Arch.D., is a SUNY Distinguished Professor of Architecture and Director of the Center for Inclusive Design and Environmental Access at the School of Architecture, University at Buffalo, State University of New York. His research interests include accessibility, universal design, and design for aging. He is a co-author of *Universal Design: Creating Inclusive Environments*. He is currently engaged in research and public education on design for gender diversity.

Magda Szarota is a human rights advocate and disability studies scholar. She is affiliated with the Centre for Disability Research at Lancaster University and the Cross-national Studies: Interdisciplinary Research and Training Program (CONSIRT) at Ohio University. She has published in *The Palgrave Encyclopedia of the Possible*, *Disability Studies Quarterly*, *Review of Disability Studies: An International Journal*, Ms. *Magazine* among others.

Introduction

Rethinking citizenship and disability

Inger Marie Lid, Edward Steinfeld, and Michael Rembis

This book examines the role of disability in rights to political and social participation – rights that many people with disabilities do not enjoy. The right to participation in all aspects of society is today recognized as a democratic value and an aspect of practicing citizenship. Although experiences varied across time, culture, and geographic location, many people living in the past who today would be defined as disabled were excluded from participation in society. A central feature of the modern era was the practice of institutionalization, which excluded a broad range of disabled people from public spaces. In the latter half of the 20th century, the practice of institutionalization was widely discredited, and many institutions were dismantled. Yet we continue to live with the legacies of institutionalization and the far-reaching effects of eugenics and medicalized understandings of disability. In many parts of the world, disabled people remain isolated or incarcerated in various settings. Others live in poverty.

The implementation of human rights laws designed to increase social and political participation of people with disabilities has led to the increased presence of some disabled people in society, but the effects of interventions made in the name of human rights have been experienced unevenly both within and among the various countries throughout the world that have adopted and implemented human rights measures. The global disability rights movement has helped to provide a better understanding of the barriers facing disabled people. Developments in the 21st century, especially the creation of information and communications technology, have broadened the reach of disability rights activism. They have also created new challenges.

Although public policy in many countries calls for inclusion and equal status, in reality public space, educational institutions, and workplaces are not always accessible due to many types of barriers. Achieving full and effective inclusion in society requires a foundation of knowledge to understand the nature of these barriers and contemplate possible solutions. This volume contributes to the growing body of knowledge that supports efforts to create a just society by situating access to participation and equal status within a human rights perspective and by arguing that full participation in society is essentially about citizenship. Although one volume cannot capture all the accomplishments of disabled people or address the full nature of the challenges still facing the global

DOI: 10.4324/9781003052708-1

community, our hope is that this book will provide an introduction to many of the issues that arise when we begin to think about disability rights from an international perspective, stimulate future work on this topic, and identify models and methods for future research. We will use the United Nations Convention on the Rights of Persons with Disabilities (CRPD) as a reference point because it is the most widely accepted statement of disability rights. Thus, it represents current conceptions of disability rights and also serves as a benchmark to identify new directions for conceiving citizenship for people with disabilities. Our hope is that this book will strengthen the global dialogue on how best to achieve the real-world participation of disabled people in society.

Implemented to varying degrees at different times, early disability rights legislation most often focused on access to the physical spaces of a community through the elimination of institutionalization and the removal of physical barriers. Pushed by disability rights activists and their allies, lawmakers came to realize what disabled people already knew – that social participation had to go beyond interventions in physical space and the provision of services, to include a recognition of rights and responsibilities, as well as access to cultural, intellectual, virtual, and social spaces at the local and global levels. Some leaders within the disability community have described this orientation as disability justice and have aligned themselves with broader social and environmental justice movements.

It is important in any discussion of disability citizenship to clarify how the citizen is envisioned in the human rights corpus. In the CRPD, as in other conventions, citizenship is defined implicitly rather than explicitly. The term *citizenship* is not mentioned in the articles or in the preamble of the CRPD. In contrast to other conventions, the term *accessibility* or *access* in the CRPD forms a bridge between having rights and duties and being able to enjoy one's rights and carry out one's duties. Recognizing disability as part of human diversity, the CRPD does not envision the individual as self-sufficient and independent but rather as embedded in social and material contexts. Thus, it implies that disability rights are relational, subject to cultural, institutional, and social forces.

In many current contexts, access is restricted based most often on economics and prior qualifications. One can attend a football match if one buys a ticket. One can enroll in university only if one has successfully obtained an education at the primary and secondary school levels. One can practice a profession only if one demonstrates competencies in a particular field. One can take communion if one has been baptized – and so on. It seems that such restrictions on participation in society have face value. If they were not useful, businesses would not be sustainable, communication of knowledge would suffer, professional qualifications would cease to be meaningful. But unnecessary structural barriers also restrict access to participation in society. For example, excluding wheelchair users from a football stadium because there are stairs; excluding people with no leg function (or no legs) from renting a car when hand controls are available to enable that person to drive; or, excluding a blind person from the legal profession because they cannot read the licensing examination when the exam materials could be provided in braille or text to speech software all unnecessarily prevent people from participating in society. As our knowledge of how to provide access and our political will to build access into the societies we create improves, disability (i.e., embodiment) becomes less of a barrier to participation. Disability rights activists, especially those who identify as part of the newly emergent disability justice movement, challenge these and other unnecessary barriers to participation. To understand these critiques *and* contemplate what full participation might mean in a fundamentally reformulated world, it is necessary to discuss what undergirds the notion of a valid restriction on access and what does not; only then will we achieve meaningful change.

The intention of the CRPD is to counteract disability-based discrimination. Lack of accessibility, or poor access, is one of the most common forms of disability-based discrimination. However, given different cultural contexts, and the situations of individuals, it might be difficult to determine whether discrimination based on disability has actually occurred, or whether some other reason for restricting access is in play. For example, if someone with a learning disability cannot pass a professional licensing exam, are they suffering discrimination or do they lack the qualifications to be a licensed professional? Are there ways in which we could envision this situation differently? Recognizing differences in impairments, as well as structural, cultural, and historical barriers to social participation, is of critical importance for identifying and dismantling the obstacles that continue to constrain disabled people from achieving equal citizenship. Ultimately, the question of citizenship must focus more on what *ability* means for participation in society rather than disability. A new understanding of citizenship enables re-thinking what participation itself might mean. Is one form of participation more valued than another? These are some of the questions with which the authors included in this volume grapple.

Looking to the future, a different set of questions become evident. It is likely that bionic prosthetics, chemical and anatomical interventions, and AI systems that enhance performance will provide advantages to the point that the majority population will adopt these interventions. What will disability mean in such a world? How will society react to the emergence of cyborgs and other "enhanced" humans? Issues of citizenship are already charged with a fear of unfair competition. Will people be excluded from participation because they are judged "not fully human" or "no longer human," recalling some of the most egregious examples of prejudice and bigotry in the past? Will people be refused access to technology or medical or genetic interventions to enforce definitions of humanness based on ideology, or worse, to maintain the dominance of social and political elites? Questions like these demonstrate that a discourse on the role of ability in citizenship is not only timely but also essential to the advancement of human rights in the future. This tension between ability and disability animates the material presented in this book.

Historically, disability has been aligned conceptually and politically with monstrosity or defect so that disabled bodies are valued less than non-disabled bodies. Such beliefs underpin a system of ableism at a structural level that demands various means of empowerment, as well as systems of protection that establish and maintain the human rights of people with different bodies. But ultimately, the conceptual link between disability and defect can only be changed by a *different definition of ability* articulated within the space of human rights, one that is based on the potential of individuals rather than the limitations of bodies. Although the CRPD promotes the idea that differences in ability should not restrict social and political participation, definitions and real-life experiences of social participation and citizenship must be transformed to meet the needs and aspirations of all citizens – and non-citizens alike – in the 21st century.

The CRPD implies a right to participation in all domains of life. But rights, as defined by treaties like the CRPD are not sufficient to ensure it. The type of social participation to which the CRPD aspires requires that disabled people have *equal access* with other citizens. Clearly, there are vast differences in resources, physical environments, ways of life, and social relations across societies. Indeed, the definition of disability and rights may vary from one place to another. A culture of accessibility is thus likely to evolve in many ways. Activists and professionals are just starting to explore how social and physical context plays a role in the realization of equal access and participation in society. Any future discussion of rights must be informed by this emerging conversation.

This book contains eight chapters that address broad concerns and interests within the global disability rights and disability studies communities. In Chapter 1, Inger Marie Lid considers the importance of the CRPD and universal design in facilitating equal access for all citizens and the critical role that political and institutional mechanisms play in implementing equal access at different scales of social life. In Chapter 2, Halvor Hanisch asks: *How do states come to provide rehabilitation services?* In answering this question, Hanisch invokes the innovative concept of "acceptance of liability," and argues that the provision of rehabilitation should be considered as a premium or compensation for citizenship. In Chapter 3, Jan Grue offers a discussion of the ways in which post- and trans-humanist perspectives are changing ideas about the "typical human" and how these changes have enabled a questioning of the norms of valuation that are implicit in, and perhaps intrinsic to, the CRPD's vision of equality and inclusion. In Chapter 4, Michael Rembis focuses on the efforts of people who identify as users and survivors of psychiatric services and people living with psychosocial disabilities to use the CRPD to combat the largely unchecked expansion of western, global north bio-psychiatry and take control of their own treatment and care.

While the authors of the first four chapters focus more globally – either conceptually or geographically – on the CRPD, citizenship, and human rights, the remaining four chapters take a more localized approach to thinking about these issues. In Chapter 5, Dmitry Lukash and Anna Chalachanová explore the meanings of religious citizenship for people with intellectual disabilities in Norway and Slovakia. In Chapter 6, Edward Steinfeld uses a study of accessibility practices in the United States to think about how access is culturally determined and how this, in turn, means that it will vary from one culture to the next. In Chapter 7, Ingunn Moser and Inger Marie Lid examine how three Norwegian diaconal non-profit service providers who deliver welfare services to people with disabilities respond to the obligations and duties which follow from ratifying the CRPD. In the last chapter, Korydon Smith utilizes four brief case studies from the Great Lakes Region of central and eastern Africa to think about how the local wisdom of Global South communities interacts with and can ultimately help to shape larger global considerations and conversations related to disability, access, and human rights.

We have also included three interludes written by disability rights activists and other people at various stages in their lives who are working on the ground in different geographical contexts. By integrating these interludes with the more formally academic and analytical chapters in the book, we hope to bring to readers a sense of how the politics of disability and citizenship get played out in the everyday lives of disabled people and their allies, while at the same time expose readers to the vanguard of disability activism and scholarship. The interludes also enable us, as editors, to expand the geographic reach of this book to more, and often less recognized, parts of the world, which is critically important in the study of disability. Disability affects every human on the planet, and as such, requires expansive analysis. The postscript features a conversation between Inger Marie Lid and Rosemarie Garland Thomson in which they contemplate issues and themes addressed in the book.

As the chapters , interludes and postscript reveal, this book approaches citizenship in a multi-dimensional way. It accounts for individual perspectives and experiences while also focusing on the responsibility of states and other governmental and non-governmental actors to facilitate citizenship. At the same time, it acknowledges and engages with disability at the level of social justice, which attends to the intersection of disability with other dimensions of discrimination, such as income, gender, age, culture, and ethnicity. This book demonstrates that access to citizenship must be emphasized and practiced comprehensively and diligently to address the political contexts, cultural priorities, and economic and human resources of any community.

Taken together, the chapters and interludes in this volume encourage readers to think about both the possibilities and the limits of a document such as the UN Convention on the Rights of Persons with Disabilities. Always open to interpretation and varying levels of implementation and enforcement, the CRPD provides a powerful but incomplete framework for achieving the inclusion and full citizenship of disabled people at multiple levels of social organization and interaction. This book emphasizes that we must think both locally and globally as we work to establish and protect the human rights of disabled people and, at the same time, to redefine and reconstruct the relationship between disability and citizenship.

Part I

1 Citizenship and universal design

Inger Marie Lid

Introduction

This chapter seeks to lay out the epistemological and normative foundations for universal design as a human rights concept and a strategy that supports equal access to citizenship. I begin by providing a brief historical background on disability and human rights and a concise description of the Norwegian context. Thereafter, I examine the normative foundations of universal design and accessibility and discuss the CRPD as a mechanism aimed at recognizing persons with disability as equal-rights-having subjects. Differences between citizenship and human rights are also addressed. Next, I discuss the epistemological framing of universal design and suggest a stratified approach to implementing universal design in different local and national contexts. I conclude by stating that universal design together with reasonable accommodation have the potential to underpin affirmative strategies and contribute to what Nancy Mairs (1997) refers to as "habitable worlds."

This chapter situates disability as both conception and lived experience within a human rights perspective. According to the United Nations (UN) Convention on the Rights of Persons with Disabilities (CRPD), disability is best understood as an evolving concept, and "disability results from the interaction between persons with impairments and attitudinal and environmental barriers" (United Nations, 1948, 2008, preamble e). The human rights principles are presented as universal and indivisible. As a human rights treaty, the CRPD is an international political document that articulates policy and universal values, and a practical document aimed at the implementation of the value-based policy in very different local and national contexts. Universal design is defined by the UN as "the design of products, environments, programmes, and services to be usable by all persons to the greatest extent possible" (UN, 2008, Article 2). Barriers in built environments can be seen as discrimination (Degener, 2016).

Universal design in the CRPD is linked to disability, as disability is part of human diversity. Thus, universal design as a design concept is responsive toward the discrimination experienced by persons with impairments when facing barriers in architecture and the environment. Universal design signifies an approach to design that recognizes human diversity, focusing on usability (Nilsson, 2018).

DOI: 10.4324/9781003052708-3

As the CRPD recognizes that universal design alone does not dismantle all barriers for all persons, reasonable accommodation and discrimination are addressed (UN, 2008, Article 2). The inherent structure of the CRPD can be analyzed as a tripartite involving discrimination, reasonable accommodation, and universal design. The CRPD defines in Article 2 reasonable accommodation as necessary and appropriate modification and adjustments; followed by a brief statement that reasonable accommodation should not impose undue burden (UN, 2008, Article 2). Denial of reasonable accommodation can be seen as discrimination. There are dilemmas in the CRPDs definitions regarding how "all persons to the greatest extent possible" as target group for universal design is understood, and how far the responsibility for reasonable accommodation goes.

Disability is situational, meaning temporally situated and context sensitive. The understandings of disability have changed over time, as have the political measures that governments take to respond to disability as a human condition. Changes in politics may have real effects on persons' lives. Therefore, implementation of universal design at the institutional level is crucial – this is how universal design can impact citizen's lives. I propose a stratified implementation of universal design at three different political levels: the micro level, meso level, and macro level. The micro level is where people live their lives as citizens in local communities. At the meso level, politics are implemented in institutions such as schools, workplaces, public transportation, and civic life. The macro level is where values and overall politics are adopted, such as the UN Sustainable Development Goals (SDG), the CRPD, and national constitutions. I argue that the implementation of universal design must involve all these political (administrative) levels in order to be efficient. The CRPD is an instrument that can be used to increase the agency of persons with disabilities; awareness of that agency helps to avoid the risk of social determinism when explaining disability history (Shah & Priestley, 2011, p. 13). For the CRPD to strengthen the agency of persons with disabilities, the transition from words in a document to practical politics is fundamental. As such, the implementation of the CRPD is important, as it entails translating universal articles into practical politics in different political contexts.

Background and context

Dignity is a fundamental concept in the UN's human rights treaties. Indeed, it is stated in the first paragraph of the 1948 Human Rights Declaration: "All human beings are born free and equal in dignity and rights" (UN, 1948, Article 1). By being included in this political document, dignity became a political concept rather than merely ethical (Habermas, 2010; Degener, 2016). Respect for human dignity became fundamental in the human rights corpus and is a response to the atrocities of the Nazi regime before and during the Second World War (Degener, 2016). Persons with disabilities were invisible citizens for the UN's first 25 years (Degener & Begg, 2017). As the UN's (1948) Universal Declaration of

Human Rights does not include disability or impairment, these categories are referred to as "other status" in Article 2 of the declaration.

Dignity is also prominent in the CRPD, stated in Article 1 as "inherent dignity." The CRPD aims to promote respect for the inherent dignity of persons with disabilities, who have been excluded from equal status in most societies. Persons with disabilities have long been met with stigma and prejudice (World Health Organisation & World Bank, 2011; Bariffi, 2018). Being recognized as equal citizens is therefore important to the defense of human welfare and dignity (Cooper, 2018). Feminist and disability studies scholars have argued that the conceptualization of "citizen" is heavily influenced by traditional male stereotypes (Kittay, 1999; Nussbaum, 2007). As such, it must be reformulated in consideration of an empirically inclusive conception of human diversity, including disability as part of human diversity. Since having rights and duties is a foundation for citizenship, the CRPD strengthens the citizenship of persons with disabilities.

The states parties to the CRPD are responsible toward one another to support equal citizenship for all citizens. I write this chapter from the perspective of the Norwegian welfare state. Norway is one of five nations in the Nordic region of Europe. All five Nordic states have ratified the CRPD, and Denmark, Sweden and Finland have also ratified the CRPD Protocol. The Nordic welfare states are considered comprehensive and supportive, meaning that inhabitants have a multitude of rights in areas such as health, including reproductive health, welfare, and education. The other side of this coin, however, is that the terminology regarding disability is characterized by medical models, and services, individual assistive devices, and pedagogical accommodations are provided with reference to medical conditions (e.g., diagnoses). It was precisely this medical framing of disability that was identified and criticized by the CRPD Committee when assessing the implementation of the CRPD in Norway (Committe on the Rights of Persons with Disabilities, 2019). This means that the citizenship and rights perspective may be less acknowledged in the Norwegian context.

Norway adopted its first discrimination and accessibility act in 2008. Its implementation has been slow, supported by action plans and strategies with little practical impact. For example, public transportation, which is used by many inhabitants of the capital of Norway (Oslo), is inaccessible for most persons with disabilities for both technical and service-related reasons. Yet, it was not until 2022 that this was recognized as an issue of discrimination.

Disability, in the context of human rights, demands implementation of strategies to dismantle barriers by focusing on equal rights, accessibility, universal design, discrimination, and reasonable accommodation. However, to realize that a barrier exists, we need to raise awareness of the material dimension of citizenship. I focus here on the responsibility of the government at national, regional, and local levels to be aware of the role environmental access plays in the everyday life of persons with disabilities. Steinfeld discusses the role of a wider range of spatial practices in this respect in Chapter 6 of this volume.

Normative foundation of citizenship and universal design

The rights of a person must be guaranteed and supported by a responsible state, if they are to be real political rights (Arendt, 2004). The ratification and implementation of the CRPD is therefore important. Moreover, using the Convention in practical politics is a necessary condition for it to be effective. According to the philosopher Paul Ricoeur, humans are ethical beings, with an ethical intention toward a good human life – with and for others – in just institutions (Ricoeur, 1992). Ricoeur offers here an anthropology that understands human beings as aiming for a good life in social relations and in political institutions. National and transnational bodies have built many institutions (e.g., the UN) to support the good life for citizens. We can interpret the CRPD as an example of a shared ethical intention at the macro- and meso level, the purpose of which is to concretize how institutions can support and mainstream equal rights for persons with disabilities.

Seen through the lens of Ricoeur, the aim of the stakeholders (when writing) and of the states (in ratifying and implementing) the CRPD is to facilitate and support the good life for persons with disabilities, so they are able to live with and for others in just institutions. As a multi-national convention, the state parties to the CRPD are responsible for contextualizing the Convention within the relevant legal and political contexts. It is however also necessary to be aware of a risk built into political and institutional systems that they may be unjust and support oppressive regimes. Here we face a limit inherent in the supra-national convention that has already been identified and discussed by Hannah Arendt (2004). The supra-national system of human rights does not in itself hinder unjust political systems at a national level.

While international human rights are regarded as innate and inalienable, the rights of citizens are created by states (Isin & Turner, 2007). Human rights are the rights of citizens in a society and are more than the rights as a formal citizen and member of a nation-state. Hannah Arendt is perhaps the political philosopher who sees this distinction most clearly. As she was outside formal national membership after her flight from Nazi Germany, she was also outside formal citizenship for 12 years – first in France and then in the United States (Arendt, 2004, p. i). This personal experience provided her with insights into the importance of the institutional support of individual persons as rights-havers, regardless of their formal status as citizens of a nation-state. Citizenship is therefore an aspect of human rights, but the person with rights needs to be recognized as such by political institutions.

Refugees, undocumented immigrants, and persons with disabilities all remain vulnerable to misrecognition of their citizenship, and thus also misrecognition as rights-having persons. Hannah Arendt (2004) argues that belonging to a well-ordered society is a precondition for recognition as a person with the right to have rights (Isin & Turner, 2007). The mismatch between the imprescriptible rights of the human being and the exclusive rights of the citizen can only be managed by anchoring human rights in a political context. Citizenship entails membership in a political unit (Cooper, 2018). By recognizing the individual as a citizen, their dignity is also acknowledged, which influences institutions' responsibilities regarding respecting human dignity (Cooper, 2018). Human rights are therefore guaranteed not by abstract ideas but by a responsive state.

There is thus a link between human rights and citizenship. Being recognized as a person with rights and duties, as a rights-having subject, is fundamental for being recognized as a citizen. The role of the local and national institutions, then, is to support welfare and a good human life for all citizens. These institutions support human rights at a local level. As such, access to individual welfare services is, at the local micro level, a condition for persons with disabilities to be able to live as citizens. The CRPD Committee's critique of Norway's practice of building on medical models of disability rather than human rights models is thus a critique of how nation-states contextualize the universal policy as it is written in the Convention's articles and preamble.

As pointed out earlier, Ricoeur argues that there is an ethical intention toward a good human life in just institutions that can be seen in human activity. I propose that his analysis of such an ethical intention and such a concept of just institutions is relevant for envisioning what the CRPD may actually entail when implemented. The CRPD makes it explicitly clear that persons with disability have the same inherent dignity as all persons. Thus, when aiming for justice, state institutions must not exclude persons with disabilities from citizenship. Here, citizenship has a material dimension, a practical political dimension, and an ethical dimension. Universal design – together with individual accommodation – touches upon each of these levels. I will now move forward by discussing the epistemological framing of universal design and individual accommodation.

Epistemological framing of universal design and reasonable accommodation

In Article 2 of the CRPD, "universal design" refers to products, programs, services, and the environment. "Reasonable accommodation" refers to the needs of different individuals, and "discrimination" refers to socio-political situations, i.e., what happens in context. The definition of universal design in the CRPD can be seen as mere technical. However, together with two other definitions in the same paragraph – for discrimination and for reasonable accommodation – universal design is part of an overall strategy for equal status and equal rights and calls for a normative grounding and epistemological framing. These three concepts together, discrimination, reasonable accommodation and universal design, indicate a complex conception of the person, the environment, and the person-environment interaction. The person-environment interaction is where barriers and accessibility emerge and can be negotiated and dismantled.

According to the social models, disability is a social construct that can be managed through changes in the environment (Degener, 2016). Our human experiences, however, tell us that embodiment and impairment is also relevant when barriers emerge. Embodied limits, pain, and fatigue are real, and are not always managed by external measures such as anti-discrimination laws and accessibility standards; moreover, not all barriers can be removed according to all citizens' needs. It is for example often easier to install a ramp than to accommodate the accessibility needs of persons with intellectual disabilities.

It has been argued that the CRPD is anchored in the social model of disability (Kakoullis & Ikeehara, 2018; Degener, 2016), the main feature of which is the understanding of disability as a social construct. However, the human rights model goes beyond the social model (Degener, 2016). The CRPD treaty text and preamble represent a more relational approach to disability as a phenomenon, focusing on the interaction between the embodied person and the environment. In a British context, this is referred to as social-relational (Thomas, 2012), and in a Nordic context, this is referred to as a relational approach, conceptualized as a gap or mismatch between the individual's abilities and the expectations of an individual's functioning inscribed in (built, social, and cultural) environments.[1] This gap can be diminished by changing the socio-material environment and strengthening the individual's abilities, for example, by offering individual devices such as wheelchairs, mobility sticks, rehabilitation and habilitation, and economic support. The gap seldom disappears but can be negotiated and managed.

I here argue that the implementation of universal design should be framed as a relational, rather than social, model of disability. One reason for this is that a relational model best supports making contextual analytical distinctions between universal design and reasonable accommodation. I agree with Degener (2016) that the social model does not pay attention to the individual dimensions of disability, such as pain, health problems, and assistance needs. I contend however that relational models are more suitable for merging the individual and environmental factors. Individual factors include embodiment, and embodied experiences such as pain and medical diagnosis. Human rights, then, is a political perspective on disability rather than a model. Disability is a human rights topic and persons with disability are persons with rights and duties on par with others. The human rights perspective includes both individual and environmental dimensions. Disability, in the Convention and the preamble, is thus understood as a product of interaction, the model of disability referred to in the treaty and preamble is a relational – or interactional model (Bickenbach, 2012; Lid, 2014).

Critical realism is a theoretical approach that can help make sense of this complexity. Critical realism is a philosophy that insists reality is real, and that phenomena such as disability and disabling barriers are also real (Shakespeare, 2014, p. 73). Phenomena that exist in the world can be analyzed as a level-structured or stratified reality (Danermark & Gellerstedt, 2004). According to the epistemology of critical realism, disability can be analyzed as a multi-layered concept (Bhaskar & Danermark, 2006). Dimensions of disability may be medically, socially, and culturally constructed, such as people's attitudes toward and expectations of persons with disability. One example is the chronic disease

Multiple Sclerosis, which is a medical diagnosis that has very different effect on the person on the one hand and often leads to disability-based discrimination due to negative public attitude toward the disease that may affect upon employment opportunities on the other.

Following a critical realist position, the individual level is real. The person is, for example, a wheelchair user. The architectural, material barriers faced by this person are real barriers. However, there are also barriers that are socially constructed and result from other people's attitudes. For instance, low expectations for the achievements of persons with disabilities often hinder access to education and job opportunities; these are attitudinal barriers (Wolfensberger, 2011).

The status of the body is contested in disability studies (Vehmas & Mäkelä, 2009; Hughes & Paterson, 1997; Wendell, 1996). Two oppositional theoretical positions are represented by social constructivism on the one hand and realism on the other (Hacking, 1999). Critical realism is the mediating position, to some extent bridging the gap between the two positions. The theoretical discussion on the meaning of the body is important for universal design research and practice. Universal design is an a-contextual concept expected to be possible to implement in different national and local contexts. When implementing universal design in a specific context, both impairments, the individual embodiment, and the object of universal design are of importance, and the context itself. If universal design is interpreted and implemented regardless of human embodied diversity, the strategy risks being reduced to a minimum threshold level of access.

In a social constructivist approach, disability as a social phenomenon is in focus and the embodied difference is paid less attention to. In contrast, in a realist approach, the cultural and social dimensions (e.g., prejudices and ableism/disableism) are toned down. Disability as part of human diversity is recognized, what is the state responsibility as a signatory to the CRPD, is to reduce the discriminatory effects of disability through planning and designing environments that meet the needs of a diverse population. Recognizing disability as a dimension of human diversity implies that the built environment, including products, services, and programs, is usable for different persons with different needs and abilities. For this reason, the knowledge base supporting universal design strategies must include interdisciplinary knowledge on human diversity including impairment, environments, and the human-environment interaction.

The dispute between different perspectives on disability is thus highly relevant when struggling with uncover and dismantle discriminatory barriers and building accessibility for persons with different abilities. Put simply, universal design is all about planning, designing, and modifying the environment to meet the needs of individuals with different abilities using different individual devices. Thus, the knowledge base supporting universal design strategies comprises generating knowledge from the individual medical perspective, from the perspective of the socio-cultural and architectural and technical disciplines. When universal design is included in the CRPD, it is closely linked to disability and becomes a human rights concept.

A critical realist approach is critical to a one-dimensional understanding of disability. Disability is, according to critical realism, a complex phenomenon involving culture, body, politics, and health (Shakespeare, 2018). Critical realism considers interdisciplinary research as productive and deals with real-life problems, such as spatial planning and urban research (Næss, 2015). Anchoring the strategy and concept of universal design in a critical realist approach means that architectural barriers are recognized as real and as excluding persons from participation. This epistemological framing of the strategy is also highly relevant, as critical realism is well-suited to real-life research (Næss, 2015).

Universal design can be implemented as a means by which to reach the goal of supporting access to equal citizenship for persons with disabilities. However, the theoretical models of disability must then be revisited. Here I argue that the model of disability to underpin universal design strategies must conceptualize disability as an interaction and a human-environment relationship.

The CRPD's Article 9 on accessibility is both comprehensive and novel and therefore has received attention from scholars (Lawson, 2018; Lid, 2010; Turner, 2006). However, access always relates to something valued – be it access to social roles or to places and buildings. These are intertwined, as access to social roles has spatial dimensions. For example, does access to the social role as a parent presuppose access to privacy and a supportive home environment sometimes also including personal assistance. Access is thus not understood as a separate and novel human right but rather as a bridge between having rights and being able to make use of one's rights. Moreover, by focusing on accessibility, the CRPD has the potential to strengthen human rights altogether. There are manifold physical barriers, information barriers, attitudinal barriers, and more that hamper the equal right to political and social participation, and thus citizenship, for persons with disabilities. Therefore, accessibility is crucial for persons with disabilities (Lawson, 2018, p. 259).

Discrimination on the basis of disability

The human rights situation for persons with disabilities is changing at a political level. The implicit conception of citizenship inherent in the Convention displays a comparative dimension. The phrase "on an equal basis with others" is used almost like a mantra in the Convention: 31 times throughout the CRPD text (Nilsson, 2018). Does this imply a comparative dimension or a strategy of normalization? One reason for the frequent use of this terminology is that a citizen in one nation-state, for example, the United States, must recognize that the Convention cannot be used to claim rights that other US citizens do not have.

Consider the right to work, as included in Article 27 of the CRPD: according to this article, state parties recognize the right of persons with disabilities to work on an equal basis with others. This means that the person with a disability in Norway has the right to apply for a job but does not have the right to be employed in a position, as no citizens in Norway have the right to employment.

A person with a disability without a paid job is therefore not entitled to employment any more than are other citizens in Norway. However, as discriminatory practices do occur in recruitment processes and because persons with disability often have poorer access to education (primary, secondary, and postsecondary), citizens with disability might have, *de facto*, less access to employment than their fellow citizens due to disabling barriers.

The recognition that disability-based discrimination exists is critical for full implementation of human rights for persons with disabilities. Discrimination is defined in Article 2 of the CRPD, and is a key concept used in Articles 3 and 4. The Convention protects persons with disabilities against discrimination on any ground, with a special focus on disability-based discrimination. This includes denial of reasonable accommodation. Yet, in Norway, people with disabilities are still subject to discrimination and have not been recognized as equal citizens. Disabled persons are more likely than nondisabled people to be victims of hate speech (Sherry et al., 2020).

It is important to note that persons with different impairments experience disability-based discrimination differently. For a wheelchair user, access is often a question of materiality and architectural barriers, whereas a person with intellectual disabilities faces disability-based discrimination as paternalistic service-provision, institutionalization, poor educational opportunities, or restrictions on self-determination. For citizens with intellectual disability, guardianship also can be a hindrance for equal citizenship. From a national level, full compliance with the CRPD cannot be achieved without addressing the full range of disability-related discrimination.

Social and spatial justice

Shifting the concept of disability from a medical to a socio-political context affects understandings of social justice and participation. The role of embodiment is, as pointed out earlier, an element of the relational model of disability. A relational or inter-actional model makes sense of the fact that social life has a spatial dimension (Soja, 2010). This may seem trivial but is fundamental seen from a disability perspective. Most of the built environment is planned and built to meet the needs of "the ordinary person," by Rosemarie Garland-Thomson referred to as "the normate" (Garland-Thomson, 1997). Institutionalization politics is a reason for this, as persons with disabilities since the beginning of the development of the modern world have been removed from their local communities.

Soja refers to the urbanist Henri Lefebvre (2006), who argued that the right to the city should be understood as a right to urban life, and thus to everyday human life in urban materiality. Universal design can invigorate the conception of social justice by addressing the material dimension of the right to live among others, and the importance of the human-environment interaction for social justice in both the political arena and lived practice. Nancy Mairs has analyzed the consequence of a built environment as built for able citizens and called for not a limited access to some spaces but rather "a world that wants me in it" (Mairs, 1997). Mairs identified the world as built not for her, and thus found ableist elements in a world facilitating for some bodies and rejecting other bodies.

Mairs is implicitly addressing one fundamental absence in social models of disability, the absence of embodiment. Many scholars have addressed this, and the problem of the absent body is a problem in universal design research and practice because social justice cannot be reduced to a theoretical concept but is always also a practical experience. Nancy Mairs' experience when interacting with a world not built for a person as herself is political, epistemological and ethical. The concept of ableism was described for the first time in 1981 (Campbell, 2019). The concept is analytically efficient to understand that attitudinal and material barriers are not always accidental but may be intentional.

Social justice involves equal status, equal access, social participation, human rights, and citizenship. Both Martha Nussbaum and Iris M. Young consider justice for persons in marginal positions and persons with disabilities as important (Nussbaum, 2007; Young, 2000). In the following sections, when I present examples on the implementation of universal design in local contexts, the examples are framed in a human rights perspective. Disability-based discrimination as described in the CRPD is still new, and there is so far little international experience in counteracting this form of discrimination. In the Norwegian context, the convention is ratified and still not incorporated. The national application of laws is characterized by little use of international juridical documents (Hellum & Strand, 2022). This means that the CRPD is very seldom used in cases handled by the discrimination committee and tribunal.

The gap between national legislation and human rights policies is especially prominent with regard to the implementation of universal design. The human rights dimension of the strategy is often neglected and what is implemented is a technical specification of limited access. Even if denial of reasonable accommodation according to the CRPD's Article 2 can be understood as disability-based discrimination, the social justice element of equal access is often overlooked. Therefore, a more material and spatial interpretation of justice can uncover the barriers that hinder social participation in real life. Soja addresses spatial injustice in urban areas; in the context of this chapter, spatial justice refers to the socio-materiality of the planned and built environment, and to services and products such as public transportation. The crucial factor here is access (Egard et al, 2021). Lack of access to public transportation on equal terms with other citizens is discrimination. It is important to note that this notion of "equal terms with other citizens" is a comparative phrase indicating that it is possible to compare one person's access to public transportation with another person's access. This is not always easy, as the individual conditions and use of individual assistive devices represent a richness of variety.

Macro-, meso-, and micro-scale stratification of institutional responsibilities for implementation

Accessibility is never general but is situated within and concerns the congruity between individual capacities and preconditions and environmental demands (Lid & Solvang, 2016). This person-environment interaction is often characterized by friction and mismatch. Examples from the macro-, the meso-, and micro level can help to illustrate the interplay between individual and environment, and how universal design can be used to achieve social justice for all citizens.

The macro level concerns universal values and is often characterized by strong consensus among actors (Lid, 2016). In democratic contexts, it is seldom argued that persons with disabilities are of lesser inherent value than citizens without disabilities and therefore should not have equal access to places and resources. This agreement on universal democratic values is reflected in the comprehensive international support of the CRPD. Thus far, 184 countries have signed and ratified the CRPD, and are therefore parties to the Convention (UN CRPD, 2021). Thus, the strong international support for the CRPD demonstrates support for equal human rights for persons with disabilities. At the national level, this implied support is not always reflected in actual policy. For example, the incorporation of the CRPD into Norwegian human rights law was turned down by the parliament three times – most recently, in March 2021 (Vik, 2021). The case of the CRPD's incorporation in Norway is thus an example of disagreement at the macro level in the Norwegian welfare state.

The design of welfare services is a good example at the meso level. The CRPD's Article 19 stipulates the right to live in local communities and experience belonging to a society and community like other citizens. The Swedish scholar Niklas Altermark (2017) argues that "people with intellectual disabilities are today provided with services that shall serve for their independence and self-determination, whilst, in practice, these services often continue to constrain how members of this group are allowed to live their lives" (p. 1316). This argument is also valid in the Norwegian context, where de-institutionalization has failed to provide equal status and rights for persons with intellectual disabilities.

In the Norwegian context, welfare reform for persons with intellectual disabilities was carried out in 1991 (Tideman & Tøssebro, 2002). The 2021 report from the Equality and Anti-Discrimination Ombud in Norway (LDO), "Right to self-determination: from guardianship to supported decision-making," shows that the design of services was not in accordance with the political goals of equal status and citizenship. Persons with intellectual disabilities are still under guardianship in Norway. This report from the LDO concludes that guardianship does not fulfill the responsibilities stipulated in Articles 3, 12, and 19 of the CRPD. The lives of these citizens are administered lives, and their situation has worsened in recent years (LDO, 2021). De-institutionalization has not improved the right to self-determination for these persons; instead, institutional logic structures the governing of their everyday lives, even if it is in smaller institutions and co-living facilities. Access to self-determination and the equal right to make one's own choices would imply a structure supporting choice-making for each person, which is referred to as supported decision-making (Blanck, 2021). At the local level, the implementation of universal design in spatial and social planning could support the right of persons with disabilities to live in and belong to local communities.

Equal access to public places in the local neighborhood is an example from the micro level. The *neighborhood* as a mediator between individual experience and community inclusion is rarely considered in Norwegian practice (for exceptions, see Lid and Solvang, 2016). There are many barriers for persons with disabilities in most neighborhoods (Jackson, 2018). The Norwegian author and professor Jan Grue, who is a wheelchair user, describes in his memoir that, as a child, he played with his friends in a neighborhood playground called Eventyrplassen, where his friends could go places he could not (Grue, 2021). He had to stay in the flat area while they were on top of the small hill; they could come to him, but he could not go where they were. In another section, he writes that this public space was covered with ice during wintertime. Now, his wheelchair became a desired plaything for his friends, as he could move smoothly and rapidly over the ice, and his companions could hang from his chair, following along behind him like a long chain of pearls. Grue notes that he felt so free when moving around and at the center of social play, i.e., included.

These examples show, albeit the last instance of participation, that despite the fact that Norway has adopted the CRPD, and seemingly has agreement with the CRPD from a political perspective, there seems to be an everyday resistance to implementation at all three levels. There is no consistent policy, service practice, or local design to support equality and social justice. Even after 50 years of policy development, the barriers are largely the same (Grue, 2021; tenBroek, 1966).

Discrimination is experienced at the micro level, by individual persons. It is, however, disputed what is to be understood as disability-based discrimination. These three examples indicate that correlation between the macro-, meso-, and micro level can have an effect upon what is seen as discrimination and what is not. In a well-organized welfare state, as the Norwegian, it is contested if and how international law should be implemented in national politics.

Affirmative strategies

I have argued earlier that universal design and reasonable accommodation should be anchored in a relational understanding of disability comprising both the individual and the environment, together with the interaction between the two. In 2000, Swain and French developed what they referred to as an affirmative model of disability. This is a non-tragic view on disability that calls for forming of positive social identities both at individual and collective scale (Swain & French, 2000). The affirmative model is promising in its critique of negative understandings of impairment, but the potential is not yet realized in terms of societal implications, such as building spaces that recognizes disability as inherent in the human condition. The aforementioned example of a child (Jan Grue) using wheelchair playing with other children on the ice is illustrating regarding understanding how spatial factors and individual factors in interaction can give freedom and playful joy. The CRPD provides a source for further developing the affirmative model, which I see as consistent with relational models of disability comprehensively understood, including both space, technology, and persons.

By including persons with disability as rights-having subjects, the exclusion shifts to inclusion, and citizenship is strived for at a political level and in different local contexts. Participating in democratic processes is a fundamental aspect of human rights. Such participation is a recognition of stakeholders and representatives of advocacy groups as citizens. Rosemarie Garland-Thomson (2009) discusses what recognition can imply in urban public areas. Drawing on Nancy Fraser, Garland-Thomson links recognition to *being present* and to *seeing* one another. Being present in urban public areas means being present in diversity. Garland-Thomson describes the trajectory of recognition in the following manner: I recognize you by seeing your similarity and your difference to me, and then I make our strangeness familiar. In other words, I see you as you are (Garland-Thomson, 2009, p. 158).

Conclusion

In this chapter, I have focused on the internal relationship between the concepts of accessibility, universal design, and reasonable accommodation, all included in Articles 2 and 3 of the CRPD. I have anchored the interpretation of these concepts in the idea of inherent dignity, as included in Article 1, and in an understanding of discrimination on the basis of disability. The concept of "person" must include disability as a human condition, and thus implies changing political and institutional mechanisms to support a workable conception of diverse citizenship that is fully inclusive.

Universal design, as conceived in the CRPD, falls short in supporting citizenship as a strategy for achieving equality and social justice. It lacks both a theoretical foundation and a means to apply it to different contexts – at the macro-, meso-, and micro level. I have therefore suggested critical realism as a theory that can support and underpin universal design as a human rights concept and strategy. Based on this theoretical perspective, however, universal design could be defined and applied in a broader manner to develop a conception of social justice. With the illustrative examples provided in this chapter, I have sought to pinpoint why and how.

Note

1 I wish to thank Anna Chalachanová for pointing out this difference between the British and Nordic context in her trial lecture for her PhD thesis on November 29, 2021.

References

Altermark, N. (2017). The post-institutional era: Visions of history in research on intellectual disability. *Disability & Society*, *32*(9), 1315–1332.

Arendt, H. (1998). *The human condition*. Chicago, IL: University of Chicago Press.

Arendt, H. (2004). *The origins of totalitarianism*. New York; NY: Schocken.

Bariffi, F. (2018). "Article 8: Awareness-Rising". In Bantekas, I., Stein, M. A., & Anastasiou, D. *The UN Convention on the Rights of Persons with Disabilities: a commentary*. In Oxford commentaries on international law. pp. 229–257.

Bantekas, I., Stein, M. A., & Anastasiou, D. (Eds.). (2018). *The UN Convention on the Rights of Persons with Disabilities: A commentary*. Oxford, England: Oxford University Press.

Bhaskar, R., & Danermark, B. (2006). Metatheory, interdisciplinarity and disability research – A critical realist perspective. *Scandinavian Journal of Disability Research*, 8(4), 278–297.

Bickenbach, J. (2012). *Ethics, Law, and Policy*. Los Angeles: SAGE.

Blanck, P. (2021). Supported decision-making: Emerging paradigm in research, law, and policy. *Journal of Disability Policy Studies*. doi:10.1177/10442073211023168

Campbell, F. (2019). Precision ableism: A studies in ableism approach to developing histories of disability and abledment. *Rethinking History*, *23*(2), 138–156.

Cooper, F. (2018). *Citizenship, inequality, and difference: Historical perspectives*. Princeton, NJ: Princeton University Press.

Danermark, B., & Gellerstedt, L. C. (2004). Social justice: redistribution and recognition—a non-reductionist perspective on disability. *Disability & Society*, 19, 339–353. 10.1080/0968759041000l689458.

Degener, T. (2016). Disability in a human rights context. *Laws*, 5(3), 35. doi:10.3390/laws5030035

Degener, T., & Begg, A. (2017). From invisible citizens to agents of change: A short history of the struggle for the recognition of the rights of persons with disabilities at the United Nations. In V. Della Fina, R. Cera, & G. Palmisano (Eds.), *The United Nations Convention on the Rights of Persons with Disabilities: A commentary*. Cham, Switzerland: Springer.

Egard, H., Kristofer, H., & David, W. (2021). *Accessibility denied: Understanding inaccessibility and everyday resistance to inclusion for persons with disabilities*. London, England: Routledge.

Garland-Thomsons, R. (1997). *Extraordinary Bodies: Figuring Physical Disability in American Culture and Literature*. New York: Columbia University Press.

Garland-Thomson, R. (2009). *Staring: How we look*. Oxford, England: Oxford University Press.

Grue, J. (2021). *I Live a Life Like Yours: A Memoir*. New York: FSG Originals.

Habermas, J. (2010). The concept of human dignity and the realistic Utopia of human rights. *Metaphilosophy*, *41*, 464–480.

Hacking, I. (1999). *The social construction of what?* Cambridge, MA: Harvard University Press.

Hellum, A., & Strand, V. (2022). *Likestillings- og diskrimineringsrett* (1. utgave). Oslo: Gyldendal.

Hughes, B. & Paterson, K. (1997). The social model of disability and the disappearing body: Towards a sociology of impairment. *Disability & Society*, 12(3), 325–340.

Isin, E. F., & Turner, B. S. (2007). Investigating citizenship: An agenda for citizenship studies. *Citizenship Studies*, *11*(1), 5–17. doi:10.1080/13621020601099773

Jackson, M. (2018). Models of disability and human rights: Informing the improvement of built environment accessibility for people with disability at neighborhood scale? *Laws*, *7*(1), 10. doi:10.3390/laws7010010

Kakoullis, E., & Ikeehara, Y. (2018). Article 1: Purpose. In I. Bantekas, M. A. Stein, & D. Anastasiou (Eds.), *The UN Convention on the Rights of Persons with Disabilities: A commentary* (pp. 35–62). Oxford, England: Oxford University Press.

Kittay, E. F. (1999). *Love's Labor. Essays on Women, Equality, and Dependency*. New York: Routledge.

Lawson, A. (2018). "Article 9: Accessibility". In Bantekas, I., Stein, M. A. & Anastasiou, D. *The UN Convention on the Rights of Persons with Disabilities: a Commentary*. In Oxford Commentaries on International Law. (pp. 258–286).

Lefebvre, H. (2006). *Writings on Cities*. Selected, translated and introduced by Eleonore Kofman and Elizabeth Lebas. Oxford: Blackwell Publishers.

Lid, I. M. (2010). Accessibility as a statutory right. *Nordic Journal of Human Rights*, *28*(1), 20–38.

Lid, I. M. (2014). Universal design and disability: An interdisciplinary perspective. *Disability and Rehabilitation*, *36*(16), 1344–1349.

Lid, I. M. (2016). Implementing universal design in a Norwegian context: Balancing core values and practical priorities. *Disability Studies Quarterly*, *36*(4). doi:10.18061/dsq.v36i2.3234

Lid, I. M., & Koren Solvang, P. (2016). (Dis)ability and the experience of accessibility in the urban environment. *Alter – European Journal of Disability Research*, *10*(2), 181–194. doi:10.1016/j.alter.2015.11.003

Mairs, N. (1997). *Waist-high in the world*. Boston, MA: Beacon Press.

Nilsson, A. (2018). Article 2: Definitions. In I. Bantekas, M. A. Stein, & D. Anastasiou (Eds.), *The UN Convention on the Rights of Persons with Disabilities: A commentary* (pp. 63–83). Oxford, England: Oxford University Press.

Nussbaum, M. C. (2007). *Frontiers of Justice: Disability, Nationality, Species Membership*. Cambridge, Mass: Belknap Press of Harvard University Press.

Næss, P. (2015). Critical realism, urban planning and urban research. *European Planning Studies*, *23*(6), 1228–1244. doi:10.1080/09654313.2014.994091

Ricœur, P. (1992). *Oneself as Another*. Chicago: University of Chicago Press.

Shah, S., & Priestley, M. (2011). *Disability and social change: Private lives and public policies*. Bristol, England: Policy Press.

Shakespeare, T. (2014). *Disability rights and wrongs revisited* (2nd ed.). London, England: Routledge.

Shakespeare, T. (2018). *Disability: The basics*. London, England: Routledge.

Sherry, M., Olsen, T., Vedeler, J. S., & Eriksen, J. (2020). Introduction. In M. Sherry, T. Olsen, J. S. Vedeler, & J. Eriksen (Eds.), *Disability hate speech: Social, cultural and political contexts* (pp. 1–17). London, England: Routledge.

Soja, E. W. (2010). *Seeking spatial justice*. Minneapolis, MN: University of Minnesota Press.

Swain, J., & French, S. (2000). Towards an affirmation model of disability. *Disability & Society*, *15*(4), 569–582. doi:10.1080/09687590050058189

tenBroek, J. (1966). The right to live in the world: The disabled in the law of torts. *California Law Review*, *54*(2), 841–919.

Tideman, M., & Tøssebro, J. (2002). A comparison of living conditions for intellectually disabled people in Norway and Sweden: Present situation and changes following the national reforms in the 1990's. *Scandinavian Journal of Disability Research*, *4*(1), 23–42. doi:10.1080/15017410209510781

Thomas, C. (2012). Theorising disability and chronic illness: Where next for perspectives in medical sociology? *Social Theory and Health*, *10*(3), 209–228.

Tøssebro, J., & "Omfattende tjenester i andres hjem: brukeres, ansattes og kommuners perspektiv". (2019). *Hverdag i velferdsstatens bofellesskap*. Oslo, Norway: Universitetsforlaget.

Turner, B. S. (2006). *Vulnerability and Human Rights*. University Park, PA: Pennsylvania State University Press.

United Nations (1948). Universal Declaration of Human Rights.

United Nations (2008). *Convention on the Rights of Persons with Disabilities*. New York: United Nations.

Vehmas, S., & Mäkelä, P.(2009). The ontology of disability and impairment. A discussion of the natural and social features. In K. Kristiansen, S.Vehmas, & T. Shakespeare (Eds.), *Arguing About Disability. Philosophical Perspectives*. London: Routledge.

Vik, T. (2021). Persons with intellectual disability are still a pariah caste in Norway. *Tidsskrift for den Norske Laegeforening*, *141*(12), 1–4. doi:10.4045/tidsskr.21.0428

Wendell, S. (1996). *The Rejected Body: Feminist Philosophical Reflections on Disability*. New York: Routledge.

Wolfensberger, W. (2011, 1983). Social role valorization: A proposed new term for the principle of normalization. *Intellectual and Developmental Disabilities*, 49(6), 435–440. doi:10.1352/1934-9556-49.6.435

World Health Organisation & World Bank (2011). World report on disability. Geneva: World Health Organization.

Young, I. M. (2000). *Inclusion and Democracy*. Oxford: Oxford University Press.

Digital references

Committee on the Rights of Persons with Disabilities. (2019). *Concluding observations on the initial report of Norway*. United Nations. https://www.regjeringen.no/contentassets/26633b70910a44049dc065af217cb201/crpd-2019-concluding-observations-endelig-versjon-fra-komiteen.pdf

The Norwegian Equality and Anti-Discrimination Ombud (LDO). (2021). Report on "The right to self-determination. From guardianship to supported decision meking." https://ldo.no/en/ombudet-og-samfunnet/rapporter/selvbestemmelse/

UN CRPD Countries Party to the Convention. https://treaties.un.org/Pages/ViewDetails.aspx?src=TREATY&mtdsg_no=IV-15&chapter=4&clang=_en

2 Veterans from life

Rehabilitation as compensation

Halvor Hanisch

Introduction

We often see rehabilitation as a response to disability. It is common to assume that the existence of disability leads directly to the provision of rehabilitation, at least if these measures are likely to reduce disability and/or impairment. In short, the colloquial understanding of rehabilitation can be summed up; thus, professional efforts, in response to disability, aimed to reduce that disability.

Nevertheless, these efforts are limited. It is a fact – not only in low-income countries – that the presence of disability is often *not* met by rehabilitation efforts. Under varying social, cultural, and legal conditions, rehabilitation services are provided for some people with disabilities and not for others. Therefore, the purpose of this chapter is not to investigate why rehabilitation should be provided but rather how the provision of rehabilitation services comes to take place.

Rehabilitation services are provided in a variety of contexts. Such services relate to very different challenges. In addition to public services, rehabilitation is also provided by various non-governmental agencies – and, not least, through informal care. Since many non-state agents are nevertheless regulated, supported, or enabled by the states, I will nevertheless simplify the question and ask: *How do states come to provide rehabilitation services?*

In response to this question, this chapter makes a broader proposal that is relevant not only to the provision of rehabilitation but to many areas of research related to disability and rehabilitation: First, I propose that states come to provide disability-related services by somehow accepting responsibility. Second, I note that this acceptance began with veterans, and propose that we should consider people with disabilities *veterans from life in a disabling society*.

Accepting liability

The provision of rehabilitation services is increasingly viewed as a fulfillment of rights, typically with reference to the UN Convention on the Rights of Persons with Disabilities (CRPD; Bickenbach et al. 2021). Simultaneously, many states have accepted the International Classification of Functioning Disability and

DOI: 10.4324/9781003052708-4

Health (ICF) as the basis of both policy and practice regarding disability and rehabilitation (Stucki et al. 2002; Solvang et al. 2017). The biopsychosocial logic of the ICF gives environmental factors causal importance. Implicitly, the ICF thereby positions rehabilitation provisions as a political (or at least rights-defined) response to a "problem" that itself has both social and political aspects.

Without detailing the importance of neither the CRPD nor the ICF, this chapter argues that the provision of rehabilitation services can be understood as an acceptance of *liability*. To the extent that the state accepts liability, the provision of rehabilitation should be considered a premium or *compensation*. The policies and systems delivering the services should hence be considered systems of *insurance*. While these terms are mainly legal, I use them in a broader, more social sense (Baikovs & Zariņš 2013; Burri 2021).

This argument is also underpinned by two empirical claims. First, I claim that rehabilitation services emerged in situations where such liability was particularly explicit: First in the context of veterans, then in the context of work-related disability. Second, I argue that this link between liability and provision of rehabilitation services is not only a historical phenomenon, but still present: The term "rehabilitation" presupposes a "downfall," an adverse event or process to which the provision of rehabilitation responds.

Genealogies and archaeologies

When I try to investigate how the provision of rehabilitation services *comes about*, I am clearly investigating a social process. However, research on the underpinnings of rehabilitation services is often theoretical rather than empirical. Typically, many of these contributions have a philosophical rather than social or historical orientation (Rioux & Riddle 2010; Kim et al. 2016; Kleiner et al. 2022). This is not to say that philosophical perspectives are not important. The utilization of these theories, predominantly perspectives that essentially theorize justice, is indispensable. The provision of rehabilitation services *is* a "disability equality issue" (Shakespeare et al. 2018).

This chapter, however, aims to be both theoretically informed and empirically based. Hence, it is necessary to acknowledge a methodological starting point: Although the purpose of this chapter is conceptual rather than historical, the interpretative mode is inspired by the concepts of genealogical and archaeological analyses, as developed by Michel Foucault in *Discipline and Punish* (first published 1975).

The remainder of this chapter falls into two parts. First, I investigate historical trajectories or genealogies. According to Foucault, a genealogy is a "complex web of continuities and discontinuities" (Foucault 1977:x) that is produced by varying social and political conditions. Beginning with the continuities, I emphasize the special role of veterans in the history of rehabilitation.

Second, after an explication of the concept of liability, I investigate what Foucault called archaeologies: Investigations of discourses as such, emphasizing the underlying structures he once called the "positive unconscious of knowledge" (Foucault 1992:xi). While the genealogical analyses investigate manifest historical changes – be they political, institutional, or terminological – archaeological analyses deal with logics or connections that are decisive to the phenomena we investigate without being fully expressed.

First genealogy: The particular importance of veterans

Throughout history, states have mostly been un-compellable, or at least un-compelled, to provide rehabilitation services. While this suggests that the provision of rehabilitation is what Foucault called a discontinuity, there is at least one important exception: Veterans. While disability has not always warranted services or benefits, the acquired disabilities of veterans have consistently warranted compensation throughout Western history (Ridgway 2011:137–139).

Several systematic reviews of historical research also detail how veterans play a particular role in the history of rehabilitation medicine: "Rehabilitation services have developed partly in association with war and the experience of rehabilitating war casualties supplied valuable principles and practices to the broader practice of rehabilitation medicine" (Eldar & Jelić 2003:1019). While this is not the place for broad discussions – as the history and social significance is a complex theme in its own right, both in rehabilitation research and in disability studies, it is nevertheless useful to look briefly at three genealogical examples.

First, it is useful to look at the history of rehabilitation hospitals. Opened in 1671 and still a site of rehabilitation services 350 years later, the *Hotel des Invalides* in Paris has a wide institutional and political *Wirkungsgeschichte*, not least since many other hospitals were "modeled upon" this throughout the 17th, 18th, and 19th centuries (England 1944). Examples include various European and American institutions such as the *Royal Hospital for Seamen* founded in 1691 (Hudson 2007:256–258), and the Pennsylvania Hospital founded in 1752 (Baker 2008:3). This monumental hospital also has a prominent place in the history of rehabilitation medicine, housing important pioneers like Dominique Jean Larrey, but is not located alongside other medical services. Instead, it is located next to the mausoleum for French military leaders (Bold 2001). In this historical situation, rehabilitation services were provided in response only to disabilities related to war. This had at least two implications: The presence of disability was not sufficient to belong in the *Hotel des Invalides*, and services were provided to veterans at the same time as they were withheld from other people with disabilities even if those were in greater need than (some of) the veterans.

Second, it is interesting to analyze the history of disability sports, particularly the "early" periods before disability issues were politicized in the 1970s. From an institutional standpoint, it is rooted in the establishment of sports rehabilitation after WW1 (Orr 1981). While this early era is often overlooked, it nevertheless testifies to a special relation among war, disability, and sports. According to

Reismüller and Parry, this "pre-history" is effectively "evidence of sporting activity in response to the exigencies of the First World War" (2017:82). After a decline in the 1930s, disability sports regained prominence after WW2. Regarding the history of disability sports in Europe, and not least the history of the Paralympics, the games at Stoke Mandeville hospital (first held in 1948) are crucial. The first games were held in 1948, only 4 years after Ludwig Guttman established a new clinical unit to "provide cutting-edge clinical treatment and rehabilitation for servicemen and servicewomen who sustained spinal cord injuries during World War II" (Wedgwood 2014:130). It is also worth noting that the most important US organization, the National Wheelchair Athletic Association, was founded by WW2 veterans and given a more formal status after the Korean War in 1956 (Fleming 1984). It is no doubt that these developments – *the days of Jim Winthers*, so to speak – helped to create what is now a very important arena for many groups of people with disabilities. From a genealogical perspective, however, it is worth remembering how veterans "were the only disabled skiers in those days" (Pringle 1999:44).

Third, veterans are also important in the historical development of an important example of assistive technology: Motorized wheelchairs. The first modern electric wheelchair was developed by the Canadian engineer George Klein, who specifically developed it for WW2 veterans (Woods & Watson 2003). From a political standpoint, it is worth noting that this technology was neither owned nor funded by health- or disability-related agencies. Instead, both innovation and results were the property of the Canadian Department of Veteran Affairs. The wheelchair manufacturer, Everest & Jennings, was also heavily involved in programs for WW2 veterans (Tremblay 1996).

In line with the increasing politicization of disability issues from 1960 onward, electric wheelchairs became more associated with participation, community, and even pride, and less associated with health-related contexts. From the 1960s, and still today, the electric wheelchair is often considered "a symbol of freedom" (Stenberg et al. 2016:388). While the aesthetics of mobility devices moved away from a traditional "medical" style, and increasingly resembled motorbikes or leisure vehicles, Karen Fritch still documents that the research and development in this period was "prompted" by "the impaired veterans of the Vietnam War in the 1960s and 1970s" (2013:138). Like many technologies, rehabilitation technologies developed out of the trials of war.

In a time when disability issues are increasingly "universalized" or "mainstreamed," for instance in light of the CRPD, it is also worth noting that veterans continue to hold special importance. Even if there are very few clinical indicators that set veterans apart from related groups such as people with multitrauma from accidents, the particular role of veterans remains throughout the provision of medical rehabilitation services. According to their webpage, Veterans Administration (VA) medical facilities remain "the United States' largest integrated health care system." Similarly, veterans continue to hold special importance for disability sports in the United States: Move United (the present name of the NWAA) delivers a specific program for veterans – the

Move United Warfighters Ambassador program – and the National Veterans Wheelchair Games is still in operation. Finally, the VA and other military entities continue to be an important funding source for research on electric wheelchairs and other forms of mobility technology (Kelleher et al. 2017; Candiotti et al. 2019).

Specific systems notwithstanding, the world of rehabilitation has arguably left behind the stage where veterans were more "worthy" than other people with disabilities. Nevertheless, genealogies have considerable *inertia*: They continue to shape understanding and practices, even if we try to change their direction. Hence, I argue that (1) the notion of the veteran continues to be important, and (2) it can inform our understanding of several underexplored aspects of the world of rehabilitation.

Second genealogy: Disability as a welfare state category

If the provision of rehabilitation is a form of compensation, then the welfare state somehow accepts responsibility. Hence, the analysis of how states come to provide rehabilitation services is effectively an analysis of the workings of the welfare state. Without moving too deep into the genealogy of welfare states, which is too wide a subject for this context, it is nevertheless useful to make a few connections to a cornerstone in the study of that genealogy: Deborah Stone's now canonical *The Disabled State* (1984).

Most of all, Stone demonstrates the importance of the category of disability: "it is something like a keystone that allows the other supporting structures of the welfare system and, in some sense, the economy at large to remain in place" (1984:12). Moreover, she also relates the development of welfare states to liability:

> Disability programs are at bottom a social mechanism for compensating people in need. There are basically two ways society can compensate people it deems needy: it can impose liability, which means identifying someone as responsible for the need and shifting the costs to that party; or it can set up public insurance or welfare programs that diffuse the costs to society at large. (1984:191–192)

Stone considers disability benefits – and, by extension, disability-related services such as rehabilitation services – in at least two ways. They can be considered as "work-based distribution" in some contexts, and as "needs-based distribution" in others. She defines the first "system" as *primary* and the latter as *secondary* (1984:10).

Stone's point here is genealogical. Rather than tracing the various responses to a "stable" phenomenon (disability), she traces the expansion of the disability category as a driving shaft in the history of the welfare states. So doing, she also emphasizes a historical and still ongoing "dynamic of definitional expansion" (1984:14). Very briefly put, she traces a 19th (and early 20th) century expansion

– including people with work-related disabilities alongside veterans – before investigating various expansions during the 20th century.

The 19th-century socio-political category of people with disabilities – and, thereby, the distribution of rehabilitation services – depended upon modes of production. Stone demonstrates that disability-related provisions were first provided not to all people who live with a disability, but to those who met two criteria: (a) a past as a non-disabled person, and (b) an onset of disability for which either the state or another party were somehow culpable.

Criterion (a) is crucial to the development. Stone details, for instance, how both German and US disability policies moved beyond veterans to include people with work-related disabilities while keeping this criterion in place until the 1960s. Criterion (b), similarly, was in operation until the reforms implemented by the Adenauer government in 1957. While it is no longer an absolute requirement, it still has gravity, there is still "[a] whole set of programs in both Europe and the United States is based on disabilities caused by work" (1984:5).

Stone explores the importance of these criteria not only by way of policy analysis but also by tracing "the transformation of the idea of 'inability to work' into the clinical concept of impairment" (1984:109). While criteria (a) and (b) are no longer absolute requirements for the provision of rehabilitation services, our categories or a "validating devices" (1984:21) are still translations of those criteria.

Stone's work demonstrates that the notion of *disabled people as veterans*, and the notion of liability, are far from specific to the context of veterans. On the contrary, the notion of veteranness was crucial to the gradual development of the welfare state in the 19th and 20th centuries and remain important today.

Disability, veterans, and liability

These genealogical variations demonstrate that rehabilitation services – and other disability-related provisions – emerged in context where a third party was somehow responsible: War is *waged by states*, who then force it upon its citizens (by conscription, mobilization, or other political and institutional arrangements). Hence, state liability (or, perhaps, state culpability) can hardly be denied. It was on this basis that veterans became "the worthiest to be relived" throughout modernity (Lagemann 2020). Similarly, rehabilitation services as work-based distribution emerged through acknowledgment of employer liability.

Since liability is primarily a legal term, I begin explicating the theoretical springboard by the often-cited definition of liability from *Black's Law Dictionary*:

1 Bound or obliged in law or equity; responsible; chargeable; answerable; compellable to make satisfaction, compensation, or restitution.
2 Exposed or subject to a given contingency, risk or casualty, which is more or less probable.

As we can see, "liability" is used in two different senses that might seem contrary to each other. On the one hand, the term denotes responsibility for some kind of adverse event (meaning 1). On the other hand, it also denotes the risk or probability of such events (meaning 2). Combining these two senses, I begin by arguing that rehabilitation comes to take place when the state becomes answerable and willing to *compensate* for an important and unpredictable "risk or casualty": Disability.

First, it is important to note that the notion of liability entails the notion of "restitution." This implies, first, that liability is more than a normative admittance of culpability: If you accept liability, you also accept responsibility for a certain social action – the compensating act that somehow restores the part at peril.

Second, the concept of liability lets us position disability as a "casualty" for which one or more parties are "chargeable," that is, *culpable*. It is also clear that the liable party is somehow "answerable." In social theory, "charges" and "answers" are most often discussed in the context of Jürgen Habermas' work (Nielsen 2012; Murphy 2020). In line with a Habermasian impulse, I interpret the "restitution" – that is, the actual provision of rehabilitation services – as a matter for deliberation: To the extent that rehabilitation is a form of compensation, that compensation is determined by various forms of dialogue or negotiation (Brodkin 2020).

Third, it is important to note the terminological roots of "liability." According to the *Oxford English Dictionary*, the term is rooted in the medieval Latin term *ligabilis*. While the OED explains the Latin term as meaning "that which can be bound," the *Oxford Latin Dictionary* demonstrates that the root – the verb *ligo* – is transitive: It denotes active acts such as "bind, tie, fasten" and "unite."

This etymology allows us to separate the specific notion of liability from general notions of culpability: Culpability follows directly from the "risk or casualty," regardless of bonds. Liability, on the other hand, takes place when an agent or entity is *made* responsible for something for which it *might not* have taken responsibility. This *binding* is often overlooked but demonstrates that the development and provision of rehabilitation services is an active and highly political choice.

First archeology: Naming rehabilitation

While Foucault's *Discipline and Punish* argues that archeology deals with the unconscious of knowledge', his later book *L'usage des Plaisirs* (1984) elaborates the notion further. Naming archeology a 'philosophical excercise', Foucault argues that thought can *think its own history* and thereby disenfranchise itself from "what it thinks silently" (1992:15). For such work, terminology is often a fruitful starting point. As many rehabilitation researchers have pointed out, the English term *rehabilitation* is rooted in the Latin noun *rehabilitatio* (Buetow et al. 2020; Timm et al. 2021), it is useful to explore these two terms.

The *Oxford English Dictionary* defines the term rehabilitation as "restoration of a person to normal health or activity after injury, illness, disablement or addiction." This definition emerged in the 19th century. It is also true that the definition applies to other domains, such as the restoration of material objects, buildings, or urban areas. The original sense of the term, however, emerged in the 15th and 16th centuries:

> The restoration of a person to former privileges, status, or possessions by official decree, declaration, etc. [...] (occasionally) *spec.* formal restoration to communion with the Roman Catholic Church.

This etymology suggests that the term rehabilitation originally denotes a response to disability as if disability was a *downfall*. Hence, the term also presupposes a hypothetical, original state of non-disability (Hanisch 2014). Even if we use the term "rehabilitation" in contexts where this downfall may seem irrelevant – for instance, in the context of pediatric rehabilitation – the prefix *re-* demonstrates that a notion of something restorative often remains.

This terminology opens at least two aspects that are often silent. First, the element of restoration unveils the importance of previous recognition. The hypothetical state of non-disability is neither universal nor socially neutral, but socially embedded: Without prior recognition, a "restoration to former privileges, status or possessions" cannot take place. In this sense, the provision of rehabilitation services depends upon both current and previous social recognition.

Second, the act of rehabilitation is itself an act of re-inclusion. *Rehabilitatio* is rooted in the adjective *habilis*. According to the *Oxford Latin Dictionary*, this term thus can be defined:

1 Able to do, possess, maintain.
2 Having the competence or power to do something.
3 Suitable, fitting, apt, proper.

As the root of the English terms *able* and *ability* – and thereby of many terms surrounding disability – this Latin adjective is very important. This etymology indicates that ability – the goal of rehabilitation, but also the opposite of disability – is a matter of match between a person and a situation. In other words, the provision of rehabilitation – which traditionally or "consciously" is seen as an instrumentalist and individualized act – is a relational matter of *making fit*.

The tree senses of the Latin adjective correspond to common terms in rehabilitation research: The ability "to do, possess, maintain" resembles *self-efficacy* (Picha & Howell 2018). To give "competence or power to do something" points toward *empowerment* (Dastyar & Mohammadi 2019). Finally, the notion of people with disabilities becoming "suitable" or "fitting" echoes the so-called *social turn* in rehabilitation, wherein services are provided with the ambition of "designing physical and social environments that welcome diversity in human functioning" (Solvang et al. 2017:1983).

This archeology is, perhaps, easy to dismiss: At least in the more "critical" strands of rehabilitation research, one might argue that this is an archeology of *repairment*, and hence ends up reinforcing the traditional understanding of rehabilitation as an instrumentalist and individualized act. However, I argue that both terms (the English *rehabilitation* and the Latin *rehabilitatio*) encompass a view of rehabilitation as welcoming someone or allowing someone to be *in the right place*. This etymology suggests that rehabilitation is not only about "repairment" or "improvement," but about facilitating belonging.

Second archeology: Naming welfare state services

Often modeled after Bismarck's *Krankenversicherungsgesetz*, most welfare states developed and became rights-based under the name of *insurance*. While this might seem as little more than a terminological remainder, linking contemporary services to the earlier history of European welfare states, it is worth noting that it is remarkably persistent: Across otherwise very different welfare states, the welfare states define their provisions as "disability insurance" in English, "Krankenversicherung" in German, or "asurance invalidité" in French. Even the Norwegian welfare state, which is often considered particularly "universalist" in its approach to both rehabilitation and welfare provisions in general, links its disability-related benefits to "Membership in the National Insurance Scheme" (NAV 2021). To the extent that rehabilitation is funded and provided within these schemes of insurance, the rehabilitation services are examples of *premium*.

In legal theory, insurance is fundamentally related to liability: The "satisfaction, compensation or restitution" that liability entails are normally regulated by contractual relations. It is, therefore, useful to return to *Black's Law Dictionary*, which identifies insurance as:

> A contract by which one party (the *insurer*) undertakes to indemnify another party (the *insured*) against the risk of loss, damage or liability arising from the occurrence of some specified contingency. [...] the agreed consideration [is often called] the "premium"; the written contract, a "policy"; the events insured against, "risks" or "perils"; and the subject, right, or interest to be protected, the "insurable interest."

To some extent, disability can be considered a "specified contingency," and there is no doubt that life with a disability sometimes entails *perils*. And it is equally clear that important aspects of the good life with a disability – such as social participation, or some other realization of citizenship – are an *insurable interest*.

The notion of insurance allows us to shed light on the importance of political recognition. By providing rehabilitation services, the state does more than "indemnify" the various problems that characterize life with a disability. The state also makes people with disabilities "the *insured*" by way of a contract. Hence, the provision depends upon "policy," both in the legal and in the more general sense.

Finally, the notion of specified contingency does more than position people with disabilities as people living with *perils*. However embryonic, this word allows us to de-naturalize the "problems," "challenges," or "troubles" often associated with disabilities. According to the *Oxford English Dictionary*, a peril is a danger or risk – something that, depending upon situational circumstances – might or might not take place.

When most countries name rehabilitation services insurance provisions, or locate them within systems named "insurance" in various ways, which is far from coincidental. In short, terminological "unconscious aspects" give two clues as to how the provision of rehabilitation services comes about: (1) Rehabilitation responds to what rehabilitation professionals call "functional problems," but unconsciously not least to *risks*, and (2) Rehabilitation expresses not only the recognition of needs but also the recognition of "original" – "pre-disability" – aspects of each person. The latter clue points towards intersectional aspects: As rehabilitation researchers, we must acknowledge that rehabilitation responds not only to disability but also to the loss of "privileges, status, or possessions" that other social markers indicate.

Provision and non-provision

In order to understand how rehabilitation services take place we must also understand how they often do not take place. The definition of insurance from *Black's Law Dictionary* is even more useful in that respect: The notions of liability and insurance shed light not only on the provision but also on the non-provision of rehabilitation. To explore this relation – in effect, cases where disability warrants rehabilitation services to a lesser degree than one might expect – at least three indications are worth mentioning.

First, the notion of state liability – as a situation where the state is "chargeable; answerable; [or] compellable" to provide rehabilitation services – implies that the state may deny responsibility: Empirical research confirms that denial of state responsibility or societal culpability does influence the provision of rehabilitation services. Disabilities related to so-called "lifestyle diseases" tend to have a particularly low "illness prestige" (Grue et al. 2015), and the people living with these less "communicable" disabilities have less access to rehabilitation than comparable groups (Wiklund 2016; Garg et al. 2020). Moreover, systematic reviews demonstrate that refugees and immigrants are provided with a lower level of rehabilitation services (Klein & von dem Knesebeck 2018; Shabnam et al. 2022) – almost as if the culpability of another state or society would make the present society less "answerable."

Second, the notion of "specified contingency" suggests that some situations might fall outside the contractual relation through which the state accepts liability and thereby comes to provide rehabilitation services. In my view, this is exactly what happens when the lack of medical "specification" – that is, diagnosis, prognosis, medical explanation, etc. – leads to a lack of services: It is well known that the so-called "medically unexplained" disabilities such as fibromyalgia or chronic fatigue syndrome are less addressed by rehabilitation services than otherwise comparable problems (Wiklund et al. 2016; Deslauriers et al. 2019).

Third, the insurance concept of "insurable interest" might suggest that you get more compensation if there is *more at stake*. When the *Oxford English Dictionary* defines rehabilitation as the restoration "to former privileges, status, or possessions," we can glimpse that the provision of rehabilitation services is bound up with larger patterns of social injustice. It is well documented, for instance, that social class influences the provision of rehabilitation services (OECD 2019; Bystrup et al. 2022). Similarly, we know that people with learning disabilities have less access to medical rehabilitation than others, likely due to the low social status associated with cognitive impairments (Gibson & O'Connor 2010; Bright & Kuper 2018).

These three examples indicate that the provision of rehabilitation services can be considered a "premium" that compensates for the "specified contingency" we call disability. Moreover, they indicate that these provisions are not "automatic" – in the sense that they follow directly from disability or challenges in one's life – but depend upon negotiations within a social and political contract. These negotiations are not only historical preconditions (as in genealogical analyses) or underlying conditions (as in archeological analyses). In my view, they are ongoing practices that continue to shape the provision of rehabilitation services.

Conclusion: Rehabilitation is compensation for the perils of a disabling society

The genealogical and archaeological analyses allow me to formulate the argument of this chapter in a way that is simultaneously more technical and more explicit:

1. The historical development of rehabilitation services seems to depend upon the state becoming answerable, first in the case of veterans and then in the context of work-related disability.
2. Disability does not become grounds for rehabilitation as an embodied *fact*, but as a contingent relational phenomenon.
3. Crucially, the understanding of contingency also implies that someone or something might be culpable.
4. This requirement comes to light not only as rehabilitation services are provided but also when they are not provided.

So far, I have tried to unearth theoretical terms that are not particularly "critical" – it is my argument that they can be supported by way of "ordinary" terms, be they legal or historical.

However, this is not to set this argument apart from more canonical traditions or arguments in disability studies. To demonstrate this, it is sufficient to relate the argument to the roots of the UK social model of disability, the UPIAS *Fundamental Principles of Disability* (1976). There, disability is defined:

> In our view it is society which disables physically impaired people. Disability is something imposed on top of our impairments by the way we are unnecessarily isolated and excluded from full participation in society. [...] Thus, we define [...] disability as the disadvantage or restriction of activity caused by a contemporary social organisation which takes no or little account of people who have physical impairments and thus excludes them from the mainstream of social activities. (UPIAS 1976:14–15).

Building on the argument presented in this chapter, I also argue that this tradition constitutes a liability argument. This is important, not least since the UK social model tradition continues to hold importance for such diverse and influential scholars as Karen Whalley Hammell (2015), Carol Thomas (Simpson & Thomas 2015), and Jan D. Reinhard (Solvang et al. 2017).

UPIAS' concept of "a contemporary social organisation" is explicitly a concept of contingency. Hence, it dovetails with liability-related notions such as "a given contingency, risk or casualty" in *Black's Law Dictionary*. Moreover, the words "unnecessarily isolated and excluded" imply that disability and disabling processes are not only *unfortunate* but an unnecessary phenomenon for which something or someone is culpable.

UPIAS also underlines how the contemporary social organization (or structure) "takes no or little account of people who have physical impairments." These terms suggest that UPIAS – and many contributions in the following decades – give social structures some kind of active agency. This rhetorical figure, a *prosopopoeia*, sheds light on how liability becomes liable. Even if different research frontiers related in vocabulary and theoretical organizations, they all use terminologies where the contemporary social organization – sometimes known as "society," "context," or "environment" – becomes *a party*. Thereby, society (represented by the state) also becomes liable and "compellable to make satisfaction, compensation or restitution" in the form of rehabilitation services.

This resonance with the disability studies canon allows for a crucial and final point, which is not necessarily dependent upon the concept of liability: People with disabilities are not only veterans from life in a disabling society. People with disabilities are also veterans of life in a society that could have been different, meaning that the social majority is *answerable* for the society's disabling structure. It is in this sense that the social majority can recognize its culpability, and thereby institutionalize rehabilitation as the stable systems we know today.

References

Buetow, S. A., Kapur, N., & Wolbring, G. (2020). From rehabilitation to ultrabilitation: Moving forward, *Disability and Rehabilitation*, 42(11), 1487–1489. doi:10.1080/09638288.2019.1620873

Baikovs, A., & Zariņš, I. (2013). Philosophical, legal and general issues of legal liability. *Entrepreneurship and Sustainability Issues*, 1(1), 23–36.

Baker, R. R. (2008). Benefits for veterans: A historical context and overview of the current situation. In N. D. Ainspan & W. E. Penk (eds.), *Returning wars' wounded, injured and ill: A reference handbook*. Westport: Praeger International.

Bickenbach, J., Sabariego, C., & Stucki, G. (2021). Beneficiaries of Rehabilitation. *Archives of Physical Medicine and Rehabilitation*, 102(3), 543–548. doi:10.1016/j.apmr.2020.09.392

Bold, J. (2001). Comparable institutions: The Royal Hospital for Seamen and the Hôtel des Invalides. *Architectural History*, 44, 136–144.

Bright, T., & Kuper, H. (2018). A systematic review of access to general healthcare services for people with disabilities in low- and middle-income countries. *International Journal of Environmental Research and Public Health*, 15(9), 1879. doi:10.3390/ijerph15091879

Brodkin, E. Z. (2020). Discretion in the welfare state. In T. Evans & P. Hupe (eds.), *Discretion and the Quest for Controlled Freedom*. Cham: Palgrave Macmillan. doi:10.1007/978-3-030-19566-3_5

Burri, S. (2021). Defensive liability: A matter of rights enforcement, not distributive justice. *Criminal Law, Philosophy*. doi:10.1007/s11572-021-09591-8

Bystrup, M. R., Hindhede, A. L., Pallesen, H., Aadal, L., & Larsen, K. (2022). Unequal neurorehabilitation trajectories – a longitudinal case study combining field structures with social class–based capital conversion. *Health Sociology Review*. doi:10.1080/14461242.2021.2007161

Candiotti, J. L., Kamaraj, D. C., Daveler, B., Chung, C.-S., Grindle, G. G., Cooper, R., & Cooper, R. A. (2019). Usability evaluation of a novel robotic power wheelchair for indoor and outdoor navigation. *Archives of Physical Medicine and Rehabilitation*, 100 (4), 627–637. doi:10.1016/j.apmr.2018.07.432

Dastyar, V., & Mohammadi, A. (2019). Investigating the empowerment of the physically-handicapped people and its related factors: A cross-sectional analytical study in Kohgiluyeh and Boyer-Ahmad Province in 2015. *jrehab*, 19(4), 354–369.

Deslauriers, S., Roy, J. S., Bernatsky, S., Feldman, D. E., Pinard, A. M., Desmeules, F., Fitzcharles, M. A., & Perreault, K. (2019, July 30). Factors associated with waiting times for persons with rheumatic conditions in multidisciplinary pain treatment facilities. *Journal of Pain Research*, 12, 2379–2390. doi: 10.2147/JPR.S206519

Eldar, R., & Jelić, M. (2003). The association of rehabilitation and war. *Disability and Rehabilitation*, 25(18), 1019–1023. doi:10.1080/0963828031000137739

Foucault, M. (1977). *Discipline and punish: The birth of the prison*. New York: Random House.

Foucault, M. (1992). *The history of sexuality volume 2: The use of pleasure*. London: Penguin Books.

Fleming, A. (1984). The national wheelchair athletic association. *Journal of Physical Education, Recreation & Dance*, 55(2), 38–39.

Garg, A., Skempes, D., & Bickenbach, J. (2020). Legal and regulatory approaches to rehabilitation planning: A concise overview of current laws and policies addressing access to rehabilitation in five European countries. *International Journal of Environmental Research and Public Health*, 17(12), 4363. doi:10.3390/ijerph17124363

Gibson, J., & O'Connor, R. (2010). Access to health care for disabled people: A systematic review. *Social Care and Neurodisability*, 1(3), 21–31. doi:10.5042/scn.2010.0599

Grue, J., Johannessen, L. E. F., & Rasmussen, E. F. (2015). Prestige rankings of chronic diseases and disabilities. A survey among professionals in the disability field. *Social Science & Medicine*, 124, 180–186.

Hammell, K. W. (2015), Quality of life, participation and occupational rights: A capabilities perspective. *Australian Occupational Therapy Journal*, 62, 78–85. doi:10.1111/1440-1630.12183

Hanisch, H. (2014). Recognizing disability. In J. E. Bickenback, F. Felder, & B. Schmitz (eds.), *Disability and the good human life*. Cambridge: Cambridge University Press.

Hudson, G. L. (2007). Internal influences in the making of the english military hospital: The early-eighteenth-century Greenwich.*In British Military and Naval Medicine, 1600–1830*. (pp. 253–272). Brill.

Kelleher, A., Dicianno, B. E., Eckstein, S., Schein, R., Pearlman, J., & Cooper, R. A. (2017). Consumer feedback to steer the future of assistive technology research and development: A pilot study. *Topics in Spinal Cord Injury Rehabilitation*, 23(2), 89–97. doi:10.1310/sci2302-89

Kim, J. H., McMahon, B. T., Hawley, C. *et al.* (2016). Psychosocial adaptation to chronic illness and disability: A virtue based model. *Journal of Occupational Rehabilitation*, 26, 45–55. doi:10.1007/s10926-015-9622-1

Klein, J., & von dem Knesebeck, O. (2018). Inequalities in health care utilization among migrants and non-migrants in Germany: A systematic review. *International Journal for Equity in Health*, 17, 160. doi:10.1186/s12939-018-0876-z

Kleiner, M. J., Kinsella, E. A., Miciak, M., Teachman, G., & Walton, D. M. (2022). "Passion to do the right thing": searching for the 'good' in physiotherapist practice. *Physiotherapy Theory and Practice*, 1–16. 10.1080/09593985.2022.2116740

Lagemann, A. (2020). The worthiest to be relieved disabled veterans in England, c. 1580–1630. In D. Hitchcock & J. McClure (eds.), *The Routledge history of poverty, c.1450–1800* (1st ed.). Routledge. doi:10.4324/9781315149271

Martin, F. W. (1975). A philosophical perspective on leisure services for the disabled. *Journal of Physical Education and Recreation*, 46(5), 25–27. doi:10.1080/00971170.1975.10610878

Murphy, M. (2020). Public sector accountability and the contradictions of the regulatory state. *Administrative Theory & Praxis*, 42(4), 517–530. doi:10.1080/10841806.2019.1700455

NAV (Arbeid- og velferdsetaten). (2021). https://www.nav.no/en/home/rules-and-regulations/membership-of-the-national-insurance-scheme

Nielsen, G. M. (2012). *The norms of answerability. Social theory between Bakhtin and Habermas*. New York: SUNY Press.

OECD. (2019). *Health for everyone?: Social inequalities in health and health systems*. OECD Health Policy Studies.

Orr, R. E. (1981). Changing attitudes: Toward wheelchair ahletics. *Journal of Physical Education and Recreation*, 52(6), 40-41.

Picha, K. J., & Howell, D. M. (2018). A model to increase rehabilitation adherence to home exercise programmes in patients with varying levels of self-efficacy. *Musculoskeletal Care*, 16, 233–237. doi:10.1002/msc.1194

Pringle, D. (1999). Skiing for individuals with disabilities–A beginning, *Palaestra*, 15, 1.

Rioux, M. H. & Riddle, C. A. (2010). Values in disability policy and law: Equality. *In Critical Perspectives on Human Rights and Disability Law* (pp. 37-55). Brill Nijhoff.

Ridgway, J. D. (2011). The splendid isolation revisited: Lessons from the history of veterans' benefits before judicial review. *The Veterans Law Review*, 3, 135.

Shabnam, J., Timm, H. U., & Nielsen, D. S. *et al*. (2022). Palliative care utilization among non-Western migrants in Europe: A systematic review. *Journal of Immigrant and Minority Health*, 24, 237–255. doi:10.1007/s10903-021-01302-8

Shakespeare, T., Cooper, H., Bezmez, D., & Poland, F. (2018). Rehabilitation as a disability equality issue: A conceptual shift for disability studies?, *Social Inclusion*, 6(1), 61–72. doi:10.17645/si.v6i1.1175

Simpson, J. & Thomas, C. (2015). Clinical psychology and disability studies: Bridging the disciplinary divide on mental health and disability. *Disability and Rehabilitation*, 37(14), 1299–1304. doi:10.3109/09638288.2014.961656

Solvang, P. K., Hanisch, H., & Reinhardt, J. D. (2017). The rehabilitation research matrix: Producing knowledge at micro, meso, and macro levels. *Disability and Rehabilitation*, 39(19), 1983–1989. doi:10.1080/09638288.2016.1212115

Stenberg, G., Henje, C., Levi, R., & Lindström, M. (2016). Living with an electric wheelchair – the user perspective. *Disability and Rehabilitation*: Assistive Technology, 11(5), 385–394. doi:10.3109/17483107.2014.968811

Stucki, G., Ewert, T., & Cieza, A. (2002). Value and application of the ICF in rehabilitation medicine. *Disability and Rehabilitation*, 24(17), 932–938. doi:10.1080/09638280210148594

Timm H., Thuesen J., & Clark D. (2021, July 2). Rehabilitation and palliative care: Histories, dialectics and challenges. *Wellcome Open Research*, 6, 171. doi:10.12688/wellcomeopenres.16979.1

Tremblay, M. (1996). Going back to Civvy street: A historical account of the impact of the Everest and Jennings wheelchair for Canadian World War II veterans with spinal cord injury. *Disability & Society*, 11(2), 149–170. doi:10.1080/09687599650023209

Wedgwood, N. (2014). Hahn versus Guttmann: Revisiting 'sports and the political movement of disabled persons'. *Disability & Society*, 29(1), 129–142. doi:10.1080/09687599.2013.776488

Wiklund, M., Fjellman-Wiklund, A., Stålnacke, B.-M., Hammarström, A., & Lehti, A. (2016). Access to rehabilitation: Patient perceptions of inequalities in access to specialty pain rehabilitation from a gender and intersectional perspective. *Global Health Action*, 9(1). doi:10.3402/gha.v9.31542

Woods, B., & Watson, N. (2003). A short history of powered wheelchairs. *Assistive Technology*, 15(2), 164–180. doi:10.1080/10400435.2003.10131900

Interlude 1
Life is possible

Stig Langvad

When I was 16, my life took a dramatic change because of a traumatic spinal cord injury after a traffic accident in 1973. Life looked bad. Looking back over almost 50 years, I can say life has been okay and perhaps more than just okay. The main reason has been the availability of new necessary individual support.

I was born in 1956 by parents from the low working class who were excellent parents but not financially well off. My father was often unemployed. My mother stayed home and took care of us two children. She did not enter the labor market before the late 1960s. She was only employed halftime. Most of the time we had meat to eat, but it did not happen every day. Nothing indicated that the direction of my life would be any different from my personal ambition of becoming an aircraft mechanic after elementary school.

On August 11, 1973 at 11:35 PM, I crashed on my small motorbike without license plate and no driving license. I had a little alcohol in my blood after some beers. I knew it was stupid and against the law, but I was young and thought I was invulnerable and could conquer the world. Because of the accident, I had a spinal cord injury (C4), not 100% complete. My life turned upside down.

My new life started hospitalized for 12 months in a special rehab center for persons with spinal cord injury; and coming out from rehab being able to stand a little but not use my arms or hands very much. I became a full-time user of a power wheelchair and required support 24/7. Now life really began. Everything was new. I felt alone, even though everyone and especially my parents supported me at this stage.

All the big questions came up. How does life look from the perspective of a young boy at 16 years and with a brand new spinal cord injury?

The first major questions were where to live, with whom to live, and how to live? – not many options in Denmark. An independent living scheme (IL) was not available. I could choose to live with my mum and dad, which they actually and luckily thought would be a very bad idea. I could get a two-room sheltered flat with attached staff at the local nursing home together with a high number of very old persons. The third option was a 12-m^2 room at an institution for young persons with mobility impairment, no individual toilet

DOI: 10.4324/9781003052708-5

and shower. I choose to live in an institution for young persons. Here I could find assistance 24/7 but only after sharing with 25 others. I could participate in leisure activities but usually in a group with all or some of the others from the institution. I could get up in the morning and go to bed in the evening; but always coordinated with what others wanted and the staff was able to provide. It was a life of structure and limitations, but it was not all bad. I stayed there 3½ years, from August 1, 1974 to January 14, 1978. This date is my liberation date.

A few days after moving in at the institution, I started high school. It was the only accessible high school in my hometown at that time! It was an ordinary but scary moment. I was a new student and with a mobility impairment, delivered at the gate by the driver from the institution, without knowing anyone and not having someone accompanying me. It looked scary but became a time that I look back upon with great satisfaction. Reflecting after almost 50 years, it might have been my luck not to have an "outsider" assisting me. Being alone and depending on assistance from other students eliminated the establishment of psychological barriers between us – they simply had to assist me. I was indeed feeling included in both study and leisure activities. Assistance was available when, for example, I needed to go pee; I did not wait, as far as I remember. Today it would not be possible to live the life that I do without my IL (24/7), but back then, I strongly believe that it could have created an invisible wall between me and the other classmates. I even had my first girlfriend after the injury, one of the young girls from my class. A very nice and good-looking girl. It was not all a walk in the park. The rest of my day was very institutionalized and limited in self-control and possibilities.

In June 1977, I graduated high school and had to decide where and what to study. In September 1977, I started studying Political Science at the University of Aarhus. It was new for me. It was new for the faculty. It was necessary to create a new pathway through the park to get around without using the stairs; and there was a need for establishing an accessible toilet (in the basement next to the parked bicycles). Studying at university was quite different from following classes in high school. Much more to read. Mixed teams of classmates depending on the subject of classes. Less structure of the day. All of us had grown older and we had become more settled in life. Life in an institution no longer fulfilled my needs. My room was too small. My life was much more unstructured and spontaneous. My fellow students were less familiar to me and thereby not to the same extent available for assistance. My life needed a change.

The Municipality of Aarhus had luckily developed an IL available for persons with extensive mobility impairment. On January 14, 1978, I moved to my own-room flat with my own IL. I needed 8 hours of assistance during the day. Today, I need 24/7/365. I was for the first time able to choose who should assist me, for what purpose and when. Life became much more flexible and self-determined.

The fight for improvement of IL has always been one of my main objectives in my disability political career. The wages and working conditions were in the beginning very bad for the personal assistants; but during the last 50 years, they have been equalizing compared to the rest of the labor market. We are not there yet, but things have improved over time. In the beginning, IL was only for the few and somehow it has not been possible to ensure IL for all of those who need it to live the life they want and with necessary support. IL has lost political momentum. Politicians and civil servants are challenging IL. They do not see personal potential but only public expenditures. In the 1970s, politicians and civil servants were proud of IL; now they only see limitations and the disability movement is not able to find the right arguments for maintaining and improving IL. On September 11, 2001, my municipality negotiated the first agreement on standardized and reasonable wage and work conditions. This agreement covered all municipalities in Denmark.

Being able to live independently turned the world upside down and made it possible for me to continue to study and graduate after almost 7 years with a Master of Political Science. I was ready to go to work where they wanted my competences and personality. I knew it would probably not be easy to get employment; but I never doubted that I would succeed; and on January 2, 1985, I got my first job in the Department for Social Affairs but in my municipality as political adviser to the "Social Mayor." I have been in the labor market ever since.

With my personal assistants, I could perform as anyone else in a similar job position. I achieved respect for filling the position and being able to meet and be active in all parts of the municipality and within the majority of its office buildings. I remember once having a discussion with my secretary at the office on persons with disability where she claimed: "They have a disability but you do not!" She did not see mine any more.

I resigned my municipality employment on April 30, 1997 because I was feeling more and more physically fatigued, which had been the situation since I came back from a trip lasting 3 weeks to Japan in spring 1996 followed by a trip of 3 weeks to the United States in autumn 1996.

I thought that my working life had ended, and I was feeling sad. Then something turned up which changed my life. I became more engaged in national disability politics through Disabled Peoples' Organisations Denmark (DPOD). In May 1998, I became vice chair to DPOD and in 2000 chair. DPOD represents all kinds of disabilities in Denmark. It has been around since 1934. The position demanded that I live 3 days a week in Copenhagen and 4 days in Aarhus, and was a significant change in life routines. Not just for me but also for my wife, whom I married in 2002, my stepson, and very differently for my dedicated personal assistants. Life became busy. Many political meetings in the Danish Parliament, ministries, regions, municipalities, European Disability Forum, the European Parliament and Commission and at the central and decentralized level within DPOD and its member organizations and local branches. Almost never a day off. No one knew when the day would end or what challenges it would bring.

In late 1980s, the United Nations (UN) rejected proposals from Italy and Sweden on establishing a convention ensuring persons with disabilities their human rights. In 2001 on the initiative of Mexico at the World Conference on Racism, a working group was set up to investigate pros and cons of a convention ensuring the human rights of persons with disabilities. This decision came as a surprise to everyone including the state parties. I decided to do my best to ensure success of the working group and participated in the first three meetings in New York. There were many from the disability movement participating in influencing the working group composed of UN representatives. I think that the number of persons with disabilities present and visible in the basement of the UN building made the difference for the decision on continuing upon the work of the working group. My ambition was the best possible convention. I participated as a member of the official Danish delegation but also as a link between civil society and UN representatives. From late 2000 forward to the Danish ratification of the CRPD, I had to convince my member organizations to change to and support the non-discrimination approach, which they had opposed in the past. DPOD changed its political approach in 2006. I also had to convince the government and the Parliament on supporting and ratifying the CRPD. It was not easy. Denmark ratified the convention 2009 and the Optional Protocol in 2014. It was not me alone, but I was more than spearheading the efforts by the disability movement.

My career brought me to the nomination by the Danish Government to the unique position within the UNCRPD Committee (2010–2018). Being one of those telling State Parties how to implement human rights within their territory ensuring equal opportunities for persons with disabilities is the highlight in my life. We met twice a year for 4–5 weeks in Geneva, Switzerland, where we worked out the understanding of the CRPD.

My professional as well as private life has always demanded me to travel, luckily. I have visited almost all the European countries several times, especially Belgium, France, Switzerland, United Kingdom, and Spain. I also traveled to the United States, especially 10–12 times to New York. I have traveled to Brazil, Japan, China, South Korea, 8 times to Uganda, and 6 times to South Africa.

Learning from and experiencing other cultures have always been enlightening and encouraging to me. Looking on whales in South Africa on a Friday and meeting politicians in the South African Parliament on Monday is beneficial to both thought and mind.

I have noticed many different levels accessibility across the globe. Denmark is not on the top of my list of accessible countries. While traveling, many things have been possible because of accessibility and others not because of lack of accessibility. It is not always easy to travel having a mobility impairment. You are challenged by non-accommodating airline companies. You meet hotels without accessible facilities. Accessible transport is often 100% absent. Attitudes among those who should be assisting you are often inappropriate. At the end of the day, it is worth it to travel. You meet other people. You meet other cultures. You see solutions to bring home. Traveling is also an essential part of being a modern person and why not be modern with a mobility impairment?

Looking back, life has become easier to those being provided real inclusion, the necessary assistive devices and access to IL. The convention and development have not given equal opportunities across different kinds of impairment and within the almost 200 countries on the globe. Difference in the opportunities of life remains unequal.

Life is not always easy; but it is always worth living!

3 Rethinking utopia

Posthumanism, transhumanism, and disability

Jan Grue

Introduction: Disability and the species norm

It is a truth hiding in plain sight that disability is a concept that only makes sense relative to a *species norm*. The lack of echolocation is not judged to be a sensory impairment for a human being, and while some humans do possess the midtarsal break characteristic of prehensile feet, the vast majority that lack it are not judged to have a motor impairment. *Typical* species-specific physiology and abilities, in interaction with natural and built environments as well as cultural, social, and historical norms, serve as the basis for determining who is and who is not disabled.

Historically, of course, the concept of species itself, as well as the status of boundaries between species, is far from stable. *Atypical* embodiment was in many contexts viewed as a sign of different species membership rather than deviation from a species norm. Disability has deep connections to the monstrous, animal, and supernatural imaginaries, expressed, for example, in the folk theory that cleft palates were caused by an expectant mother looking at a hare, and in the notion that newborn "changelings" ought to be returned to their actual, non-human parents.

In the by-now conventional story, however, clear-cut relationships between impairments and species norms are established with the 19th-century emergence of statistics and the concurrent medicalization of disability. In the wake of the pioneering work of Adolphe Quetelet and Francis Galton (Davis, 1997; Grue & Heiberg, 2006), disability was no longer conceived as monstrous in the medieval or early modern sense, a category that troubled the boundaries between humans and other species, fully other modes of embodied being. Instead, it became a much more manageable category of negative deviation from an empirically grounded (though, inevitably, constructed) norm, a problem not of ontology but of physiology.

Disability nevertheless remains a *problem* – it has arguably always been conceived as a problem (Hughes, 2012) – one that was all the more pressing for having suddenly become solvable. Francis Galton's most famous coinage, "eugenics," promises a world in which disability has become a thing of the past: through positive eugenics, the average of the species has been radically shifted

DOI: 10.4324/9781003052708-6

upward, toward the normative ideal, while through negative eugenics, individual deviations from the average have been prevented.

In the 21st century, the relationship between disability and species norms is hardly resolved, partly because the concept of species norms itself has over the last few decades come under new and somewhat unexpected scrutiny. This chapter examines some aspects of these developments through the lenses of *posthumanism* and *transhumanism*. Regarding the CRPD, the chapter is less concerned with the convention as an instrument of practical inclusive and emancipatory politic, and more concerned with its utopian visions. Utopias have long had an important place in how we model and theorize disability – as ideal solutions that, in turn, suggest how we understand the problem at hand. The aim, here, is to use post- and transhumanism as frames through which the utopian visions of the CRPD can be seen more clearly – including their implications for how the convention currently understands and represents disability.

Disability and the posthuman

My starting point, posthumanism, can be viewed as a multiform, rhizomatic project that, not unlike poststructuralism, has grown out of and affected a number of interrelated fields of academic inquiry, shifting their perspectives and questioning the validity of some of their central concepts. The fields most directly affected by the posthumanist turn may be philosophy, metaphysics, critical theory, but not least ethics (Braidotti, 2013; Castree & Nash, 2004; Wolfe, 2010), as posthumanism is concerned with how "the human" is construed and how it is used for purposes of legitimation. A full account of posthumanism is beyond the scope of this chapter. It can be and has been defined in many ways – as an example, Wikipedia (2019) counts seven main definitions – but across those definitions a family resemblance exists that links posthumanism to a questioning of certain core assumptions of traditional humanism.

One analytical aspect of the posthumanist project can play out along historical or contemporary lines, as a deconstruction of "the human." In fields as different as art, architecture, and medicine, "the human" is often found to be a false universalization of much more narrow aspects of human experience – usually that of white, non-disabled, heterosexual, adult males. In the field of human rights, this view applies to the historical process through which the Universal Declaration of Human Rights in 1948 was supplemented by, among other key documents, the Convention on the Elimination of All Forms of Discrimination Against Women in 1981, the Convention on the Rights of the Child in 1990, and the CRPD in 2007. From a posthumanist perspective, the inadequacies of the original framing of "human rights" can be viewed as a consequence of the deficiencies of Enlightenment humanism's gendered, ableist, and racialized conception of "universal man."

Another, related line of inquiry focuses on the normative function of "the human," and how exclusion either from "the human" is used to legitimize symbolic and physical violence as well as oppression. Here, posthumanism unites the concerns of, e.g., feminist studies, gender studies, and critical race theory, in exploring how "full humanity" has been a restricted and closely guarded quality along many dimensions.

Against this background, it is perhaps not surprising that the intersection of disability studies with posthumanism and the posthuman has proved productive in recent years. Disability studies has long been concerned with what it means to be included in or excluded from full membership in human society, or indeed in the human species, and the historical investigations of disability studies have often dealt with dehumanization as a philosophical and political tool for the oppression of disabled people, as well as with the questioning of disabled people's humanity as a prelude to violence. Arguing that disability and posthumanism are conceptually at ease because "disability has always contravened the traditional classical humanist conception of what it means to be human," Goodley et al. (2014, p. 342) view posthuman thought as a productive and potentially liberating contribution to disability studies because of its potential for destabilizing the grounds for ableist norms.

The core of this position is the argument that humanism, while in many ways a positive force, has always played the role of gatekeeper. Humanism "invites some into its fold while banishing others" (Goodley et al., 2014, p. 343). In contrast, posthumanism represents a potential for playfulness and exploration, for going beyond the normative constraints of a narrowly conceived vision of humanity. It stresses the interdependent nature of existence – not just the interdependence of humans upon humans, but of humans upon *others*, whether in the form of technology, "non-human entities, communication streams and people and non-peopled networks" (Goodley et al., 2014, p. 348).

Two questions that remain unanswered, however, are (1) whether posthumanist perspectives offer new and valuable insight for disability studies and (2) whether the posthuman turn is a good thing politically for disabled people.

These two questions are often entangled, reflecting the generally uneasy relationship that posthumanism has with normativity. The argument that "the human" often represents a false universalization can be made on very solid empirical grounds. It is hard, too, to dispute that its role as a standard of value and as a guarantor of rights is problematic and inherently exclusionary. The problem, which posthumanism has yet to resolve, is what may be offered instead.

It seems likely that most posthumanists embrace some form progressive politics, wishing for true egalitarianism, and to expand the circle of moral concern beyond the boundaries that have traditionally been drawn by humanism – both inside and beyond species boundaries. Stressing the potential for alliances, alignment, and the recognition of interdependence, however, posthumanist analysis tends to avoid the topics of conflict of interest and prioritization. In the field of disability studies, there is considerable resistance to the posthumanist turn (Vehmas & Watson, 2016) on the grounds that the erasure of "the human" as an indicator of intrinsic value mostly represents a risk for disabled people, and a danger that outweighs, e.g., the potential alliances between the struggles for disability liberation and animal liberation suggested by Sunaura Taylor (2018).

Questions of this nature must necessarily be tested in practical politics. In the next section, I will focus, rather, on the grounds for a normative posthumanist critique of documents such as the CRPD, and that posthumanist perspectives have an important contribution to make in foregrounding the limitations of the classically humanist rights-based approach to disability. Subsequently, however, I will argue that the normative evasions of much of posthumanism means that the critique becomes stuck at the level of problematization. Somewhat surprisingly, it is the peculiar branch of posthumanism known as transhumanism that offers the most interesting insight – namely that the CRPD, and by extension much of the current human rights approach to disability, has a strong tendency toward *utopian medicalization*.

Posthumanism and the CRPD: Pluralism versus hierarchization?

The most obvious basis for a posthumanist critique of the CRPD lies, as Goodley et al. point out, in examining and questioning the normative status of the average human being for disabled people, and to make the case for normatively recognizing a fuller range of human experience. In Article 1, the CRPD states that its purpose is to

> [...] promote, protect and ensure the full and equal enjoyment of all human rights and fundamental freedoms by all persons with disabilities, and to promote respect for their inherent dignity. Persons with disabilities include those who have long-term physical, mental, intellectual or sensory impairments which in interaction with various barriers may hinder their full and effective participation in society on an equal basis with others.

The salient link made here is that between impairment and marginality, i.e., the notion, familiar from medicalization and personal tragedy theory (Oliver & Barnes, 2012) that it is one's embodiment that is the ultimate cause of exclusion. If disabled people constitute a naturally distinct class of people, naturally pre-excluded from society (albeit through interaction with "barriers"), then it is also logical to assess their lives *relative to* the lives of their non-disabled peers – it is the non-disabled population that provides the baseline for a "successfully included" disabled person, someone who can be provisionally granted full membership in society. In this reading, there is an underlying presumption to the CRPD of a binary division of humanity – those with problematic impairments and those without, i.e., "normal" human beings. From a posthumanist point of view, a plurality of modes of being should first be acknowledged, not the single goal shaped by "humanistic values of independence and autonomy" (Goodley et al., 2014, p. 349).

I find this critique relevant, insofar as it exposes the way in which the CRPD is embedded in the long intellectual tradition of framing and conceptualizing disability as an ontological problem. This framing is distinct from that of viewing disability as pragmatically or empirically problematic. While almost all approaches to disability assume, explicitly or not (Vehmas & Watson, 2016), the normative position that disability as disadvantage is a bad thing, not all approaches treat the existence of disabled people as the ontological locus of the problem. There are alternative visions, not least those developed from within disability studies, that reframe it as an aspect of natural human variation. But the history of disability is dominated by the "problem" frame, as is most policy on disability. This is not surprising, since there are many *secondary* problems linked to disability, including poverty, inequality of opportunity, shorter life expectancy, exclusion, and marginalization. The questions at stake are, rather, (a) whether the problem frame is *intrinsic* to disability as a concept, and (b) what the problem frame implies in terms of *solutions*.

Arguably, the CRPD falls into the "ontological problem" category of approaches by construing disabled people as a group that will be validated only by participation "on an equal basis with others." As an overarching goal, this is *prima facie* fine; it only becomes problematic in a particular context. The field of work and working life is a case in point. Full and effective participation *on an equal basis with others* is here a highly ambitious and potentially unreachable goal, given the severity of some impairments and the near impossibility of eliminating every structure that constitutes a "barrier" to participation – not to mention the ideologically charged status of work as a source of value to begin with (Taylor, 2004).

In this view, moreover, impairments are discrete and consistently identifiable features of individuals. This position has considerable intuitive appeal, but impairments, too, are not always simple physiological givens; many are socially constructed, in that points along the continuum of human capabilities only become impairments under certain circumstances, which must in turn be understood in the context of (variable) natural and built environments.

The argument about discreteness is grounded in a critical analysis of the history of normality and statistics (Canguilhem, 1991; Davis, 1997; Grue & Heiberg, 2006; Moser, 2000), which points out that many "problems" of body structure or functioning can be more neutrally described as significant deviation from the mean. While human capabilities can be described dichotomously – seeing/not seeing, walking/not walking – the continuum is a more accurate representation. Terms such as "legal blindness" or even "blindness" do not imply a complete lack of visual perception. The cut-off point for when a certain level of ability becomes definable as an impairment is neither wholly arbitrary nor wholly deterministic; it is a matter of complex negotiations, explored (aside from in disability studies) in the sociology of diagnosis (Brown, 1995; Conrad, 2008; Jutel, 2011, 2015).

Generalizing from this example, one can delineate in the provisions of the CRPD a particular solution to the problem of disability; compensatory inclusionary action that is conceptually dependent upon hierarchization. The phrase "equal basis" is introduced in Article 2 of the Convention and recurs frequently in the text, informing the right to accessibility, recognition before the law, home and family life, etc. It is of course a pragmatic solution to the problem of how to establish a satisfactory or even minimal standard of inclusion. However, for Goodley et al., as for many writers and scholars who have embraced the posthuman turn, the point is to ontologically validate disabled embodiment by recognizing incommensurable and non-hierarchical *difference*. The CRPD seeks to further the rights of disabled people to be compensated and provisionally included; from a posthumanist perspective, this reifies the framing of disability as negative deviation from an unproblematized notion of human normality.

This contrast of frameworks is not unique to the intersection of the CRPD with posthumanism. The problem/solution frame occurs both outside and inside disability studies, that is, it is common both in schools of thought that deploy the concept of disability more or less uncritically, and in those that try very hard to destabilize and critique it. As an example, early versions of the British Social Model (BSM) of disability explicitly compartmentalized the concepts of "impairment" and "disability" so that while impairments were viewed as unproblematic, even neutral aspects of human variation, disability was defined as a socio-economically created problem of oppression and marginalization, i.e., of forced hierarchization (Oliver, 1990; Oliver & Barnes, 2012; Shakespeare, 1996, 2013).

For some BSM scholars and activists, the solution to the political problem of disability was the reorganization of the built environment and social structures so that individual impairment no longer mattered, that is, to obviate the hierarchy by leveling the playing field. But this school of thought also had room for ironic subversion. A fable famously told by Vic Finkelstein (1988) sketched out a village adapted to its wheelchair user residents, making a problem out of the *walking* residents, having them bump into doorways, and so forth. In a very different vein, the US disability activist Harriet McBryde Johnson's novel *Accidents of Nature*, set at a summer camp for children with disabilities, features the image of a "reverse telethon" – hosted for the benefit of "Norms" rather than "Crips" (Johnson, 2006). The point, of course, is to suggest that any singular form of embodiment will become problematic as soon as it becomes narrowly normative, whether applied to the built environment or to sociocultural practices.

To acknowledge and validate the lives of people with disabilities, then, may well involve the subversion or inversion of hierarchies of ability, in favor of variation. But such imaginings have a distinctly utopian flair. They either envision a world in which disability has ceased to matter. In practical politics it matters a great deal, and the strongest arguments for changing society in the areas that matter most depend very much upon a hierarchical logic.

While the CRPD, like other documents of its kind, points toward an egalitarian utopia, it depends in pragmatic terms upon the recognition of hierarchical difference and a reasonably demarcated standard of comparison – the unproblematically normal "others" to which Article 1 refers. This implies a conceptual hierarchy that disabled people can never really extricate themselves from, but may well be dependent upon for political change. If disability, ontologically speaking, simply represents neutral difference rather than disadvantage, why should society change in order to accommodate disabled people, beyond symbolically acknowledging their particular forms of embodiment? If there is no real basis for hierarchical comparison – a group-level difference in levels of education, levels of employment, or socio-economic status, for instance – then neither are there grounds for group-level political intervention.

From descriptive posthumanism to normative transhumanism: Reaching for the stars

If we shift our attention from the CRPD back to posthumanism, we will see that the problem of normativity and hierarchization has generated both non-answers and a very clear answer indeed. While some posthumanist scholars work very hard to avoid the hierarchical element (Braidotti, 2006, 2013; Wolfe, 2010, 2013), there is still, within the posthumanist family of analytical approaches, an ineluctable element of normative ranking of forms of embodiment. That element, the *transhumanist* element, is explicitly disavowed by much of what we might call ecumenical posthumanism. Nevertheless, I will argue, it has many features in common with posthumanism, and its rigidly hierarchical vision of human and non-human embodiment cannot, given a posthumanist starting point, be easily avoided.

By the lights of one of its central proponents, the philosopher Nick Bostrom (2004, 2005a, 2005b), parts of the transhumanist imaginary are as old as human culture's capacity for storytelling and systematic thought. Its dream of immortal existence animates the *Gilgamesh* epic, and reoccurs throughout the literary canon and the history of philosophy; it appears whenever humanity tries to think beyond the limitations of its embodiment.

Transhumanist thought can, as I have argued elsewhere, be potentially both an expansive and a narrowing force of the imaginary, with fascinating ideological subtleties to be explored in the realms of, e.g., science fiction and superhero narratives (Grue, 2020, 2021). Modern transhumanism, though, is also a postwar ideological phenomenon influenced by real-world developments in, cybernetics, artificial intelligence, and genetic science. It is, moreover, a political movement that is moving rapidly from fringe to mainstream. A transhumanist candidate named Zoltan Istvan campaigned in the 2016 presidential election in the United States, and although he was perceived as quixotic, his exploits saw coverage in *The New Yorker* (Marantz, 2016). Transhumanist advocates in academia such as Nick Bostrom participate in serious debates on key technological developments, while Ray Kurzweil, the most well-known proponent of the "Singularity" idea, is also, at the time of writing, Director of Engineering at Google Inc., with a purview including machine learning and artificial intelligence.

Genealogically speaking, if posthumanism can be said to have been birthed by Foucault's image, at the very end of *The Order of Things* (Foucault, 1970), of a face drawn in sand, washed away by the waves, then modern transhumanism emerges from Julian Huxley's (1968) image of "man" (sic) taking charge of his own evolution and striving for the Godhead. If Foucault infused posthumanism with a nihilist melancholia to temper its ostensible exuberance for every form of embodied life, then Huxley gifted transhumanism with a triumphalist, techno-utopian fervor tempered by very little.

By one measure, it should be said, transhumanism is non-hierarchical. From its view of consciousness and life, respectively, as first and foremost *information systems*, derives the possibility of transcending entirely the constraints of human embodiment as we currently know it. To transhumanism, as to much of posthumanism, there is nothing especially valuable about being human. Consciousness can be moved from one material substratum to another; as long as the pattern can be recreated, the epiphenomenon of personal identity can be preserved.

Crucially, however, transhumanism hierarchizes consciousness itself, largely along neo-Platonist and Christian eschatological lines (Gray, 2018; Tirosh-Samuelson, 2012). It eschews lowly embodiment and dreams of the arrival of the millennium – ideally through personal immortality either in a biological but flawless body or in a disembodied, digital, oceanic environment. Here, "the human" represents first and foremost the mortal coil.

An oft-cited precursor of transhumanism is Pierre Teilhard de Chardin, a Jesuit who attempted to integrated Catholicism with evolution, and came up with the idea of the Omega point, effectively a Godhead emerged from the natural universe, with the human race as a waystation (Steinhart, 2008; Teilhard de Chardin, 1960). This is the kind of utopia suggested through Julian Huxley's original coining of transhumanism: of the universe becoming aware of itself (Huxley, 1957). It is a fantasy of human empowerment, achieved by leaving present humanity behind.

From the point of view of disability studies, transhumanism is equally interesting for its fears and for its desires, and even more so for its normative stance. What it seeks to escape are those troublesome aspects of human existence – in particular, suffering – that have always been the target of ameliorative politics, but transhumanism takes the stance that the suffering caused by embodiment simply should not exist, and that this problem must be resolved both on a species level and an individual level. In this aim, transhumanism clearly aligns with the old ideals of eugenics, albeit augmented by high hopes for the potential of artificial intelligence.

Transhumanism distinguishes itself from posthumanism not only by choosing convergence into the Godhead over divergence into incommensurable forms of life, by choosing the celestial over the chthonic, but also by its explicit normativity. Transhumanist thought has a philosophical as well as an ideological face. It speculates about the capabilities and implications of future technology, particularly information technology and biomedicine. But it also states what *ought* to be the case, i.e., what kind of technology should exist and how it should be used. It seeks influence on policy through normative positions, and though it is less concerned with descriptive *or* normative analysis of social structures or organization, its techno-utopian ambitions have unavoidable reactionary implications for these. Yuval Harari's pop-science best sellers (Harari, 2014, 2015) are among the critiques that point out the implications of this dynamic for social organization: they align very well with a kind of extreme capitalist ideology where resources may be concentrated in the hands of a very small number of people who have nothing left to achieve except personal immortality. The increasing political footprint of the transhumanist movement can probably be explained largely by the degree to which it resonates in the power centers of Silicon Valley.

Another way of seeing things, however, is that transhumanism has stepped into a normative space that was co-explored with posthumanism, which then abandoned it. If posthumanism studiously avoids making normative judgments of its own, seeking only to deconstruct those made by classical humanism, then transhumanism accepts the premises of critique – there is nothing intrinsically valuable about human existence or human embodiment – while moving to an entirely logical conclusion: the only relevant norm does not derive from any animal, material species, but from the realm of ideas. From this follows a fundamental devaluation of any form of embodiment deemed intellectually inferior, whether inferiority is associated with animality or disability.

Embodied utopias

Needless to say, human rights occupies a thoroughly problematic space in the transhumanist imaginary. Transhumanism vacillates between addressing the concerns of "humanity" and of individual humans, allowing for the reading that while "humanity" will be left behind, *individual* humans may transcend the human condition and become, through enhancement, the first transhumans. At this moment, in which a new and better species emerges, humanity as we know can best be described as obsolete. "Full and equal participation" in society will be a moot point, since society as we know it will no longer have a function. The novelist Michel Houellebecq satirizes this aspect of transhumanism in *The Possibility of an Island* (2006); here, in the far future, a "neo-human" narrator tries, in vain, to understand the strange, ape-like creatures from which he descended.

These are fantastical ideas, yet relevant to our contemporary concerns because they help magnify and clarify the conceptual weaknesses in our current human rights framework – no less utopian, in its way, than the science fiction scenarios of transhumanism or the rhizomatic inter-species alliances of posthumanism. The distance between utopias is always shorter than the distance between any given utopia and the world as it is.

As an example, consider how contemporary society is suffused with discourses of *healthism* and *medicalization*. The extent of these tendencies is by now well appreciated, in work going back decades (Crawford, 1980; Zola, 1977). What is less recognized is the radical implications of their conceptualization of human embodiment, and the extent to which their conceptualizations align with transhumanist ideology.

The utopian imaginary is more or less an intrinsic feature of the modern ideology of human health. At its inception, the World Health Organization famously defined health as a "state of complete physical, mental, and social well-being, and not merely the absence of disease and infirmity" (World Health Organization, 1948). It has become a commonplace or *locus communis* in the literature that this perfectionistic definition has long been roundly criticized, just as it is obligatory to note that it endures in the face of criticism. But on the WHO's online "frequently asked questions" page, the original definition endures as the touchstone of the organization's principles and mission. Why, when health as the WHO defines it, appears singularly unattainable? Callahan (1973, p. 77) suggests that it endures *because* of its unreality; it is "the perfect straw man" that nevertheless continues to defeat all comers. It remains attractive for the reason that so many visions of humanity in the postwar years remain attractive: it has the appeal of Utopia. Everyone knows it is unattainable; therefore, it provides a goal worth striving for.

Not all of medicine subscribes to the utopian, perfectionistic view of health. A widely cited review in the *British Medical Journal* (Huber et al., 2011) notes with some exasperation that the WHO definition is no longer "fit for purpose," and proposes that "the ability to adapt and self-manage" is a better way to approach human health. In particular, such an approach can explain the "disability paradox," the fact that impaired functioning does not necessarily change a person's perceived quality of life. This new approach to defining health has clear advantages on the criteria of realism and pragmatism; it would appear to be more flexible and more sensitive to environmental constrains, suggesting collaborative and ongoing work to create a *habitable world*.

Both these definitions of and approaches to health require ongoing, never-ending effort. The most important difference is teleological, in that the perfectionistic vision places its goal in the future, while the adaptive vision places the goal squarely in the present. While these goals may not be mutually exclusive, they are often in conflict. A blinkered orientation toward the future may undercut concern about the present, particularly regarding the matter of whom society is *for*: all of the people who are here, now, or the people who will inherit it tomorrow.

As every reader of science fiction knows, every utopia is mirrored by a dystopia. Sometimes it is difficult to tell the two apart. Aldous Huxley's *Brave New World*, rivaled only by Orwell's *Nineteen Eighty-Four* as the most significant dystopian novel of the modern age, came about as an inversion of contemporary utopian visions: technocratic solutionism, eugenics, Fordism or socialism, depending on one's ideological bugbear of choice. Nearly a decade ago, the argument was made that a *re*-inversion of the eugenic project is well under way (Raz, 2009); utopia or dystopia is at least in part a matter of one's political stance and visions of the future.

As it happens, the utopian/dystopian vision suggested by the WHO definition of health is intimately linked with Aldous' brother Julian, the father of modern transhumanism. His thoughts on human embodiment and human progress simply take *very seriously* the postwar promise of complete physical and mental, though possibly not of social (Tennison, 2012), wellbeing.

Transhumanism recognizes perfectly that utopias such as those suggested by the WHO definition of health cannot be attained by humans as we know them (Bishop, 2010). That realization is in fact expressed through the very name *transhumanism*, which suggest that the point of contemporary society is to advance beyond humanity, to manufacture an escape hatch from the human condition.

As we have seen, transhumanism can appear quixotic in the extreme. That is why this article began in a more familiar place, with the world's best known and internationally most acknowledged definition of health. We argue here that even the quotidian may be deeply linked to utopias and visions of the future, which in turn have important implications and potential consequences for the lives we lead in the present. Transhumanism, not in spite of but because of its outlandish elements, helps explain these implications. Transhumanism's utopian vision, radical though it appears, is in fact the logical consequence of a number of ideological currents that run much wider, and deeper, than is generally acknowledged. In its way, it represents the *id* of late modern technocratic solutionism, exposing, as such, the impossible desires and inherent contradictions of an ostensibly rational system of governance grounded in Enlightenment thought (Hughes, 2010).

Now consider the utopia proposed by the CRPD. Its goal of "full and effective participation on an equal basis with others" is intended to be achieved through "reasonable accommodation," defined in Article 2 as "necessary and appropriate modification and adjustments not imposing a disproportionate or undue burden."

There is a fundamental incompatibility between the first and second articles of the convention, as disability is conceived both as a signifier of fundamental difference, distinguishing a part of humanity in need of a distinct convention or its protection, *and* as a group whose inclusion may be achieved through relatively minor adjustments to society as we know it.

Remaining human, remaining disabled?

Post- and transhumanist perspectives on issues of human rights can be confusing as well as bracing. The contrast between transhumanism and posthumanism has to do not only with their different stances toward embodiment – posthumanism embracing embodied vulnerability and transhumanism rejecting it – but with the strategies and standards of valuation that make reading, interpretation, and meaning possible. Transhumanism insists upon a Sidgwickian "point of view of the universe" in which nothing is intrinsically valuable, while posthumanism generally attempts to balance inherently incompatible standards of valuation for different kinds of lives – what might be termed incommensurable species norms.

The transhumanist imaginary insists upon the *absolute*. It envisions absolute freedom from suffering, infirmity, and, ultimately, mortality. The posthumanist imaginary attempts to incorporate variously enmeshed modes of embodiment – of *kinship*, in Donna Haraway's (2003, 2015) terminology. The dream of kinship across experiential boundaries, even across species boundaries, recurs in its relationship to meaning and the possibility of meaning-making, including through language and the language of rights. These perspectives thus force us to think through, quite carefully, what standards we set and how we set them. Through their explicitly utopian imaginaries, too, they draw out the utopias implicit in ostensibly more worldly ideologies and imaginaries.

Medicalization and healthism are functions of the epistemologically as well as institutionally crucial position medicine in modern society. Through its capacities for improving health, extending life, and managing complaints, medicine serves critical functions for most people, certainly in the industrialized world. Attendant with these functions, medical institutions have important, even crucial tasks in terms of *certification* and *justification*; medicine has for a very long time provided legitimacy for mechanisms of economic redistribution and social justice. Through indicators such as *quality-adjusted life years* (Nord, 1992), medicine also provides *valuation standards* and *valuation hierarchies* (Carr-Hill, 1991). Sometimes framed "merely" as technical instruments, the quantitative and discrete assessment tools of medicine tend to generate strong implications about which lives are good or bad; ultimately about which lives are worth or not worth living.

Transhumanism takes these tendencies one step further. By assuming that a WHO definition of health is attainable, in the future, for some very fortunate (trans)humans, it takes as a norm what was initially presented as an ideal. This interpretive shift and slippage is familiar from the history of normality; what is first introduced as an unreal and unattainable form of perfection can all too easily become a normative standard from which deviation is inherently negative.

From this perspective, the utopia suggested by the CRPD is *prima facie* egalitarian, but the hierarchies suggested here, and the attendant valuation criteria, remain intact. Disability remains an object of inclusion – an example of the always-already excluded – rather than an expression of the natural range of variation in human capabilities. This framing, of course, makes it much easier to conceive of a practical politics of inclusion, a not unimportant function of an international convention on human rights. What the perspectives of post- and transhumanism offer, then, is not really a critique of the CRPD's proposed means, but of their ends. The recognition that the CRPD is not only a pragmatic document but a utopian one forces a reckoning with that utopia, and the question of whether the human rights approach to disability, in certain ways, serves to reify and preserve the familiar and reactionary framing of disability as an individual deficit that it ostensibly tries to challenge and overcome.

References

Bishop, J. P. (2010). Transhumanism, metaphysics, and the posthuman god. *Journal of Medicine and Philosophy*, *35*(6), 700–720.

Bostrom, N. (2004). Transhumanism: The world's most dangerous idea? https://nickbostrom.com/papers/dangerous

Bostrom, N. (2005a). A history of transhumanist thought. *Journal of Evolution and Technology*, 14, 1–25.

Bostrom, N. (2005b). Transhumanist values. *Journal of Philosophical Research*, 4, 3–14.

Braidotti, R. (2006). Posthuman, all too human. *Theory, Culture & Society*, *23*(7–8), 197–208. doi:10.1177/0263276406069232

Braidotti, R. (2013). *The Posthuman*. London: Polity Press.

Brown, P. (1995). Naming and framing: The social construction of diagnosis and illness. *Journal of Health and Social Behavior*, *35*(Special issue), 34–52.

Callahan, D. (1973). The WHO definition of "health". *The Hastings Center Studies*, *1*(3), 77. doi:10.2307/3527467

Canguilhem, G. (1991). *The Normal and the Pathological*. New York: Zone Books.

Carr-Hill, R. A. (1991). Allocating resources to health care: Is the QALY (Quality Adjusted Life Year) a technical solution to a political problem? *International Journal of Health Services*, *21*(2), 351–363. doi:10.2190/HPLM-EGXV-BWKY-5XBN

Castree, N., & Nash, C. (2004). Mapping posthumanism: An exchange. *Environment and Planning A*, *36*(8), 1341–1363. doi:10.1068/a37127

Conrad, P. (2008). *The Medicalization of Society: On the Transformation of Human Conditions into Treatable Disorders*. JHU Press.

Crawford, R. (1980). Healthism and the medicalization of everyday life. *International Journal of Health Services*, *10*(3), 365–388. doi:10.2190/3H2H-3XJN-3KAY-G9NY

Davis, L. (1997). Constructing normalcy. The Bell curve, the novel, and the invention of the disabled body in the nineteenth century. In L. J. Davis (Ed.), *The Disability Studies Reader*. New York: Routledge.

Finkelstein, V. (1988). To deny or not to deny disability - what is disability? *Physiotherapy*, *74*(12), 650–651.

Foucault, M. (1970). *The Order of Things*. London: Routledge.

Goodley, D., Lawthom, R., & Runswick Cole, K. (2014). Posthuman disability studies. *Subjectivity*, *7*(4), 342–361. doi:10.1057/sub.2014.15

Gray, J. (2018). *Seven Types of Atheism*. New York: Farrar, Straus, and Giroux.

Grue, J. (2020). On the transhumanist imaginary and the biopolitics of contingent embodiment. *New Literary History*, *51*(4), 805–823.

Grue, J. (2021). Ablenationalists assemble: On disability in the Marvel Cinematic Universe. *Journal of Literary & Cultural Disability Studies*, *15*(1), 1–17.

Grue, L., & Heiberg, A. (2006). Notes on the history of normality - Reflections on the work of Quetelet and Galton. *Scandinavian Journal of Disability Research*, 8(4), 232–246.

Harari, Y. N. (2014). *Sapiens: A Brief History of Humanity*. New York: Harper.

Harari, Y. N. (2015). *Homo Deus: A Brief History of Tomorrow*. New York: Harvill Secker.

Haraway, D. (2015). Anthropocene, capitalocene, plantationocene, chthulucene: Making kin. *Environmental Humanities*, 6(1), 159–165.

Haraway, D. (2003). *The Companion Species Manifesto: Dogs, People, and Significant Otherness*. Chicago: Prickly Paradigm Press.

Houellebecq, M. (2006). *The Possibility of an Island*. New York: Alfred A. Knopf.

Huber, M., Knottnerus, J. A., Green, L., van der Horst, H., Jadad, A. R., Kromhout, D., …, & Smid, H. (2011). How should we define health? *BMJ (Clinical Research Ed.)*, *343*, d4163. doi:10.1136/bmj.d4163

Hughes, B. (2012). Civilising modernity and the ontological invalidation of disabled people. *Disability and Social Theory: New Developments and Directions*, *17*, 17–32. https://monthlyreview.org/2004/03/01/the-right-not-to-work-power-and-disability/

Hughes, J. (2010). Contradictions from the enlightenment roots of transhumanism. *Journal of Medicine and Philosophy*, *35*(6), 622–640.

Huxley, J. (1957). *New Bottles for New Wine. Essays*. London: Chatto and Windus.

Huxley, J. (1968). Transhumanism. *Journal of Humanistic Psychology*, 8(1), 73–76.

Johnson, H. M. (2006). *Accidents of Nature*. New York: Henry Holt.

Jutel, A. (2011). *Putting a Name to It: Diagnosis in Contemporary Society*. JHU Press.

Jutel, A. (2015). Beyond the sociology of diagnosis. *Sociology Compass*, 9(9), 841–852.

Marantz, A. (2016). The transhumanists' nominee for president. *The New Yorker*.

Moser, I. (2000). Against normalisation: Subverting norms of ability and disability. *Science as Culture*, 9(2), 198–240.

Nord, E. (1992). Methods for quality adjustment of life years. *Social Science & Medicine*, *34*(5), 559–569.

Oliver, M. (1990). *The Politics of Disablement. Critical Texts in Social Work and the Welfare State*. London: MacMillan Press.

Oliver, M., & Barnes, C. (2012). *The New Politics of Disablement*. London: Palgrave Macmillan.

Raz, A. E. (2009). Eugenic utopias/dystopias, reprogenetics, and community genetics. *Sociology of Health & Illness*, *31*(4), 602–616. doi:10.1111/j.1467-9566.2009.01160.x

Shakespeare, T. (1996). Disability, identity and difference. In C. Barnes & G. Mercer (Eds.), *Exploring the Divide*. Leeds: The Disability Press.

Shakespeare, T. (2013). *Disability Rights and Wrongs Revisited*. London: Routledge.

Steinhart, E. (2008). Teilhard de Chardin and transhumanism. *Journal of Evolution and Technology*, *20*(1), 1–22.

Taylor, S. (2004). The right not to work: Power and disability. *Monthly Review*, *55*(10).

Taylor, S. (2018). *Beasts of Burden: Animal and Disability Liberation*. New York: The New Press.

Teilhard de Chardin, P. (1960). *The Phenomenon of Man*. New York: Collins.

Tennison, M. N. (2012). Moral transhumanism: The next step. *Journal of Medicine and Philosophy*, *37*(4), 405–416.

Tirosh-Samuelson, H. (2012). Transhumanism as a secularist faith. *Zygon®*, *47*(4), 710–734. doi:10.1111/j.1467-9744.2012.01288.x

Vehmas, S., & Watson, N. (2016). Exploring normativity in disability studies. *Disability & Society*, *31*(1), 1–16. doi:10.1080/09687599.2015.1120657

Wikipedia. (2019). Posthumanism. https://en.wikipedia.org/wiki/Posthumanism downloaded/checked on Feb 2, 2023

Wolfe, C. (2010). *What Is Posthumanism? What Is Posthumanism*, Vol. 8. Minneapolis: University of Minnesota Press.

Wolfe, C. (2013). *Before the Law: Humans and Other Animals in a Biopolitical Frame*. Chicago: University of Chicago Press.

World Health Organization. (1948). Preamble to the Constitution of the World Health Organization as adopted by the International Health Conference, New York, 19–22 June, 1946; signed on 22 July 1946 by the representatives of 61 States (Official Records of the World Health Organization).

Zola, I. K. (1977). Healthism and disabling medicalization. In I. Illich (Ed.), *Disabling Professions* (pp. 41–67). London: Marion Boyars.

4 Mad citizenship

Michael Rembis

As other scholars have noted, the creation of the Convention on the Rights of Persons with Disabilities (CRPD) marked a paradigm shift in global disability politics. For the first time in history, disabled people played key roles in drafting a UN convention that, once ratified, could significantly affect their daily lived experiences. Lucy Series (2020) writes in her discussion of disability and human rights that the CRPD was drafted by disabled people for disabled people.

Given its unique history, the CRPD has become "fertile terrain" for all types of disability scholarship (Series 2020, 72). In this chapter, I engage with some of that literature. I focus on the work of survivors and users of psychiatry, and people who identify as psychosocially disabled. Psychiatrized people played key roles in drafting the CRPD and in its ratification and implementation. Although they critique the "strong" or British social model of disability, most survivors, users, and psychosocially disabled people align themselves with the disability rights movement and strongly support the CRPD. They see the CRPD as the best way to protect their rights and prevent the imposition of western, global north bio-psychiatry into their lives. Throughout this chapter, I use the terms "users," "survivors," "mad," "people living with psychosocial disabilities," "psychosocially disabled," and "psychiatrized" interchangeably to identify a broad and growing global community of people who experience mental troubles, who have had encounters with various *psy* professionals, and who are working to use the CRPD and other tools to transform mental health care.

This chapter is divided into three sections. In the first section, I highlight the role of mad activists in drafting the CRPD. I focus on their relationship to the disability rights movement and their specific contributions to the CRPD. The second section presents the mad critique of the globalization of bio-psychiatry or what some critics refer to as "psychocentric discourse" (Rimke 2016). As efforts to expand and protect the rights of people with disabilities have increased, so too have efforts to export western, global north – particularly US – notions of and treatments for madness and distress. Some of these measures have been met with resistance by people with psychosocial disabilities living in the global north and the global south who challenge the legitimacy of bio-psychiatry and consider many of its prescribed interventions – everything from psychopharmaceuticals to electroconvulsive therapy (ECT) to forced commitment – a

DOI: 10.4324/9781003052708-7

violation of their rights under the CRPD. In the third section, I assess the ways in which physicians and other advocates for the expansion of bio-psychiatry have responded to critiques made against it.

Drafting the CRPD

Although many people who identify as users and survivors of psychiatry, as well as people who identify as psychosocially disabled, take a more nuanced approach to thinking about impairment than the early, largely white, cis-male wheelchair users who created the "strong" or British social model of disability, they generally align themselves with the disability rights movement. Lawyer and mad activist, Tina Minkowitz, who was instrumental in drafting the CRPD, explains that she and other mad people advocate for disability rights, because they have, for decades, been legally and socially regarded as having a disability (Spandler et al. 2015). Minkowitz adds that in some countries, psychosocially disabled people can receive disability pensions and they are protected against disability-based discrimination. Users and survivors of psychiatry, and other people living with psychosocial disabilities, have been included in previous UN resolutions on disability. And like other disabled people, they have historically, and in more recent times, been marked (labeled, diagnosed), subjected to commitment to institutions, and forced to endure sometimes violent intrusions into their bodies. Mad people also face the disabling effects of medical diagnosis and the creation of a medical case file, which they often have little input in creating and which can stay with them for the rest of their life (Wilson and Beresford 2002). When the call went out early in the new millennium for disability rights leaders to convene in Beijing to draft the CRPD, Minkowitz and other mad activists from around the world saw an opportunity to enact real, lasting change that would correct decades of abuse and neglect, and move beyond the mental health law reform that had taken place in the UK, the United States, Canada, and elsewhere.

Mad activists brought their own perspectives and goals to the creation of the CRPD. Users, survivors, and psychosocially disabled people wanted to draft a convention that would protect their right to make choices about their care, even if those choices contravened or did not conform with the recommendations of medical professionals. Minkowitz explains that the "core advocacy points" that the user/survivor/psychosocially disabled leaders brought to the CRPD were: the legal capacity to make one's own decisions; the prohibition of discriminatory detention; and the prohibition of non-consensual interventions (Spandler et al. 2015, 173). Under the CRPD, forced treatment and forced commitment to a hospital or other institution would be considered "disability discrimination" and under certain circumstances could be defined as torture (Spandler et al. 2015, 172). Minkowitz, like other survivors, as well as many users and people living with psychosocial disabilities, opposes the "quasi-state power" of psychiatrists to classify, confine, and violate the bodies of mad people (Spandler et al. 2015, 176–177). According to Minkowitz, the contributions of mad people to the CRPD were "not only integral to the treaty," they were the "most dynamic and forward-looking legal contributions" to it (Spandler et al. 2015, 173). Minkowitz believes that during the process of writing the CRPD, disability rights leaders developed a mutual respect for one another and created a working relationship that "not only incorporated the advocacy agendas of each constituency but eventually allowed [them] to find commonalities that may not have been apparent before" they came together (Spandler et al. 2015, 174).

Minkowitz and the World Network of Users and Survivors of Psychiatry (WNUSP) as well as members of the Committee on the Rights of Persons with Disabilities – the group of independent experts created by the CRPD to monitor compliance with the convention – consider the CRPD a "legal revolution" because it diverges significantly from previous mental health laws that have been based on a medical model of mental illness. According to Minkowitz, the CRPD is the only legislation in international or domestic law that guarantees the rights of people living with psychosocial disabilities "on a basis of full equality with others, and that makes no exception to legitimize acts of [state and medical] violence and abuse" of mad people, which in the past, and in more contemporary settings, have been carried out in the name of "science" and "treatment" or under the guise of "protecting" mad people or the people around them. The CRPD enables people with disabilities, including psychosocial disabilities, to make their own decisions and it provides a framework for addressing forced treatment, including forced drugging, electroshock, and involuntary commitment, as a violation of their rights (Spandler et al. 2015). Many of the most vocal activists and advocates, such as the Center for the Human Rights of Users and Survivors of Psychiatry, the Pan-African Network of People with Psychosocial Disabilities, the Trans-Asia Strategic Group of Persons with Psychosocial Disabilities, and the Global Mental Health Peer Network, value the creation of the CRPD as a means of empowering mad people and their allies to create their own systems of support and mental health care and to resist the imposition of western, global north bio-psychiatric interventions into their lives.

Resisting the globalization of bio-psychiatry

Since the adoption of the CRPD in 2006, there has been a push to expand a certain type of bio-psychiatry throughout the world. Evidence of the push to globalize bio-psychiatry can be found in the Movement for Global Mental Health (MGMH). The MGMH, which the *Lancet* commission on global mental health and sustainable development describes as a "virtual global alliance," began in 2008, the same year that the CRPD went into force (Patel et al. 2018, 1559). By the end of 2021, the MGMH had more than 230 member organizations and about 15,000 individual members "representing diverse stakeholders" (Patel et al. 2018, 1559; Sunkel 2021, 1502–1503). While it recognizes diverse perspectives on mental health care, the MGMH seeks to increase access to bio-psychiatric services for people experiencing what it calls "mental disorders" and "mental illnesses" throughout the world, but especially in low- and middle-income countries.

Users, survivors, and people living with psychosocial disabilities do not deny or minimize the need to improve access to mental health care across the globe. They do, however, take issue with the largely unchecked expansion of bio-psychiatry. Resistance to bio-psychiatry, which dates back decades, and centuries in some parts of the world, has taken on new meanings and increased intensity since the enactment of the CRPD in 2008. A growing number of activists and scholars and scholar-activists have formed sophisticated critiques of what the University of Winnipeg sociologist, Heidi Rimke (2016), calls, "psychocentric discourse." Stated plainly, the word "psychocentric" refers not to a generalized understanding of the psyche, but to specific power-knowledge systems created by western, global north bio-psychiatry; and "discourse" does not merely signal a critique of language or labeling, but of the ways in which psychiatric power gets operationalized, materialized, and deployed in and through the bodies and everyday lives of psychosocially disabled people. Critics of psychocentric discourse contend that since the 1980s, an increasingly globalized neoliberal bio-psychiatry has developed, which, according to Daley and Ross (2018), "promotes the individualization and pathologization of structurally produced mental and emotional distress, as well as the responsibilization of individuals for such distress." Stated in more direct terms, the modern power-knowledge regime that critics refer to as "bio-psychiatry" roots the cause of various "mental illnesses" and "mental disorders" in (an as yet undiscovered and unmeasurable) impairment and holds individual people responsible for their well-being. Although it acknowledges the social determinants of health, bio-psychiatry roots the cause of madness and distress in individual bodies and situates its interventions at the level of individual biochemistry. It stresses the alteration of individual biochemistry through the (compulsory if necessary) use of often debilitating psychopharmaceuticals as a means of "treatment" and control of psychiatrized people. Bio-psychiatry frames madness and distress as "disease" or "disorder" and asserts that psychiatrized people must remain chemically dependent for the remainder of their lives in order to approximate some semblance of hegemonic normality.

Drawing on decades of work, recent scholars are exposing western, global north bio-psychiatry's reliance on the deployment of dominant, hetero-normative, white-Anglo, and broadly middle class, ways of being in the world to delimit health and illness, order and disorder, normality and pathology (Daley and Ross 2018; Jacob et al. 2018; Mills 2015; Pilling et al. 2018; Van Veen et al. 2018). Numerous authors have shown the significant role that race, gender, class, sex, sexuality, and neurotypicality play in the creation of psychiatric diagnoses, which have expanded with each new edition of the American Psychiatric Association's *Diagnostic and Statistical Manual of Mental Disorders* (Horwitz 2021). Only 3–6% of mental health research published in high impact and indexed medical journals comes from low- and middle-income countries (Lancet Global Mental Health Group 2007). Although about 85% of the world's population lives outside of Europe and the United States, about 95% of the evidence used in bio-psychiatry comes from those two places (Lancet Global Mental Health Group 2007). Pereira-Sanchez et al. (2021) found that 95% of Masters programs in global health are in high-income countries, with most of them in the United States and United Kingdom. Concepts critical to the maintenance of bio-psychiatrists control over people with psychosocial disabilities, such as "insight" – the extent to which someone is aware of their "illness" – and "capacity" – the ability to make informed decisions – have been shown to have deep roots in racialized and gendered ways of understanding the world and the people in it (Daley and Ross 2018). "Insight," moreover, has been found to be positively correlated with the extent to which a "patient" accepts the bio-psychiatric narrative of their "illness" and remains "compliant" with its administration of various interventions into their bodies (Pilling et al. 2018).

Users, survivors, and psychosocially disabled people critique the *DSM* and other systems of classification, which operate on an as yet unfounded understanding of madness as an impairment rooted in the body (Brunner 2020; Russo 2016). Although it promotes a "bio-psycho-social" approach to thinking about disability and asserts that disability is the result of a dynamic interaction between the person and the environment, the International Classification of Functioning, Disability and Health (ICF), which is important in the work of the World Health Organization (WHO) and the MGMH, relies on a biomedical understanding of mental troubles and distress. The WHO states that "mental *disorders* ... have a physical basis in the brain" (Mills 2015, emphasis in original). China Mills (2015) points out that the ICF and the WHO do not "distinguish between type or cause of disability, or between mental and physical health" (205). They take the approach that "impairments are not contingent on ideology," or, in other words, on the power-knowledge systems that produce them. Instead, the ICF and the WHO operate with a rather uncritical understanding that all impairments "represent a deviation from certain general accepted population standards in the *biomedical* status of the body and its functions" and that disability is identified and measured by "those qualified to judge physical and mental functioning" (Mills 2015, 205, emphasis in original). Critics of the medical model of madness created through the *DSM*, the ICF, and the WHO challenge the notion that mental troubles and distress are biomedical impairments, which can be determined or delimited by experts who deploy dominant standards of normality.

Bio-psychiatry's interventions have also faced consistent challenges. With no clear etiology, psychiatrists, both past and present, have been able to do little more than intervene in the bodies of mad people in an effort to suppress or mask the "symptoms" or behaviors associated with madness and distress. Interventions such as restraint, seclusion, forced commitment to a hospital or other institution, forced drugging, and electroshock, many of which have been used since the early-19th century, have never been without their critics, who challenge both their efficacy and their safety (Jacob et al. 2018). Other more brutal interventions, such as transorbital lobotomy, genital mutilation, removal of sections of the colon or intestines, and extraction of some or all of the teeth, which were used in the 20th century in the United States and elsewhere, have been widely denounced for their barbarity (El-Hai 2005; Scull 2005). Some mad activists, especially those who identify as survivors, critique psychopharmaceutical interventions as well, calling them "chemical straightjackets" or "tranquil prisons" (Fabris 2011). While they do not deny the need for intervention and support in the lives of mad people, critics of bio-psychiatry challenge the often coercive, reductive, and harmful approaches to mental health care it deploys (LeFrancois et. al. 2013; Mills 2012; Morrison 2009). They instead favor community-based interventions that rely on peer support, open dialogue, and other more equitable and sustainable forms of mental health care (Kemp et al. 2019).

Activists and scholars have articulated multiple interconnected critiques of the social and structural forces that have contributed to the globalization of bio-psychiatry. They make the rather obvious argument that multinational pharmaceutical corporations stand to gain billions in added revenue if they are able to market their drugs as a first line of defense against the perceived rise in madness and distress around the world, and in some places, as the only (or perhaps least expensive and onerous) intervention into the bodies of people living with psychosocial disabilities (Mills and Davar 2016; Mills 2015). Writers also note the long history of psychiatric colonization in the global south. The colonial expansion of mental medicine that began as early as the 16th century with the construction of asylums in North and South America, and later spread to the African continent, south and east Asia, and Oceana, endures and is gaining strength in the 21st century with the expansion of bio-psychiatry throughout the world (Ablard 2008; Baum 2018; Edington 2019; Keller 2007; Leckie 2020; Ramos 2022; Watters 2011). Critics who situate the spread of bio-psychiatry within the broader context of colonial expansion are concerned that people across the globe are being told they have to think, feel, grieve, cope with natural and other disasters, manage stress, and perceive the world in certain acceptable ways if they are to be considered "normal," "healthy," and "productive" citizens.

The expansion of bio-psychiatry throughout the world has been met by growing networks of grassroots non-governmental organizations created by people living with psychosocial disabilities who have been working to develop the means to resist it. Organizations such as the Pan-African Network of People with Psychosocial Disabilities, the Bapu Trust, and the Trans-Asia Strategic Group of Persons with Psychosocial Disabilities are working to challenge, and in some cases overturn, global north, biologically based understandings of psychosocial disability and mental health care. The Bapu Trust, which was founded by Bhargavi Davar in memory of her mother, Bapu, who, according to Mills and Davar (2016), "was subjected to violent psychiatric interventions and indignity … because she heard voices," relies on the knowledge of those who experience madness or distress to create networks of support within communities (439). One of the goals of the Bapu Trust is to create the conditions needed in the community to care for people in a way that is equitable, just, and sustainable. Like a number of localized global south organizations run by people who identify as psychosocially disabled or as users or survivors, the Bapu Trust has built and nurtured relationships with the global movement to resist bio-psychiatry – representatives from the Bapu Trust helped write the CRPD – while always remaining mindful of and connected to the local communities and cultures within which it is embedded (Mills and Davar 2016).

Together, people with psychosocial disabilities are using the CRPD to expose the human rights abuses they encounter in different medical settings throughout the world (Mills and Davar 2016). The right not to have bio-psychocentric interventions imposed in the global south is increasingly being expressed by people living with psychosocial disabilities. For example, the Pan-African Network of People with Psychosocial Disabilities states that services and support must be delivered in "non-paternalistic and non-patriarchal frameworks with choices available outside of the medical framework" within the community, and that available services and supports must include "the choice not to use western medical 'solutions'" (Quoted in Mills and Davar 2016, 444). The Pan-African Network has further critiqued the World Health Organization's QualityRights tool kit, which provides countries with resources for assessing and improving quality and human rights standards in mental health and social care facilities, declaring that it does not "adequately reflect" the meaning and intent of the CRPD or the social model of disability, which they associate with non-medicalized policies and interventions and the right of disabled people to make decisions about their own lives (Mills 2015, 209). The Pan-African Network insists that there can be no mental health "without embracing our [people living with psychosocial disabilities'] expertise. We have always remained the untapped resource in mental health care" (quoted in Mills 2015, 212). Psychiatrized people throughout the world are creating local and global movements to resist the imposition of bio-psychiatry into their lives.

Although some global south activists and advocates have aligned themselves with groups such as the World Network of Users and Survivors of Psychiatry in their struggle against bio-psychiatry, there are people and organizations in the global south who refuse even to use the terms "user" and "survivor" because they consider them unrepresentative of their experiences and part of psychocentric discourse. In some places, peoples' lived experiences have not been dominated by medico-legal or colonial psychiatric systems. More often, however, people who have been made part of medico-legal and colonial *psy* systems want to reject the terms associated with them, such as "user" and "survivor." The Pan-African Network and the Trans-Asia Strategic Group of Persons with Psychosocial Disabilities are two groups that have decided not to use the terms "user" and "survivor" because those terms do not adequately represent their lived experiences, or because those terms are already too deeply embedded within psychocentric discourse (Mills and Davar 2016).

Other groups, such as the Global Mental Health Peer Network, situate themselves more firmly within the growing MGMH, but maintain a powerful critique of bio-psychiatry. Charlene Sunkel, and others who identify as people with lived experience of mental health conditions, launched the Peer Network in February 2018 at the MGMH's fifth Global Mental Health summit in Johannesburg, South Africa (Sunkel 2021). Sunkel describes the Peer Network as a "global mental health care user organization" with a "well-established and sustainable structure, that supports the recovery and person-centered approach to mental health" (Sunkel 2021, 1497). Although it uses some of the language and tools associated with psychocentric discourse, the network insists that it is founded upon an "integrated and holistic" understanding of mental health that incorporates medical and social models of madness and distress, and that it works to protect the human rights of people experiencing mental troubles. The Peer Network describes what it calls "mental health conditions" and "mental disorders" as multi-dimensional and asserts that they can affect all aspects of people's lives and occur at all stages of life. The Peer Network is founded upon the belief that mental troubles cannot be dealt with solely as a "medical problem" (Sunkel 2021, 1497–1498).

The Peer Network advocates for mental health care and service delivery that protects the rights, dignity, will, and preferences of people with lived experience. It is working to move mental health care away from a "one approach fits all" (western, global north, bio-psychiatric) model and instead utilizes an integrated and coordinated approach that involves "diverse stakeholders" (Sunkel 2021, 1502). It seeks to empower people with lived experience to "take charge" of their health and well-being. It is working to improve access to care and services and to move away from "substitute decision-making" toward "supported decision-making" (Sunkel 2021, 1502). One member of the Peer Network's executive committee, Matthew Jackman from Australia, describes the importance of peer work among people with lived experience of madness and distress (Sunkel 2021). Jackman writes that without peer work the mental health care system "will continue to implode through biomedical band aid solutions to complex socio-political structures creating collective and inter-generational mental distress" (quoted in Sunkel 2021, 1511). According to Jackman, peer work "reconstructs a human rights, social justice and natural medicine approach to clinical mental health systems often dominated by bio-medical approaches" (quoted in Sunkel 2021, 1511). While they work within clinical mental health settings and they are part of the MGMH, the Peer Network enacts systems of support and care that are in some ways a radical departure from bio-psychiatry.

The Peer Network is building a sustainable mental health movement led by people with lived experience (Sunkel 2021, 1498). Network leaders are working to create a global community of "experts by experience" who are empowered to self-advocate and to advocate on a broader scale (Sunkel 2021, 1499). The Peer Network also seeks to address "deeply entrenched systems of discrimination and exclusion" that people experiencing mental troubles and distress continue to encounter (Sunkel 2021, 1500). It is using the CRPD to eliminate stigma and to transform mental health care by improving human rights literacy across the world, but especially in low- and middle-income countries. It works to link "user groups and movements" to provide peer support, knowledge sharing, and the sharing of "evidence-based" information. The Peer Network works to create collaborative opportunities for mental healthcare users and other people with lived experience of mental troubles (Sunkel 2021, 1501). Many of the Network's activities take place online at its website (gmhpn.org) and through social media websites, such as Facebook and Twitter. The network uses these and other platforms to share written and video "recovery stories" through its "Our Global Voice Project." It incorporates the fund of knowledge created through its various platforms into its policy and mental health care advocacy work. Through its focus on sharing stories and information, building peer support, and empowering leaders with lived experience, the Peer Network is creating a space within the medically oriented MGMH where people can voice their needs, challenges, views, opinions, and perspectives and shape their individual and collective encounters with mental health care.

Activists, academics, and global leaders of organizations dedicated to advancing the rights of users, survivors, and other people living with psychosocial disabilities, are working – often with relatively little funding – to build and strengthen efforts to resist the imposition of bio-psychiatry into their lives. They oppose what some have referred to as "standardized approaches and monocultures" in favor of building diversity within their movements and within the systems of support and care available in the community (Mills and Davar 2016, 447–448). Many activists and advocates argue that working for social justice and broad structural change will help to mitigate, if not eliminate, at least some of the causes of madness and distress. Organizers insist that efforts to create and diversify coalitions and work toward social justice and structural change must include a willingness to rethink current attempts to globalize bio-psychiatry. As the work of multiple groups around the world makes clear, bio-psychiatry cannot be neatly or easily transposed onto the global south, where local histories and cultures, and global capitalism converge and interact to shape knowledge and lived experiences. Building and sustaining meaningful and effective mental health care requires local and global efforts to organize and advocate for rights and social justice led by people living with psychosocial disabilities.

Bio-psychiatry responds

As noted earlier, the MGMH emerged in 2008 in response to a call made by the *Lancet* commission on global mental health and sustainable development to "scale up" mental health care across the world, but especially in low- and middle-income countries. With more than 230 organizational members and 15,000 individual members, the movement appears to be thriving. In 2018, the *Lancet* commission on global mental health and sustainable development published its report on a decade of efforts to expand mental health awareness and services throughout the world (Patel et al. 2018, 1553). While the *Lancet* report acknowledges the concerns raised by activists and advocates, as well as their attempts to diversify mental health interventions in clinical settings, it remains deeply rooted in bio-psychocentric discourse.

It seems, on the surface, that the authors of the 2018 *Lancet* report are listening to users, survivors, and other people living with psychosocial disabilities. The report recognizes the importance of the CRPD and asserts that "mental health problems" exist on a continuum. It makes explicit the idea that mental health is "unique" and dependent upon social and environmental influences and that it can change over the course of the lifespan. It acknowledges, for example, that mental health can be affected by climate change and growing global inequality, as well as trauma and abuse. The report notes that many people living with psychosocial disabilities suffer trauma and abuse. The report encourages embracing new opportunities and perspectives on mental health care provided by "trained non-specialist individuals," "digital technologies," and the "mobilization of the voices of people with lived experience of mental disorders," as well as their families (Patel et al. 2018, 1553–1554, 1557).

It is clear, however, that the authors of the report consider much of what is being said by critics of bio-psychiatry as a threat to the expansion of a certain type of medically oriented mental health care. The authors of the report include their discussion of mounting critiques of bio-psychiatry in their section entitled, "Threats to global mental health" (Patel et al. 2018, 1559–1560). Advocacy for global mental health, the report contends, has been "threatened by fragmentation caused by diverse constituencies and scientific perspectives," which can result in a "lack of coherent plans to address mental health" (Patel et al. 2018, 1560). The report pathologizes and dismisses academic and activist concerns as a "fear" (Patel et al. 2018, 1560). It states that critics of bio-psychiatry "fear that a biomedical emphasis will take priority over indigenous traditions of healing and recovery, medicalise social suffering, and promote a western psychiatric framework dominated by pharmaceutical interventions" (Patel et al. 2018, 1560). The language in the report further undermines the work of critics of bio-psychiatry by arguing that they are "championing" a "cultural," and therefore unscientific perspective of madness and its treatment (Patel et al. 2018, 1560). The report does little to convey the earnest work being done by users, survivors, and other people living with psychosocial disabilities at the local and global levels to redefine mental troubles and distress and to provide people with meaningful, effective, and sustainable forms of intervention and support.

Instead of collective, collaborative, and structural approaches to mental health care, the *Lancet* commission calls for more individualized and widely dispersed bio-psychiatric interventions. The 2018 report privileges interventions made at the level of genes and individual biochemistry to both treat and prevent what it refers to as "mental disorders." It frames "prevention" as early interventions into the bodies of "at-risk" children, older adults, and other populations often marked by race, class, and gender. The authors of the report frame the expansion of bio-psychiatry not as the imposition of western, global north ways of knowing and treating madness, but as an historic opportunity to transform the global mental health "agenda." Access to bio-psychiatry, they declare is a "public good" and efforts should be made to improve its availability to "all populations," not merely those "affected by mental disorders." While the MGMH includes groups such as the Global Mental Health Peer Network, it remains reluctant to rethink the bio-psychocentric discourse that undergirds its work.

The *Lancet* report prioritizes the global south in its continued call to expand bio-psychiatry. The authors of the report recognize the need for improved mental health care in high-income countries, but contend that people living in middle- and low-income countries are especially vulnerable and should be given priority in global efforts to increase access to mental health care. The report highlights changes made in Brazil, India, Ghana, Sri Lanka, Rwanda, and China. It asserts, however, that much more work remains to be completed. Many people around the world go untreated or are subjected to abuse and neglect, and in India and China, where one-third of the world's population lives, 80% of people with "any mental or substance use disorder" do not "seek treatment" (Patel et al. 2018, 1559). Instead of working within local cultures and communities to create sustainable systems of support and intervention, the authors of the report envision the mental health crisis gripping much of the world as an opportunity to expand bio-psychiatry (Watters 2011).

The focus on expanding bio-psychiatry in low- and middle-income countries can be seen in Pereira-Sanchez et al. (2021). Although they acknowledge that mental health curricula and education should be "grass-rooted" and "tailored to local needs and context" (709), Pereira-Sanchez et al., who are all early career psychiatrists and psychiatric trainees, dismiss the concerns raised by critics of the globalization of bio-psychiatry in a single sentence. They make no effort to include users, survivors, and people who identify as psychosocially disabled in their call to improve and expand mental health curriculum and education. The authors make no mention of peer support or other systems of care that empower users, survivors, and people living with psychosocial disabilities (Beresford 2016; Brown and Stastny 2016; Brunner 2020; Davar 2016; Ellis et. al. 2021; Filson and Mead 2016; Jesperson 2016). Instead of immersing themselves in support and care work that might alter their views and challenge their assumptions about their own power and authority (Kemp et al. 2019), Pereira-Sanchez et al. (2021) advocate training physicians in "cultural competence" and "cultural humility" (715), which are individualized approaches meant to improve the clinical or therapeutic encounter. No effort is made by Pereira-Sanchez et al. (2021) to incorporate what Metzl and Hansen (2014) call "structural competency," which would begin to shift the focus away from individual bodies and bio-chemistry toward the social and structural determinants of health and social justice. While the approaches promoted by Pereira-Sanchez et al. (2021) may help individual physicians to be more mindful in their interactions with patients, they do not alter inequities rooted in long histories of ableism, racism, colonialism, and patriarchy, or shift the balance of power in mental health care toward users, survivors, and psychosocially disabled people.

Conclusion

Global mental health initiatives emphasize "scaling up" access to bio-psychocentric interventions, including the administration of psychopharmaceuticals and treatment in clinical mental health settings. The MGMH and the WHO use the ICF and a rather uncritical reading of essential activist-created measures such as the CRPD to legitimize their efforts to standardize bio-psychiatric mental health care across the globe. At the same time, however, there are growing groups of people living with psychosocial disabilities in the global north and in the global south who are using the CRPD to challenge the largely unchecked expansion of bio-psychiatry.

Many of the most vocal disability rights activists and advocates consider the CRPD revolutionary and want to use it, at least in part, to constrain the expansion of bio-psychocentric discourse (Minkowitz 2014). Tina Minkowitz and the Center for the Human Rights of Users and Survivors of Psychiatry, as well as the Pan-African Network of People with Psychosocial Disabilities, the Trans-Asia Strategic Group of Persons with Psychosocial Disabilities, and the Global Mental Health Peer Network see the CRPD – which disabled people helped to write – as providing them with the legal means to create local and global networks of peer support and oppose bio-psychiatric interventions such as forced drugging and compulsory commitment to hospitals or other institutions into their lives.

Critics of bio-psychiatry assert that attending to mounting global mental health concerns is essential work, but it cannot be done without the input and leadership of people living with psychosocial disabilities. They insist that although initiatives like the MGMH acknowledge diverse ways of knowing and being in the world, they are overly reliant upon a bio-psychocentric discourse that devalues the place of psychosocially disabled people in the development of effective, equitable, and sustainable mental health care. Too often the only voices and experiences the MGMH and other initiatives like it recognize are those of people whom they identify as "consumers" of psychiatric services administered by a range of mental health professionals, including psychiatrists, psychologists, nurses, general practitioners, and social workers. Innovative approaches, such as peer support and open dialogue (Kemp et al. 2019), which have their roots in communities of survivors and other people with lived experience, have the potential to transform global mental health care, but only if physicians and other professionals commit themselves to developing structural competency (Metzl and Hansen 2014) and open themselves to relinquishing at least some of the power and control they have in most mental healthcare settings.

References

Ablard, Johnathan. *Madness in Buenos Aires Patients, Psychiatrists and the Argentine State, 1880–1983*. University of Calgary Press, 2008.

Baum, Emily. *The Invention of Madness: State, Society, and the Insane in Modern China*. University of Chicago Press, 2018.

Beresford, Peter. "The role of survivor knowledge in creating alternatives to psychiatry," in Jasna Russo and Angela Sweeney, eds. *Searching for a Rose Garden: Challenging Psychiatry, Fostering Mad Studies* (PCCS Books, 2016): 25–34.

Brown, Celia and Peter Stastny. "Peer workers in the mental health system: A transformative or collusive experiment?" in Jasna Russo and Angela Sweeney, eds. *Searching for a Rose Garden: Challenging Psychiatry, Fostering Mad Studies* (PCCS Books, 2016): 183–191.

Brunner, Richard. "Critical realism as the fourth "wave": deepening and broadening social perspectives on mental distress," in Nick Watson and Simo Vehmas, eds. *Routledge Handbook of Disability Studies*, Second Edition (New York: Rutledge, 2020): 189–205.

Daley, Andrea and Lori E. Ross. "Uncovering the heteronormative order of the psychiatric institution: a queer reading of chart documentation and language use," in M. Kilty Jennifer and Erin Dej, eds. *Containing Madness: Gender and 'Psy' in Institutional Contexts* (New York: Palgrave Macmillan, 2018): 169–190.

Davar, Bhargavi. "Alternatives or a way of life?" in Jasna Russo and Angela Sweeney, eds. *Searching for a Rose Garden: Challenging Psychiatry, Fostering Mad Studies* (PCCS Books, 2016): 14–19.

Edington, Claire E. *Beyond the Asylum: Mental Illness in French Colonial Vietnam*. Ithaca, NY: Cornell University Press, 2019.

El-Hai, Jack. *The Lobotomist: A Maverick Medical Genius and His Tragic Quest to Rid the World of Mental Illness*. Hoboken, NJ: J. Wiley, 2005.

Ellis, Robert, Sarah Kendal, and Steven J. Taylor, eds. *Voices in the History of Madness: Personal and Professional Perspectives on Mental Health and Illness*. Basingstoke: Palgrave Macmillan, 2021.

Fabris, Erick. *Tranquil Prisons: Mad Peoples Experiences of Chemical Incarceration Under Community Treatment Orders*. University of Toronto Press, 2011.

Filson, Beth and Shery Mead. "Becoming part of each other's narratives: intentional peer support," in Jasna Russo and Angela Sweeney, eds. *Searching for a Rose Garden: Challenging Psychiatry, Fostering Mad Studies* (PCCS Books, 2016): 109–117.

Horwitz, Allan V. *DSM: A History of Psychiatry's Bible*. Baltimore, MD: Johns Hopkins University Press, 2021.

Jacob, Jean Daniel, Dave Holmes, Desire Rioux, and Pascale Corneau. "Patients' perspective on mechanical restraints in acute and emergency psychiatric settings: a poststructural feminist analysis," in Jennifer M. Kilty and Erin Dej, eds. *Containing Madness: Gender and 'Psy' in Institutional Contexts* (New York: Palgrave Macmillan, 2018): 93–118.

Jesperson, Maths. "The Personal Ombudsman: an example of supported decision-making," in Jasna Russo and Angela Sweeney, eds. *Searching for a Rose Garden: Challenging Psychiatry, Fostering Mad Studies* (PCCS Books, 2016): 134–141.

Keller, Richard C. *Colonial Madness: Psychiatry in French North Africa*. University of Chicago Press, 2007.

Kemp, Holly, et al. "Peer support and open dialogue: possibilities for transformation and resistance in mental health services," in Paul Rhodes, eds. *Beyond the Psychology Industry: How Else Might We Heal?* (Springer, 2019): 49–67. http://www.vlebooks.com/vleweb/product/openreader?id=none&isbn=9783030337629.

Lancet Global Mental Health Group. "Global Mental Health 6, scale up services for mental disorders: a call for action," *The Lancet*, 370 (October 6, 2007): 1245. doi:10.1016/S0140-6736(07)61242-2.

Leckie, Jacqueline. *Colonizing Madness: Asylum and Community in Fiji*. Honolulu: University of Hawai'i Press, 2020.

LeFrançois, Brenda A., Robert Menzies, and Geoffrey Reaume, eds. *Mad Matters: A Critical Reader in Canadian Mad Studies* (Canadian Scholars' Press, 2013).

Metzl, Jonathan M. and Helena Hansen. "Structural competency: theorizing a new medical engagement with stigma and inequality," *Social Science & Medicine* 103 (2014): 126–133.

Mills, China. "The global politics of disablement: assuming impairment and erasing complexity," in Helen Spandler, Jill Anderson, and Bob Sapey, eds. *Madness, Distress and the Politics of Disablement* (Bristol: Policy Press, 2015): 199–213.

Mills, China. "Live and let die: global mental health and critical disability studies," in Jill Anderson, Bob Sapey, and Helen Spandler, eds. *Distress or Disability? Proceedings of a Symposium Held at Lancaster University, 15–16 November 2011* (UK: Centre for Disability Research, Lancaster University, 2012): 57–61.

Mills, China and Bhargavi Davar. "A local critique of global mental health," in Shaun Grech and Karen Soldatic, eds. *Disability in the Global South: The Critical Handbook* (Cham: Springer International Publishing, 2016): 437–451.

Minkowitz, Tina. "Convention on the rights of persons with disabilities and liberation from psychiatric oppression," in Bonnie Burstow, Brenda A. LeFrançois, and Shaindl Diamond, eds. *Psychiatry Disrupted: Theorizing Resistance and Crafting the (R)Evolution* (McGill-Queen's University Press, 2014).

Morrison, Linda J. *Talking Back to Psychiatry: The Psychiatric Consumer/Survivor/Ex-Patient Movement*. Taylor & Francis, 2009.

Patel, Vikram, et al. "The *Lancet* Commission on global mental health and sustainable development," *Lancet* 392 (2018): 1553–1598. doi:10.1016/S0140-6736(18)31612-X.

Pereira-Sanchez, Victor, Jibril I. M. Handuleh, Justo E. Pinzón-Espinoza, and Darpan Kaur Mohinder Singh. "Developing a curriculum in global mental health: theories and models in medical education," Samuel O. Okpaku, ed. *Innovations in Global Mental Health* (Springer, 2021): 707–725. doi:10.1007/978-3-030-57296-9.

Pilling, Merrick D., Andrea Daley, Margaret F. Gibson, Lori E. Ross, and Juveria Zaheer. "Assessing 'insight', determining agency and autonomy: implicating social identities," in Jennifer M. Kilty and Erin Dej, eds. *Containing Madness: Gender and 'Psy' in Institutional Contexts* (New York: Palgrave Macmillan, 2018): 191–214.

Ramos, Christina. *Bedlam in the New World: A Mexican Madhouse in the Age of Enlightenment* (University of North Carolina Press, 2022).

Rimke, Heidi. "Introduction - mental and emotional distress as a social justice issue: beyond psychocentrism." *Studies in Social Justice* 10, 1 (2016): 4–17.

Russo, Jasna. "Towards our own framework, or reclaiming madness part two," in Jasna Russo and Angela Sweeney, eds. *Searching for a Rose Garden: Challenging Psychiatry, Fostering Mad Studies* (PCCS Books, 2016): 59–68.

Scull, Andrew T. *Madhouse: A Tragic Tale of Megalomania and Modern Medicine*. New Haven: Yale University Press, 2005.

Series, Lucy. "Disability and human rights," in Nick Watson and Simo Vehmas, eds. *Routledge Handbook of Disability Studies*, Second Edition (New York: Rutledge, 2020): 72–88.

Spandler, Helen, Jill Anderson, and Bob Sapey. "Advancing the rights of users and survivors of psychiatry using the UN Convention on the Rights of Persons with Disabilities: an interview with Tina Minkowitz," in Helen Spandler, Jill Anderson, and Bob Sapey, eds. *Madness, Distress and the Politics of Disablement* (Bristol: Policy Press, 2015): 171–182.

Sunkel, Charlene. "The global mental health peer network: the role of persons with lived experience with mental health conditions," in Samuel O. Okpaku, ed. *Innovations in Global Mental Health* (Springer, 2021): 1497–1513. doi:10.1007/978-3-030-57296-9.

Van Veen, Christopher, Mohamed Ibrahim, and Marina Morrow. "Dangerous discourses: masculinity, coercion, and psychiatry," in Jennifer M. Kilty and Erin Dej, eds. *Containing Madness: Gender and 'Psy' in Institutional Contexts* (New York: Palgrave Macmillan, 2018): 241–266.

Watters, Ethan. *Crazy Like Us: The Globalization of the American Psyche*. New York: Free Press, 2011.

Wilson, Anne and Peter Beresford. "Madness, distress and postmodernity: putting the record straight," in Mairian Corker and Tom Shakespeare, eds. *Disability/Postmodernity: Embodying Disability Theory* (London: Continuum, 2002): 143–157

Part II

5 Conditions for religious citizenship for people with intellectual disabilities

Cases from Norway and Slovakia

Dmitry Lukash and Anna Chalachanová

Religious citizenship: Delineating a concept

The notion of citizenship is elusive and manifold, in both general and scholarly usage. Its most traditional and widely used understanding is legal and political and signifies a special status of belonging to a particular nation-state. This belonging is often conceived as connected to a set of rights and corresponding duties which citizens hold (Halvorsen, Hvinden, Bickenbach, Ferri, & Rodriguez, 2017; Sépulchre, 2020). However, the concept of citizenship is used in a much wider sense, highlighting various kinds of group identity, status and belonging, as well as the rights, obligations, activities and practices connected to them (Friedman, 2005; Hirschmann & Linker, 2015). An especially fruitful way to conceptualise citizenship, at least in the context of our research, is to emphasise it as belonging to a particular community (not necessarily a nation-state), which enacts certain rights and obligations from its members (Hirschmann & Linker, 2015).

Here, it is important to note that citizenship can be understood both as belonging to or membership in a group or a community and as (active) participation in the life of the group on equal footing with other members (Isin, 2008). Both aspects are inseparable from each other. The inherent worth of a human qua humans is inseparable from being an agent, a *subject* of one's own life (Isin, 2008; Mackenzie, 2019). It entails that to exercise one's citizenship actively means not only enjoying a formal status as a member of a community with corresponding formal rights but also opportunities to realise and exercise them together with and on an equal basis with one's fellow citizens. Thus, citizenship presupposes democratic participation in social life.

While citizenship in general is a multifaceted concept, the theoretical underpinnings of the notion of religious citizenship are underdeveloped (Nyhagen, 2015). It is beyond the scope of this chapter to bridge this gap in any significant way, but we would argue that religious citizenship may also be considered a varied and multilevel concept. On the level of the nation-state, it may be understood as the constitutionally guaranteed freedom to worship and participate in religious practice, alone or in community with others. On the level of religious organisations and communities, it can be seen as

DOI: 10.4324/9781003052708-9

granting people the status of full members of these organisations on an equal basis with others.

In the research we present in this chapter, we consider religious citizenship largely from the perspective of conditions that enable people with intellectual disabilities to actively practise religion and participate in the lives of their religious communities, on their terms and an equal basis with their non-disabled fellow citizens.

Religious citizenship of people with intellectual disabilities

It is impossible to consider citizenship as practice, including religious citizenship, without taking into account disability itself, its formation and maintenance. The relational model of disability presupposes that it is formed and maintained by both intrinsic (bodily, cognitive) and extrinsic (societal) factors (on the relational model, see, for example, Broderick & Ferri, 2019; Ellingsen & Sandvin, 2014; Gustavsson et al., 2005; Shakespeare, 2005). In other words, a person's disability is caused not only by their bodily or cognitive impairments but also by social and cultural factors—like built environments, political institutions, laws and cultural attitudes—which may be organised and structured in such a way that restricts the person's ability to function (Hirschmann & Linker, 2015). This approach elucidates the implications of extrinsic factors of disability since these factors play a significant role in excluding persons with disability from exercising citizenship, or at least setting barriers for them.

Therefore, for people with intellectual disabilities, practicing citizenship entails both theoretical and practical challenges. On the practical level, it may be argued that for people with disabilities, citizenship as status was (and to a significant extent still is) separated from citizenship's practical dimension (Sépulchre, 2020). For instance, people with intellectual disabilities are legally considered citizens of their states, but in practice are often deprived of the ability to vote (e.g., due to a lack of easy-to-read support materials; Sépulchre, 2020; Glørstad, 2019). Similarly, people with physical impairments can be denied participation in elections by physical barriers which may hinder their access to polling stations. At the same time, current and widely held notions of what constitutes necessary and sufficient conditions for people to be regarded as citizens may deprive some people with intellectual disabilities from enacting their citizenship. For instance, it could be argued (indeed, quite intuitively) that to have certain rights and be able to enact them, one must possess a certain level of cognitive capacity (Skarstad, 2019; Griffin, 2009). From this point of view, to be entitled to civil and political rights requires a person to possess reasoning, self-awareness and autonomy, as well as the capability to take part in rational deliberation concerning public affairs (Lukash, 2020; Terzi, 2015). Thus, people who lack—or are assumed by others to lack—these capacities could be easily marginalised and regarded more as passive recipients of care than as active co-citizens (Lukash, 2020).

In the sphere of religious life, people with intellectual disabilities likewise encounter both obstacles for practising citizenship and factors that empower them in this activity. It is important to note that these factors unfold differently in different arenas. For instance, as we show in the next section, in the arena of international human rights law and national legislation, a person with disabilities may be entitled to full freedom of religion; at the same time, attitudes towards their capacity to be an active religious citizen—among the population in general, as well as in a specific religious community—may significantly hamper their religious citizenship.

Religious citizenship of people with ID from the perspective of human rights

The notion of religious freedom and the right to religious practice represents one of the basic human rights, and is emphasised as such in all central sources of international human rights law, such as the Universal Declaration of Human Rights (Article 18), International Covenant of Civic and Political Rights (ICCPR; Article 18), International Covenant on Economic, Social, and Cultural Rights (ICESCR; Article 18) and, regionally, the European Convention of Human Rights (ECCHR; Article 9). At the same time, two documents are dedicated solely to freedom of religion: namely, the Declaration on the Elimination of All Forms of Intolerance and of Discrimination Based on Religion or Belief, enacted by the United Nations General Assembly in 1981 (United Nations, 1981), and the General Comment on Article 18 of ICCPR, issued by the United Nations Human Rights Committee in 1993 (UN Human Rights Committee, 1993).

This body of law has a general character and prohibits all types of discrimination. It serves as a fairly strong protection for the freedom of religion of people with intellectual disabilities. Nevertheless, the Convention on the Rights of People with Disabilities (CRPD), the most central body of international law protecting the rights of people with (intellectual) disabilities, does not include freedom of religion and the right to worship. Religion *is* mentioned in the preamble, where the CRPD raises concerns about

> the difficult conditions faced by persons with disabilities who are subject to multiple or aggravated forms of discrimination on the basis of race, colour, sex, language, religion, political or other opinion, national, ethnic, indigenous or social origin, property, birth, age or other status. (United Nations, 2006, Preamble p.)

However, any specification of rights and freedoms connected to disabled people's religious practice is absent from the Convention.

At the same time, in Article 30, the Convention confirms the rights of people with intellectual disabilities to participate 'in cultural life, recreation, leisure and sport' (United Nations, 2006, 30). For instance, it specifies the rights of people with disabilities to fully participate in cultural life on an equal basis (United Nations, 2006), including having access to cultural materials, activities and performances or services, as well as the opportunity to develop and use their creative potential. Furthermore, it proclaims that people with disabilities are entitled to recognition and support of their cultural identity and heritage. All these articles may be interpreted as encompassing religious practice. However, it can be argued that, by omitting such a fundamental first-generation right as the freedom to practise religion individually and in community with others, the Convention leaves important issues unaddressed—like people with disabilities' right to (a) insist that providers of residential and medical services offer opportunities to participate in the religious life and (b) select medical and other services in accordance with their religious beliefs (Silecchia, 2014). Thus, the Convention, through its emphasis on the subjectivity and agency of people with disabilities, provides a strong moral and legal case for their citizenship; at the same time, the lack of a specific article on religious freedom and the right to practise religion may lead to situations where these rights are implemented insufficiently and potentially leave certain areas of citizenship unaddressed.

Potentials and barriers to religious citizenship: Cases from Norway and Slovakia

Setting the context: The freedom of religion and the religious landscape of Norway

Norway has ratified and/or incorporated into its domestic legislation all the aforementioned sources of international human rights law regulating freedom of religion (Human Rights Act, Article 1). In addition, these rights are included in the national Constitution (Article 19).

There is no specific domestic legislation that secures rights and freedoms, including that of religion, among people with disabilities. Norway signed the CRPD in 2007 and ratified it in 2013 (Strand, 2014); it is therefore obliged to implement its requirements. However, unlike the International Covenant on Civil and Political Rights (ICCPR), the ECCHR and the ICESCR, as well as the Convention on the Rights of the Child (CRC) and the Convention on the Elimination of All Forms of Discrimination Against Women (CEDAW), the CRPD in its official wording is included neither in the Human Rights Act (1999) nor in any other law (Strand, 2014). Thus, formally speaking, it has lower status than the aforementioned conventions and in the case of a conflict between norms, domestic legislation would have precedence over it, weakening the Conventions' position vis-à-vis domestic law (Strand, 2014).

The religious landscape of contemporary Norway is in many ways similar to other Nordic states. Historically, it was dominated by one established church, the Lutheran Church of Norway (Schmidt, 2010). At the same time, alongside other Nordic countries (except Denmark), the Church was officially separated from the State, through the constitutional amendments of 2012–2014

(Lukash, 2020; Kühle et al., 2018). However, constitutionally, the Church still retains special status as 'the established Church' (*folkekirke*), with a special provision in the Constitution (§ 16) that guarantees its state support.[1]

In recent years, the Church of Norway has lost a significant number of its members (from 85% of the population in 1994 to 68% in 2020; Østhus, 2021). Similarly, the number of baptisms and confirmations decreased from 80% of newborns and 68.3% of 15-year olds, in 2001, to 45% and 52.3% (respectively) in 2020 (Østhus, 2021). According to European Values Study data from 2008 to 2010, 54% of Norwegian respondents either never attended a church service, or had done so only on the main religious holidays (Furseth et al., 2018).

At the same time, the available data show that membership in religious societies outside the Church of Norway (Christian and others) has recently increased, from 8% in 2006 to 13% in 2020 (Statistisk Sentralbyrå, 2021). This increase in membership may, at least partly, be attributed to immigration (Østhus, 2021). Most of these organisations are Christian, including Roman Catholics and free Lutheran Churches, followed by Islamic, Buddhist, Hindu and others (Statistisk Sentralbyrå, 2021). A somewhat peculiar feature of Norway's religious landscape is its large number of organised secular humanists, represented mostly by the Norwegian Humanist Association, which is the country's third-largest faith and life-stance organisation (Statistisk Sentralbyrå, 2021).[2] In short, the Norwegian religious landscape is characterised by religious pluralism, with a growing non-Lutheran and non-Christian milieu, although the Evangelical Lutheran Church still retains the special status.

Being a faith community that claims to be open and accessible to all, the Church of Norway has not been oblivious to people with intellectual disabilities and their religious needs. Moreover, it actively involves other religious communities, as well as other organisations of civil society, in its advocacy for intellectually disabled people. For instance, in 2009, the Church Council (the Church's highest organ)—together with the Christian Council of Norway and the Council of Religious and Spiritual Communities—produced a booklet called 'Participation and Affiliation: The Inclusion of People with Disabilities into Faith and Spiritual Communities' (*Deltakelse og tilhørighet. Inkludering av mennesker med utviklingshemning i tros- og livssynssamfunn*). This text unequivocally rejects paternalistic attitudes towards people with intellectual disabilities as simple recipients of charity:

> Adults with intellectual disabilities should be treated in the same way as other adults. […] We are all fellow human beings (*medmennesker*). Nobody is an 'object of charity' for whom we have to do something. (Kirkerådet et al., 2009, pp. 10, 11)

Thus, this and other similar declarations show that, at least officially, the Church of Norway and other major religious organisations in Norway has rejected the paternalising and incapacitating view of people with intellectual disabilities as mere objects of charity, taking a clear stance towards their empowerment as equal religious citizens. Together with legal guarantees for religious freedom, these policies may contribute to setting more favourable conditions for the enactment of intellectually disabled people's religious citizenship.

Setting the context: The freedom of religion and the religious landscape of Slovakia

As an independent nation, Slovakia is rather young, having been established in 1993 as a result of former Czechoslovakia's peaceful split. Slovakia has aligned its legislation on religion with that of the European Union, of which it has been a member since 2004.

Despite the common historical and cultural heritage of Czechia and Slovakia, the contemporary religious landscapes in the two countries are significantly different. While Czechia has one of the highest percentages of people in Europe unaffiliated with any faith community (72%), Slovakia still has a majority identifying as Roman Catholic (Sčítanie Obyvateľov, Domov a Bytov, 2021). However, the latest data show a significant increase in people with no religious affiliation (from 13.4% in 2011 to 23.8% in 2021), and a decrease from 62% in 2011 to 59.8% in 2021, respectively. And in 2021, 56% declared membership in the Roman Catholic church in 2021—representing a decrease in those identified as Roman Catholic by more than 6% since 2011 (Sčítanie Obyvateľov, Domov a Bytov, 2021; Starr, 2019). The rest of the population identified themselves as Lutherans (Evangelical Church of Augsburg Confession, 5.3%), Slovak Greek Catholics (4.0%) and Calvinists (1.6%); all other religions represent less than 1% of the population (Sčítanie Obyvateľov, Domov a Bytov, 2021).

Slovakia's legal statutes guarantee religious freedom. For instance, Article 24 of the republic's Constitution guarantees freedom of thought, conscience and religion, including the right to 'freely express religion, or faith alone or together with others, privately or publicly, by means of religious services, religious acts, by observing religious rites, or to participate in the teachings thereof', as well as to change religious affiliation and persuasion or be without any (Constitution of Republic of Slovakia,1992, Article 24.1). The Constitution's Article 24.3 establishes the separation of religious communities and organisations from the state. Moreover, Slovakia is part of all international agreements that protect religious freedom and the right to worship, including the ECCHR. However, the Roman Catholic Church has a special relationship with the Slovak Republic through the 2004 Concordat, which regulates Catholic education and military chaplaincy. In addition, it should be noted that, like the Church of Norway, the Roman Catholic Church's official position strongly insists on including people with disabilities in the life of the church, including receiving the sacraments (Francis, 2020).

The different legal, political, religious and cultural contexts in Norway and Slovakia create different conditions for the enactment of religious citizenship by people with intellectual disabilities in the respective countries. While Norway and Slovakia both provide legal conditions for the enactment of religious freedom and the right to worship (through international conventions and national legislation), the religious landscapes of Norway and Slovakia significantly differ, as shown earlier—regarding the majority denomination (Lutheran and Roman Catholic), the degree and form of the majority's religiosity, the religious diversity (including the presence of non-Christian religions) and the traditions, attitudes and policies towards people with intellectual disabilities. When considering the potential for and barriers to religious citizenship for people with intellectual disabilities in these countries, these issues must be taken into account.

General presentation of the studies

Perceptions and attitudes of Norwegian social and healthcare workers towards the religiosity of people with intellectual disabilities

The first study we consider here is based upon four focus group interviews with professional caregivers employed in residential homes (shared accommodations) and day centres for people with intellectual disabilities in Oslo and South-Western Norway between 2016 and 2019. The general aim of the study was to explore how professionals understand and perceive the religiosity and religious practice of the people with intellectual disabilities with whom they work and for whom they care (Lukash, 2020). The more specific aims of the study were to determine the significance religion holds for Norwegian service providers as professionals; what they do to secure users' freedom of religion; and in what extent and form they perceive their users as religious agents and subjects—that is, as capable of practising religious citizenship (Lukash, 2020).

The focus groups consisted of four to five participants of diverse professions (social educators, social workers, nurses and milieu therapists), as well as employees with no relevant professional backgrounds; they were conducted at the participants' workplaces (Lukash, 2020). The latter had different institutional characteristics and value profiles (one was private and Christian value-based, two were public, municipal residential homes and one was a private day centre).

Participants in all groups reported that their workplaces had a connection with a local parish of the Church of Norway, independent of the location's profile and ownership. This parish appeared to be the only religious organisation that cooperated with the workplaces (Lukash, 2020). The cooperation is usually manifested in announcements about regular pastoral services and visits (Lukash, 2020). Moreover, the staff and residents engaged in traditional activities around public holidays such as Christmas, Easter and Ascension Day (Lukash, 2020). In the residential homes with a Christian profile, furthermore, devotions (*andakter*) and certain 'devotional lunches' were conducted regularly (Lukash, 2020).

However, the focus group participants noted that not all of their users belonged to the Church of Norway; some were even members of other faiths, most notably Muslims (Lukash, 2020). According to the informants, any Islamic dietary requirements were met; all other religious practices they might wish to engage in (like celebrating Eid al-Fitr) were considered the responsibility of their families (Lukash, 2020). Moreover, the staff reported that they had no organized collaboration with mosques or other Islamic institutions: everything was left to the residents' families (Lukash, 2020). The reason for this may have been the small number of users belonging to and practising other religious traditions than Norwegian Lutheranism, or the lack of initiative from their religious communities to set up such a collaboration.

The study shows that while many focus group participants acknowledged that people with intellectual disabilities in general, as well as their caretakers in particular, have or can have religious needs, many seemed to be puzzled about what these needs are and what form they may take (Lukash, 2020). For instance, some informants suggested that the users' level of religiosity and ability to be religious could be determined by their intellectual capacities—in other words, the more cognitively able a person is, the more capable they are to be religious (Lukash, 2020). Consider the following dialogue between the interviewer and three participants in the focus group at one of the municipal residential homes:

I:	What do you think religion means for your residents?
Aisha:	I think it's connected to cognitive level …, if you have a higher …
Soraya:	Cognitive functioning.
Kai:	Clearly, it is.
Aisha:	So it'll be more religious, more about religion [sic]. If they are not equally functioning, it will be in a way more cultural.
Kai (with others):	Yes.

These (and other) participants seemed to place their understanding of the users' religiosity along the lines of the religion–culture dichotomy, correlating it with the ability–disability binary, and likely even ascribing the 'religion' part a higher status than the 'culture' part (Lukash, 2020). From this point of view, the 'religious' part of the binary may represent religiosity's doctrinal and experiential dimensions, while the 'cultural' part may point towards ritual and social dimensions (Smart, 1984; Lukash, 2020).

The emphasis on the social, ritual or even practical everyday dimensions of the users' religiosity was emphasised by many group participants. Several expressed doubts that, at least for their users, religiosity means anything beyond these dimensions. In other words, activities such as visiting the church, singing Christmas carols and participating in devotions were seen by many participants as a good opportunity for residents to socialise with friends or just have a good time—and are thus similar to activities connected with Halloween or Valentine's Day. They were often described in terms of *kos* ('cosiness' and 'enjoyment'; Lukash, 2020). These attitudes seemed to be spread unequally among the different focus groups, however. Some of the participants also pointed to the importance of the existential and spiritual aspects of religiosity, which could provide meaning in a time of crisis (such as the death of a loved one). Others suggested that religious practices can give people with intellectual disabilities solace and security in their daily lives (Lukash, 2020).

The study also shows that the participants generally agreed that securing freedom of religion for people with intellectual disabilities in general, and their caretakers in particular, is important. They agreed that impeding users from practising religion or actively coercing them to do so would represent a gross violation of human rights and their professional code of conduct. Moreover, a number of the participants emphasised the need to create favourable conditions for users to enact their religious rights (Lukash, 2020). At the same time, several were quite frank that they may not be doing enough to identify the residents' religious and spiritual needs and to enable them to enact their right to worship. In fact, the staff of the Christian-value-based institution, which provided pastoral visits, devotions and other religious activities on a regular basis, were perhaps most explicit about the lack of concern about users' religious needs (Lukash, 2020).

Exploring religious themes with people with intellectual disabilities in Slovakia with the help of participatory action research

This participatory action research (PAR) study took place in 2017 in Slovakia, as part of the second author's PhD work. The study explored the following research questions: how do people with intellectual disabilities express citizenship in the stories of their everyday life? Are research circles a suitable method for exploring citizenship with people with intellectual disabilities? A research circle is a participatory approach to research, consisting of dialogical collaboration over time between academic researchers and people with experience-based competence (Cech, 2001; Luteberget, 2019; Slettebø, 2013)—in this case, people with intellectual disabilities. The research circle generally consists of two phases (Holmstrand & Härnsten, 2003; Slettebø, 2013). In the first phase, the research relationship is established, research questions defined and existing knowledge mapped. This phase is largely focused on helping the participants get to know each other and on building trust in new research relationships. The second phase is more action-oriented and highlights how the acquired knowledge from the first phase can be transferred and applied in the everyday life of participants. The present study adapted the research circle approaches of Cech (2001) and Holmstrand & Härnsten (2003).

The research circle's work was based on everyday life themes of interest to people with intellectual disabilities. The topics selected were proposed, developed and explored together with them.

Seven participants with intellectual disabilities took part in the research circle—five women and two men; all were adults in their twenties, thirties and forties and participated in a day care program operated by a centre run by a non-governmental Christian organisation. Several of the participants had practical upper secondary education in gardening, as a masseur, or in other similar vocations. None of the participants were participating in paid work. Some had previously worked at a local café that was run as a workplace for people with intellectual disabilities, but they were left without jobs after the company went bankrupt. Some worked as volunteers. All participants lived with either their parents or other family members, and they participated in daily activities related to the household. Many described going to church and participating in prayer as an important daily activity. Several had pets for whom they cared deeply. The participants said that they wanted a life with holidays, independence and their own homes, where they could have self-determination.

The working process in this research circle consisted of a total of seven meetings held approximately once a month with a duration of about three hours, from April 2017 to December 2017. Based on 'icebreaker' conversations and the common everyday-life issues discussed in the group, the participants agreed upon three topics and questions which they wanted to explore and learn more about.

The participants also decided to invite guests (e.g., professionals who were familiar with the specific topic and could serve as qualified discussion partners). The participants with disabilities asked the guests questions and were active in analytical discussions about what had been learned and how the new knowledge could be applied in participants' everyday lives. Lastly, they presented their experiences with the project in a magazine called *Integrácia* (*Integration*; Cangárová, 2017), targeted towards professionals working within the field of services for people with intellectual disabilities.

EXPLORING RELIGIOUS CITIZENSHIP ('WHAT IS HEAVEN LIKE?')

The discussions in the research circle initially centred around general questions, such as: what would you like to know more about? What are your dreams? One of the participants suggested that the circle explore what heaven is like. As there were no objections to this question, the group proceeded to hold further discussions on how it could be explored. Participants agreed to invite a nun working at the day care centre and to continue discussions with her.

As the topic of religion is considered a sensitive research topic, ethical considerations were deliberated before the exploration of the topic was continued. Here, the risk was assessed against societal benefits and the value for those who participate in the research, in accordance with National Research Ethics Committees (NESH, 2016) Following Lid and Rugseth (2019), although the participants' potential risk was contextually conditioned, it was the researcher's task to find a balance between the research project's interests and safeguarding the participants so that they were respected and not reduced simply to a means. Ultimately, the topic was considered to be valuable for participants and the group decided to move forwards with the question; the topic was to be explored on a general basis with no connection to a specific religion. The exploration of a religious theme in this study was considered significant in terms of the benefit for the participants, the field of practice and society in general, as little emphasis is currently placed on spirituality and religious needs practice (Lukash, 2020). New knowledge about religiosity developed with people with intellectual disabilities can be a resource for people with intellectual disabilities, the research community and the field of practice in general. Indeed, had this topic not been explored, this may have affirmed the position of people with intellectual disabilities as vulnerable citizens, and their position as equal partners would have been weakened (Morgan, Cuskelly, & Moni, 2014).

Moreover, in terms of participatory research, which stresses the importance of involving people with experienced-based competence, it is crucial to create a space for equal, rather than token, participation. In the meetings, space was created to talk about things and to commence and conclude discussions. Each meeting was evaluated using a simple form to provide participants with the opportunity to give constructive feedback. Before the nun visited the research circle, the group prepared questions and agreed upon who was going to ask what questions. The topic of religious practice (going to church, participating in courses and retreats, taking part in reading in the church, etc.) became a natural part of discussions in the group. Several participants talked about going to church and taking part in activities in their respective religious communities, such as readings during Easter or before Christmas. As such, the discussion expanded the original topic of what heaven is like.

The discussions in the research circle highlighted several potentials and barriers to religious citizenship for people with intellectual disabilities. Participants in the research circle expressed their wish to discuss the topic, and that everyday religious practices (such as prayer in church or religious community participation during holidays) were important for them. Religious practices were a natural part of their daily life. On the other hand, they experienced barriers in their respective religious communities, as they were not always perceived as full members. More specifically, the participants in the research circle talked about how they enjoyed participating in religious retreats organized by their local church. They described feeling excited, anxious and stressed when they read biblical texts in church, and ashamed when these undertakings highlighted their difficulties with reading. They talked about the different events and fun experiences during retreats—for instance, if there a storm suddenly arose, or the bed was too hard—but also how fun it was to spend time with others and discuss religious topics. The barriers highlighted in participants' stories of everyday life showed that they were not always perceived as equal partners in church. For instance, as one of the participants explained, 'I have asked the priest whether my boyfriend and I could get married, that we would like to formalise our relationship. But he said "No, people like you can't get married, otherwise you wouldn't be allowed to participate in the holy communion"'. They were therefore both simultaneously welcomed and excluded/marginalised in their religious communities. We discuss this further.

Discussion

The discussion draws on the findings from our two studies and indicates potentials for and barriers to religious citizenship for people with intellectual disabilities in different arenas. We argue that the studies may be seen as representing two perspectives on religious citizenship for people with intellectual disabilities: that of the professional service providers and that of the persons with intellectual disabilities themselves. The first study highlights the underlying views and attitudes of staff towards the religiosity of service users, which may influence the staff's professional practice and thus affect users' ability to practise religion on the same footing as others. The second study focuses on the users' own perspectives and experiences of practising religious citizenship. It is also important to add that while the first study aimed to explore the religious citizenship of people with intellectual disabilities, the second study did not include religion in its original design—this theme was picked up by the participants themselves during the research circle sessions. However, the fact that it was proposed by the participants themselves indicates that this issue is important to them.

While the first study emphasises the importance of professional practice towards and acknowledgment of people with intellectual disabilities and their religious needs, the second study shows that the participants in the research circle considered practising religion as a natural part of their everyday lives. However, it appears that there were significant barriers concerning practising religious citizenship, set up by the religious communities of which they were a part. Recall, for example, the priest who told one participant that she could not marry her boyfriend: this type of experience points towards paternalistic, exclusionary attitudes and, possibly, discriminatory practices and a significant barrier to disabled participants' (a) realisation of their religious citizenship and (b) participation in their religious community on an equal basis with others.[3]

In the second study, there is no indication that the participants' experience of the professional caretakers' attitudes and practices led to any significant impediment in religious citizenship. However, the first study is more ambiguous in this respect. On the one hand, no participants in that study explicitly denied the users' ability to practise religious citizenship. Indeed, many of them emphasised the importance of creating conditions that would enable users to exercise their religious citizenship. At the same time, some views and attitudes suggest impediments to citizenship. The acknowledgement among participants that they did not do enough to assess users' religious needs indicates that these needs are overlooked. This may, in turn, hamper the facilitation and empowerment of persons with intellectual disabilities in their religious practices.

The uncertainty about the nature and form of the service users' religiosity may also indicate that these issues are neglected. In addition, the staff's perceptions of the users' religiosity may have mixed implications. On the one hand, the tendency to correlate a person's ability to be religious with a higher level of cognitive functioning among some members of the staff may potentially lead to the stereotyping of people with intellectual disabilities as 'dumb', 'simple' or even 'eternal children', incapable of any 'higher' forms of religiosity (Lukash, 2020). At worst, these kinds of views may lead to ascribing the more 'functionally fit' service users with the role of active meaning makers, while others are viewed as passive, unspiritual and primitive (Lukash, 2020). Similarly, describing the residents' religiosity in terms of *kos* and mere entertainment may lead to perceiving it as something unserious and unimportant (Lukash, 2020).

However, on the other hand, one might argue that these perceptions and attitudes—for instance, the tendency to view service users' religiosity as reducible to quotidian practices or entertainment—do not necessarily devalue their agency in the eyes of the staff. Indeed, non-religious people fond of socialising with friends or having a good time are not necessarily seen as lacking agency, at least in Norway, with its significantly secular population. Moreover, the participants' views seem to point towards an area that has recently captured scholarly attention, namely the 'religion of everyday life' or 'lived religion'. By shifting focus from belief towards the practical side of religiosity, this approach challenges common binaries like religious and secular, organised and non-organised religion, and 'high' and 'low' religion (Ammerman, 2016; Henriksen, 2016). In other words, by describing religious activities in which the users participate as essentially nothing more than socialising with friends and enjoying food, the staff may have unintentionally shed light on a sphere of religious life that is worth taking seriously.

Nevertheless, some participants did seem to describe their residents' and service users' religiosity in terms of the 'religion–culture' binary, where 'religion' was essentially considered to require 'higher' cognitive abilities than 'culture'. Others, while emphasising the practical and social dimensions of the users' religiosity, tended not to consider them as religious, possibly because they did not see them as capable of understanding and appreciating religions' deeper dimensions (Lukash, 2020). This in turn holds the risk that they will be seen as one-dimensional and, at least in certain situations, may jeopardize their ability to practise religion on an equal basis with others.

Thus, the studies from Norway and Slovakia presented in this chapter highlight barriers to religious citizenship for people with intellectual disabilities that may occur in different societal arenas. The first study discusses how views, perceptions and attitudes among caregivers—mostly authorized professionals with a clear mandate from the state—may play a role in both facilitating and impeding service users' religious citizenship. The second illustrates barriers established by the religious communities, either in the form of institutional and/or doctrinal aspects, or attitudes and practices of the clergy. These studies clearly illustrate the multidimensionality and diversity of forms of religious citizenship among people with intellectual disabilities, as well as institutions, practices and attitudes on which its enactment is crucially dependent.

The many barriers to religious citizenship for people with intellectual disabilities pose a challenge when implementing the CRPD: the main legal and political instrument for the enactment of their rights. As noted earlier, the CRPD strongly affirms basic human rights but leaves religion and religious practice under-addressed. This—and the insufficient implementation of the Convention by state parties—may mean that barriers to the religious citizenship of people with intellectual disabilities remain overlooked.

Conclusion

Drawing on two studies, this chapter reflects upon potentials for and barriers to the religious citizenship of people with intellectual disabilities, from the perspective of professionals and people with intellectual disabilities.

It should be noted that the studies have limitations. First, the profound difference in research design limited our ability to make more thorough and systematic comparisons. Second, there are significant limitations regarding the number of participants, and only two countries are represented. Thus, although both studies contribute valuable knowledge about resources for and barriers to the religious citizenship of people with intellectual disabilities in two countries, the sample is too small to make generalisable conclusions about every religious community in every country.

It would be interesting to explore this topic further in future research and to include both people with intellectual disabilities and professionals. Here, a research question might target how professionals and religious communities can accommodate the exercise of religious citizenship. Cross-cultural dialogue between people who have intellectual disabilities would also be an interesting subject of study, as would ethical issues regarding the exploration of religious topics in qualitative research.

Notes

1 The term *folkekirke* is rather ambiguous and could mean slightly different things in different contexts. While the direct English translation of it should be 'folk church' or 'people's church', the English version of the Constitution translates it as 'the established church'; this may be confusing, as the latter term could be understood as synonymous with the official church. It could also be understood as the church of all, or most, Norwegians. However, this understanding is explicitly denied by the Church itself, which states that 'as a folk church [it] is not identical with the community of the people (*folkefellesskap*), but is a distinct community based on baptism and faith' (Kirkemøtet 2004, p. 4).

2 Norwegian specialised literature and official documents use the term 'faith- and life stance organisations' (*tros- og livssynsorganisasjoner*), where 'life stance' (*livssyn*) often, but not exclusively, refers to non-religious metaphysical and ethical views, often of a secular humanist character.

3 Unfortunately, the study's research design and methodology do not allow us to know to what denomination this priest or pastor belonged. This gap in our data makes it difficult to interpret this participant's experience in a wider social,

political and theological context. To be sure, as we have mentioned earlier, the official position of the dominant faith community in Slovakia, the Roman Catholic church, emphasises the importance of allowing people with disabilities (including, presumably, intellectual disabilities) to receive the sacraments (including, presumably, marriage).

References

Ammerman, N. T. (2016). Lived religion as an emerging field: An assessment of its contours and frontiers. *Nordic Journal of Religion and Society*, 29(2), 83–99. doi:10.18261/ISSN.1890-7008-2016-02-01

Broderick, A. & Ferri, D. (2019). *International and European Disability Law and Policy*. Cambridge University Press.

Cangárová, L. (2017). Občianstvo a zvládanie každodenného života. *Integrácia*, 27(3–4), 64–67.

Cech, B. N. (2001). *Pedagogik på social omsorgsrund för personer med utvecklingsstörning* [Unpublished doctoral dissertation]. Karlstad University.

Constitution of the Kingdom of Norway. *FOR-2018-06-01-788*. https://lovdata.no/dokument/NLE/lov/1814-05-17

Constitution of Republic of Slovakia. (1992). https://constituteproject.org/constitution/Slovakia_2017.pdf?lang=en

Ellingsen, K. E. & Sandvin, J. T. (2014). Utviklingshemming: funksjonsnedsettelse, miljøkrav og samfunnsreformer.. In K. E. Ellingsen (Ed.), *Utviklingshemming og deltakelse* (pp. 11–31). Oslo, Norway: Universitetsforlaget.

Francis (2020). Message of the Holy Father Francis for the International Day of Persons with Disabilities. https://www.vatican.va/content/francesco/en/messages/pont-messages/2020/documents/papa-francesco_20201203_messaggio-disabilita.html).

Friedman, M. (2005). *Women and citizenship*. Oxford University Press.

Furseth, I., Ahlin, L., Ketola, K., Leis-Peters, A., & Sigurvinsson, B. R., (2018). Changing religious landscapes in the Nordic countries. In I. Furseth (Ed.), *Religious Complexity in the Public Sphere: Comparing Nordic Countries* (pp. 31–80). London, England: Palgrave Macmillan.

Glørstad, V. (2019). 'Min stemme teller også!': personer med utviklingshemming – praktisering av politisk medborgerskap, In U. S. Goth (ed). *Verdier og visjoner: profesjonalitet i endring*. (pp. 39–62). Cappelen Damm Akademisk.

Gustavsson, A., Tøssebro, J., & Traustadottir, R. (2005). Introduction: Approaches and perspectives in Nordic disability research. In A. Gustavsson, J. Sandvin, R. Traustadottir & J. Tøssebro (Eds.), *Resistance, Reflection and Change: Nordic Disability Research* (pp. 23–46). Lund, Sweden: Studentlitteratur.

Griffin, J. (2009). On Human Rights. Oxford: Oxford University Press.

Halvorsen, R., Hvinden, B., Bickenbach, J., Ferri, D., & Rodriguez, A. M. G. (2017). *The changing disability policy system: Active citizenship and disability in Europe* (Vol. 1). Taylor & Francis.

Henriksen, J.-O. (2016). Everyday religion as orientation and transformation: A challenge to theology. *Nordic Journal of Religion and Society*, 29(1), 36–51. doi:10.18261/ISSN.1890-7008-2016-01-03

Holmstrand, L. & Härnsten, G. (2003). *Förutsättningar för forskningscirklar i skolan: En kritisk granskning*. Myndigheten för skolutveckling.

Hirschmann, N. J. & Linker, B. Disability, citizenship, and belonging: a critical introduction. In N. J. Hirschmann & B. Linker (Eds.), *Civil Disabilities: Citizenship, Membership, and Belonging* (pp. 1–21). University of Pennsylvania Press.

Isin, E. F. (2008). Theorizing acts of citizenship. In E. F. Isin & G. M. Nielsen (Eds.), *Acts of citizenship* (pp. 15–43). Palgrave Macmillan.

Kirkemøtet. (2004). Den norske kirkes identitet og oppdrag. Kirkerådet. https://kirken.no/globalassets/kirken.no/om-kirken/slik-styres-kirken/planer-visjonsdokument-og-strategier/identitet_oppdrag_2004_bokmaal.pdf

Kirkerådet. (2009). Likeverd, inkludering og tilrettelegging. In Kirkerådet (2012). *Den norske kirkes betjening av mennesker med utviklingshemning*. Den Norske kirke.

Kühle, L., Schmidt, U., Jacobsen, B. A., & Pettersson, P. (2018). Religion and state: Complexity in change. In I. Furseth (Eds.), *Religious complexity in the public sphere: Comparing Nordic spheres* (pp. 81–135). Springer.

Lukash, D. (2020). Just like everyone else? Service providers' perceptions of the religiosity of people with intellectual disabilities [Unpublished doctoral dissertation]. VID Specialized University.

Luteberget, L. (Ed.). (2019). *Forskningssirkler som modell for fagutvikling: Erfaringer fra tjenestetilbud til personer med utviklingshemming*. Universitetsforlaget.

Mackenzie, C. (2019). *Feminist innovation in philosophy: Relational autonomy and social justice*. Women's Studies International Forum.

Morgan, M. F., Cuskelly, M., & Moni, K. B. (2014). Unanticipated ethical issues in a participatory research project with individuals with intellectual disability. *Disability & Society*, 29(8), 1305–1318.

National Committee for Research Ethics in the Social Sciences and the Humanities (NESH). (2016). Guidelines for research ethics in the social sciences, humanities, law, and theology. The Norwegian National Research Ethics Committees.

Nyhagen, L. (2015). Conceptualizing lived religious citizenship: a case-study of Christian and Muslim women in Norway and the United Kingdom. *Citizenship Studies*, 19, 768–784. 10.1080/13621025.2015.1049979.

Østhus A. (2021). *Sekularisering i Norge*. Statistisk Sentralbyrå. https://www.ssb.no/kultur-og-fritid/religion-og-livssyn/artikler/sekularisering-i-norge

Schmidt, U. (2010). Religion i dagens Norge: Sekularisert? Privatisert? Pluralisert? In P. K. Botvar & U. Schmidt (Eds.), *Religion i dagens Norge* (pp. 196–203). Universitetsforlaget.

Sépulchre, M. (2020). *Disability and citizenship studies*. Routledge.

Shakespeare, T. (2005). Nordic disability research: Reflections, not conclusions. In A. Gustavsson, J. Sandvin, R. Traustadottir, & J. Tøssebro (Eds.), *Resistance, Reflection and Change: Nordic Disability Research* (pp. 205–300). Lund, Sweden: Studentlitteratur.

Silecchia, L. A. (2014). The convention on the rights of persons with disabilities: Reflections on four flaws that tarnish its promise. *Journal of Contemporary Health Law and Policy*, 30(1). https://scholarship.law.edu/jchlp/vol30/iss1/10

Slettebø, T. (2013). Forskningssirkler som Fagutvikling. In E. Døhlie & A. M. Støkken (Eds.), *Fagutvikling i velferdstjenester*. Universitetsforlaget.

Smart, N. (1984). *The religious experience of mankind* (3rd ed.). Charles Scribner's Sons.

Skarstad, K. (2019). *Funksjonshemmedes menneskerettigheter. Fra prinsipper til praksis*. Oslo: Universitetsforlaget.

Starr, K. J. (2019). *Once the same nation, the Czech Republic and Slovakia look very different religiously*. Pew Research Centre. https://www.pewresearch.org/fact-tank/2019/01/02/once-the-same-nation-the-czech-republic-and-slovakia-look-very-different-religiously/

Sčítanie Obyvateľov, Domov a Bytov. (2021). Religion. https://www.scitanie.sk/en/roman-catholics-represents-56-percent-of-the-population

Statistisk sentralbyrå. (2021). *Trus- og livssynssamfunn utanfor Den norske kyrkja*. https://www.ssb.no/kultur-og-fritid/religion-og-livssyn/statistikk/trus-og-livssynssamfunn-utanfor-den-norske-kyrkja

Strand, V. B. (2014). Norway's ratification of the UN Convention on the Rights of Persons with Disabilities: Highlighting current discourses in the field of human rights in Norway. *Nordic Journal of Human Rights*, 32(1), 75–83. doi:10.1080/18918131.2013.878894

Terzi, L. (2015). Cognitive disability, capability equality, and citizenship. In N. J. Hirschmann & B. Linker (Eds.), *Civil Disabilities: Citizenship, membership, and belonging* (pp. 186–204). University of Pennsylvania Press.

United Nations. (1981). *Declaration on the elimination of all forms of intolerance and of discrimination based on religion or belief*. https://www.ohchr.org/en/instruments-mechanisms/instruments/declaration-elimination-all-forms-intolerance-and-discrimination

United Nations. (2006). *Convention on the rights of persons with disabilities (CRPD)*. http://www.un.org/disabilities/documents/convention/convoptprot-e.pdf

UN Human Rights Committee. (1993). CCPR general comment no. 22: Article 18 (Freedom of Thought, Conscience or Religion), 30 July 1993, CCPR/C/21/Rev.1/Add.4, https://www.refworld.org/docid/453883fb22.html

Interlude 2
"Symbiotic citizenship" and a struggle for the right of life as frames for interpreting the 40-day disability protest in the Polish Parliament

Natalia Pamula and Magda Szarota

The year 2018 was an extraordinary year in the history of the Polish disability community. On 18 April, disabled people and their caregivers started a 40-day occupation of the Parliament in Warsaw. They had two demands: "bringing the social allowance into line with the lowest rate of the full incapacity allowance; [and the] introduction of a monthly rehabilitation allowance of 500 PLN [$111,02] to adults whose disabilities have been assessed [as] severe."[1] Only the latter demand was fulfilled by the government. The protest was suspended after 40 days because of the physically and mentally taxing conditions of living in the halls of Parliament with restricted access to bathrooms, outdoors, and physical therapists.[2] This has been, probably, the biggest disability protest in Polish history. Its significance extends beyond Polish or Eastern European history. We claim that this occupation is a part of global disability history. In other words, one of the aims of this interlude is to insert the protest into global disability history and outline its possible interpretations. Our writing is motivated by both activist and academic impulses.

We offer close readings of the statements made by the protesters to answer how disability citizenship operates in Poland and, equally important, think of the role the Convention on the Rights of Persons with Disabilities (CRPD) plays in disability communities here. While we attempt to open up some new avenues of thinking about the protest, citizenship, and the CRPD in Poland, our text does not pretend to offer a broad and detailed analysis neither of the 2018 protest nor its consequences. Rather, it forms an invitation to look for disability histories in the so-called "second world" and their resonances with disability movements in other parts of the world.

The 2018 protest and, in particular, the statements made by caregivers – mothers who participated in the Parliament occupation – reveal that disabled subjects and their mothers are bound together in what we call a "symbiotic citizenship." In other words, we claim that a liberal citizenship understood as an individual right to participate in the life of a society and have access to the state's resources might be unavailable at least for some segments of the disabled

DOI: 10.4324/9781003052708-10

population in Poland. The liberal and individualistic citizenship is replaced by a more familial or, precisely, symbiotic citizenship. In order to explain what we understand as symbiotic citizenship and demonstrate its workings, we offer a close reading of two short statements made by Iwona Hartwich and Anna Glinka who together with their sons Jakub Hartwich (24 years old at the time) and Adrian Glinka (22 years old at the time) were among the leaders of the Parliament occupation.

On 18 April, the day of the inauguration of the protest, Iwona Hartwich said that "today we are our children's voice. They are disabled, some of them intellectually, some of them use wheelchairs. They cannot go and protest on their own."[3] The mothers then are the conduits for their "voiceless" children; they mediate their communication with other people and as such enable their civic disobedience. It is unclear here who, or what, renders disabled people voiceless: disability? Structural inequities? However, if mothers, according to Hartwich, are their children's voices, do they retain their own voice or do they simply speak on behalf of their children? Undoubtedly, Hartwich's words highlight that women's rights, in particular mother's rights, are intimately interwoven with their disabled children's rights. They also remind us of the very material – corporeal – dependence of a disabled child on her mother in Poland (no matter the child's age). Moreover, these words testify to disabled and gendered loss: a loss of individual voice which might represent here a loss of autonomy and subjectivity for both a disabled subject and a nondisabled mother. Symbiotic citizenship is then a result of this loss. But this loss, even if naturalized by the Polish state and a large part of Polish society, is not natural. Rather, it stems from structural deficiencies and cultural expectations that a mother should be the primary caretaker of her disabled child throughout her/his entire life. In other words, these losses could have been avoided, were the state involved in providing services to the disabled population on a large scale and in a systemic way.

Two days later, on 20 April, Anna Glinka said, "together with Adrian we have participated in disability protests since 2015. We are always together. I take care of my son every day, since the day he was born, without a single day off."[4] This is an important passage for a few reasons: first, it emphasizes – similar to what Hartwich said – that a mother and her disabled son are literally bound together. As a result, sanctioned and upheld by the state's disablist discourses and practices such as the inadequate provision of already scarce resources and services for disabled populations cancel the possibility of autonomy for a disabled child and her mother. Disability is synonymous with a lack of separation (and participation) because of the state's withdrawal from the sphere of assistance and because of its lack of interest in developing independent living centers and/or community living arrangements.

The forced togetherness of mothers and their disabled children is oppressive here and results from both ableist and patriarchal assumptions, structures, and practices. The nearly universal and uninterrupted togetherness of mothers and their disabled children is rarely engaged in out of free will. Rather, it is an effect of oppressive and disablist state policies, or, alternatively, a lack of adequate systems of support. Second, Glinka's statement comments – albeit indirectly – on disability temporality. By making references to the past and bringing up the present (which does not differ much from the past), it can be concluded that the future, similar to the past and present, is marked by togetherness and forms an extended version of the present. The past, present, and future are collapsed into one. We understand the protest as an attempt to interrupt the continuity of the past and the future, as a fight for a different future. By adding that she did not have a single day off since her son was born, Glinka recognizes the practice of care as labor (and since care here is not provided necessarily only out of free choice it can be seen as a form of forced labor). Protesting then is both a continuation of care – they protest together, she cannot leave him for the period of the occupation – but also directed against the symbiotic citizenship forced upon them. We read her short statement as a reminder that a caregiver's subjectivity and autonomy might be just as fraught as a disabled person's autonomy and subjectivity. Symbiotic citizenship is a result of the privatization of disability care, as well as the negation of disabled lives, and the disregard for both women's and disabled people's rights.

Yet symbiotic citizenship violates the very principles the CRPD is based on, including respect for inherent dignity, individual autonomy and independence of disabled people, their full and effective participation in society, nondiscrimination, equal opportunity, and accessibility (Article 3 of CRPD). In 2006, the United Nations enacted the CRPD. Through ratification, in 2012, the CRPD became a part of the Polish legal system, and it obligates the Polish state to implement disability human rights set out in the Convention. The 2018 protest worked to expose the void between the Convention and the day-to-day lives of disabled people in Poland not only to the authorities but also to Polish society. As protesters were present in the Parliament for 40 days, their protest was extensively covered by the press. It could not be ignored by the broader society, which was forced to note and reflect on the inhuman circumstances experienced by disabled people (especially those with "severe" conditions) and their caregivers. The protest received the support of numerous disability and disabled people's organizations and circles, but it also was joined by nondisabled human rights and social justice activists, feminists, mothers of nondisabled children, etc. "Listening to the comments around the protest, one could get the impression that, for the general public, this was a turning point (…)"[5] wrote journalist and researcher, Rafał Bakalarczyk. He expressed the expectation that the protest triggered a permanent shift of perspective "in societal consciousness."[6] We suggest – along with some other scholars and disability activists – that this shift may be correctly framed as an important step toward a disability discourse recognizing and respecting Polish disabled people's human rights set out in the CRPD. While the CRPD and the social model of disability underlying the Convention are known in progressive disability activist circles in Poland, the protest allowed them to move beyond the narrow disabled people's community.

However, the protesters did not foreground the CRPD, independent living, nor any other of the Convention's rights, or the social model conception of disability. Their narrative predominantly focused on financial benefits for disabled people with "severe" conditions and their caregivers. In Poland, welfare benefits and services for these groups are such that people permanently find themselves in a life-endangering situation. Hartwich stated, "We are starving on the provisions that we receive" – and she meant that literally rather than in some figurative sense. Hence, we would argue that the protesters' direct motivation was not so much a struggle for independent living, inclusion in the community, or even better living conditions – rather they protested for their survival and against their demise. This was expressed quite dramatically by one of the caregivers, Katarzyna Milewicz, as she cried out: "Then what are we to do? [Should the government fail to meet our request] the best thing would be to let our disabled children die in gas chambers like dogs." These words exemplify that the support provided to at least some Polish disabled people is on a eugenic level. Their living situation may be described as a constant humanitarian crisis. Hence, in our view, the 2018 protest should be reframed as – first and foremost – a struggle for the right to life, a basic human right, and a disability human right reaffirmed in Article 10 of the CRPD. In Poland, this must not be suppressed from or unacknowledged in political debates about disability. It must be prioritized according to the urgency and gravity of the situation, which is one of basic survival.

On the heels of the 2018 protest, there was an evaluation of Poland's progress in the implementation of the CRPD. A United Nations special committee tasked with monitoring the CRPD's realization by the Convention's member states found that the human rights of disabled people are not respected in Poland.[7] In its 2018 "Concluding Observations," the committee particularly emphasized violations of two of the Convention's articles by Poland: the right of disabled people to independent living (Article 19 of CRPD); and the rights of disabled women subjected to multiple forms of discrimination (Article 6 of CRPD). Since the beginning of the work leading up to the CRPD's ratification by Poland, Article 19 of the CRPD requiring states to provide independent living solutions was treated as a beacon of hope by the Polish disability community. Both 2018 events – the committee's evaluation of Poland and the 2018 disabled people's protest – vividly demonstrate how much the Convention's principles still remain in the realm of hope. Until the human rights of disabled people are recognized and upheld in Poland, Polish citizens will be forced to live in an oppressive and abusive symbiotic citizenship.

Bios

Natalia Pamula is an assistant professor at the American Studies Center at the University of Warsaw. She received her PhD from the Comparative Literature Department at SUNY Buffalo in 2018. She studies disability discourses and representations in Polish socialist and postsocialist culture. Her work has appeared, among others, in *Aspasia*, *East European Politics and Societies: And Cultures*, and *Re/Imaginations of Disability in State Socialism: Visions, Promises, Frustrations*.

Magda Szarota is a disability and human rights advocate and consultant, disability studies researcher, NGO executive, and photographer. She has lived, studied, and worked in Europe, the United States, and Asia. She is considered one of the pioneers of the disabled women's movement in the post-socialist Poland. She serves as a Member of the Board of Humanity in Action Poland; Member of the Steering Committee of the Feminist Alliance for Rights at the Center for Women's Global Leadership, Rutgers University; a Founding Member of Article 6, a Polish feminist disability rights collective. She is affiliated with the Centre for Disability Research at Lancaster University and the Cross-national Studies: Interdisciplinary Research and Training Program (CONSIRT) at Ohio University. Magda is a network member of the Disability Studies in Eastern Europe – Reconfigurations research platform at Jagiellonian University. She is a recipient of numerous merit-based scholarships including those awarded by the Kosciuszko Foundation and by the Yale University. Magda co-authored the first shadow report to the UN CRPD Committee about Polish girls and women with disabilities, and successfully advocated on their behalf during the 20th session in Geneva in 2018. She has published in *The Palgrave Encyclopedia of the Possible*, *Disability Studies Quarterly*, *Review of Disability Studies: An International Journal*, among others. In 2018, she co-edited, with Dr Natalia Pamuła and Dr Marta Usiekniewicz, a special issue of *Studia de Cultura* devoted to disability studies in Poland. In 2021, she co-wrote, with Dr Marta Sałkowska, Magdalena Kocejko, and Angelika Greniuk, a book *The (Non)Attendance List: Disability in School Textbooks* (publisher Collegium Civitas). Her op-eds appeared in Ms. Magazine (co-written with Suzannah Phillips), ngo.pl, niepelnosprawni.pl, OKO.press, among others. In 2019, she received a title of a UN CRPD Ambassador – an award, which was presented by the Polish Ombudsman, Professor Adam Bodnar, for "educational, scholarly and activist initiatives aimed at advancement of human rights and the United Nation Convention on the Rights of Persons with Disabilities."

Notes

1 Kubicki, P., Bakalarczyk, R., Mackiewicz-Ziccardi, M. (2019). Protests of people with disabilities as examples of fledgling disability activism in Poland. *Canadian Journal of Disability Studies*, 8.5.

2 In the beginning of the protest, physical therapists had access to the protesters; however, as the protest continued the conditions worsened: physical therapists were denied access to the building, the protesters could no longer go for a walk to the Parliament gardens. The lights in the halls where protesters slept were not turned off for the night and there was a limited bathroom access. The protest was suspended precisely because of the difficult conditions in the Parliament; or, rather, they were made to suspend the protest, which attracted enormous media attention and mobilized many people to protest outside the Parliament to show their support.

3 https://oko.press/wznawiaja-strajk-okupacyjny-sejmu-rodzice-doroslych-niepelnosprawnych-w-2014-r-prezes-kaczynski-calowal-nas-po-dloniach-a-dzis-jestesmy-sami/, access: 07/04/2022

4 https://krytykapolityczna.pl/kraj/protest-rodzicow-osob-niepelnosprawnych-sejm-2018/, access: 07/04/2022

5 https://krytykapolityczna.pl/kraj/niepelnosprawni-w-sejmie-czyli-tym-razem-cos-peklo-cos-sie-zmienilo/, access: 07/03/2022

6 https://oko.press/wznawiaja-strajk-okupacyjny-sejmu-rodzice-doroslych-niepelnosprawnych-w-2014-r-prezes-kaczynski-calowal-nas-po-dloniach-a-dzis-jestesmy-sami/, access: 07/03/2022

7 https://www.ohchr.org/en/documents/concluding-observations/crpdcpolco1-concluding-observations-initial-report-poland?fbclid=IwAR0PNPmO_yy5EY5MwOKvqIt2eCbRqp_9z-tZEjYtUNQgVsJZlMy2AkWb1Lw, access: 07/04/2022

6 The space of accessibility and universal design

Edward Steinfeld

Introduction

Accessibility, as articulated in the Convention on the Rights of People with Disabilities (CRPD), is a compensatory strategy and is focused primarily on the functional aspects of design. Politically, it is implemented as a top-down activity, prescribed by standards and laws, and enforced by a government regulatory agency. This emphasis implies that those who create the built environment need to be policed and that societal resources need to be redistributed to accommodate a specific population (Whyte and Ingstad 1995). In comparison, universal design seeks to change the consciousness of designers so that they will take disabled bodies and abilities into account and reduce the need for oversight. It avoids positioning disability as a "counterpoint to normality" (Murphy 1995). It represents a different paradigm about design for disability, although the two are certainly not incompatible. What unites them both is the focus on inclusion. The accessibility paradigm seeks to *adjust* a world that is designed to exclude the disabled body. The universal design paradigm, in contrast, seeks to *construct* a world to support life with a disability.

Ron Mace, an architect and disability rights advocate who lived with a disability, is credited with the first articulation of universal design (Mace 1985; Hamraie 2017; Williamson 2019). He noticed a fundamental problem with the accessibility paradigm. Barriers to access only exist because those who design and build the physical environment do not consider and prioritize the needs of people with disabilities. Thus, the effort to remove barriers is a rearguard action needed to overcome that neglect. He used the term "universal design" to represent the conscious attempt to design for a broader range of abilities. From his education as an architect, he viewed aesthetics as an important element in the acceptance of accessible design. He argued that universal design would not only improve accessibility and usability for people with disabilities but lead to better design for everyone else as well, including the production of accessible products and places that are also more aesthetically pleasing than the clinical look of accessible design at the time. While Mace and his colleagues were developing the idea of universal design in the United States, in Europe, similar concepts, "design for all" and "inclusive design," were emerging. But, by the

DOI: 10.4324/9781003052708-11

early 21st century, universal design had become the dominant term used worldwide for this paradigm and thus found its way into the CRPD.

The concept of universal design shifts the focus of accessibility from a pragmatic vision, "how can we get this fixed" to a more theoretical perspective, "why is it that barriers exist in the first place?" Metaphorically, the accessibility paradigm is about getting into the door while universal design is about getting into the mind of the designer. That is not to say that universal design supplants accessibility. Laws and standards make sure that people with disabilities are visible, an essential first step. And there is truth to the belief that designers need to be policed. But laws and standards are negotiated with many stakeholders and thus will always be a compromise from higher aspirations. They incorporate cultural beliefs about disability that caused exclusion in the first place. Further, they provide little of value to other stakeholders in the design process. In fact, they are viewed negatively by designers and building owners as constraints that restrict them from achieving other goals, such as cost effectiveness, beauty, or sustainability. Universal design is more aspirational, challenges the prevailing cultural beliefs, and provides a framework to address the relationship between design for disability and other goals of cultural change such as racial equity, gender equality, and social sustainability.

Figure 6.1 demonstrates the difference between accessible design and universal design. In the 21st century, after 40 years of experience with legal mandates for accessibility, enlightened campus planners realize that universal design can improve the livability of campuses for everyone in the university community. This represents a major change in consciousness. Some critics argue that universal design is a "first world" concept and costs too much to implement in low-income countries. But consider that the cost of creating Entry B would not be substantially greater than Entry A if done from the start. The difference between the two is more about value than cost.

While the inclusion of universal design in the CRPD acknowledges the new paradigm, the focus of Article 9 on barrier removal situates the Convention solidly within the frame of the accessibility paradigm. As such the document is a snapshot of the times. It represents a period of transition between two ways of understanding the role of the environment in disability rights. Although some authors argue that universal design is a departure from the critical practice of accessibility which foregrounded disability (Hamraie 2017; Williamson 2019), I hope to demonstrate that it is the opposite, a more powerful tool for critical practice and a way to advance disability rights further and faster. In fact, the Convention, in its emphasis on equal opportunity, autonomy, fairness, and dignity, implies a broader set of goals than a purely functionalist approach to access. Thus, it incorporates the vision of universal design despite its explicit emphasis on the accessibility paradigm.

The sociologist Henri Lefebvre developed a conceptual framework of space that is useful for studying the relationship of disability and the physical world. He viewed space as a dynamic and charged reality that is actively "produced" (Lefebvre 1991; Merrifield 2006). He brought together separate concepts of

Figure 6.1 Two entries designed to provide access to older academic buildings on university campuses in the U.S.

Source: © E. Steinfeld, 2022

physical space, mental space, and social space with his conception of a "spatial triad." Representations of space (conceived space) is the space constructed by professionals and scientists such as planners, architects, and geographers. It is characterized by abstractions, codes, and jargon and is the dominant mental space of a society. The space of representation (lived space) is the space of everyday experience, the space of inhabitants or "users." Spatial practices (perceived space) mediate between the conceived and the lived.[1] They structure lived reality by supporting access, usability, a sense of orientation, and the ways in which people act, including social relations. These three aspects of space are closely related, overlap, and work together to produce the known space of disability. In the rest of this chapter, I will analyze how the spatial practices of accessibility and universal design change the way we perceive space, the way we represent it, and how we live in it. The focus will be on the content of accessibility standards, the standard development process, the regulation of accessibility, and the emergence and evolution of universal design in the United States. I have been a participant in these activities for over 50 years, so this is both a reflective analysis and an eye-witness account. Of course, every observer sees things with some bias, so I would not deny that there may be other perspectives. But I hope my insights might help advance the field using a theoretical lens. I am not advocating for adoption of US practices. Rather, I present this case study to demonstrate how the path toward an accessible society is culturally determined, and how a critical analysis of cultural practices can help to advance our understanding of the role that the physical environment plays in disability.

The space of accessibility standards

In the United States, accessibility standards are adopted in both real estate laws (e.g., local and state building codes) and human rights laws (e.g., the Americans with Disabilities Act). But the content of the standards used is quite similar. They describe the minimum building features required to meet the laws by specifying geometry, scalar dimensions, and other quantitative criteria. When standards developers in the United States discuss accessibility, they focus almost exclusively on abstract conceptions of space, e.g., the slope of a ramp, the width of a door, the volume of an emergency alarm, the roughness of a ground surface, how many accessible entries should be provided, how large braille and raised letters should be on signs. These are parameters that can be prescribed and measured by technical standards and guidelines. In Lefebvre's terms, such standards are a form of conceived space. As such, they are a reductionist view of space because they do not incorporate information on the space of experience and the space of perception.

Figure 6.2 represents the content in accessibility standards in the United States. It includes an illustration of accessible toilet compartments with the

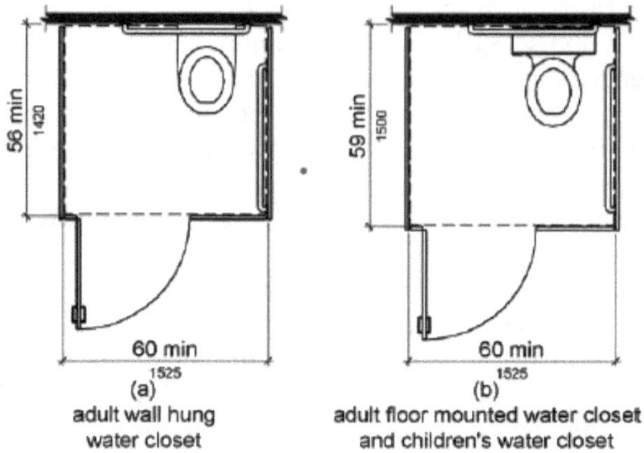

604.8.1.1 Size. Wheelchair accessible compartments shall be 60 inches (1525 mm) wide minimum measured perpendicular to the side wall, and 56 inches (1420 mm) deep minimum for wall hung water closets and 59 inches (1500 mm) deep minimum for floor mounted water closets measured perpendicular to the rear wall. Wheelchair accessible compartments for children's use shall be 60 inches (1525 mm) wide minimum measured perpendicular to the side wall, and 59 inches (1500 mm) deep minimum for wall hung and floor mounted water closets measured perpendicular to the rear wall.

Figure 6.2 Excerpt from ADA Standards for Accessible Design 2010.

Source: https://www.ada.gov/regs2010/2010ADAStandards/2010ADAstandards.htm#c6, public domain.

accompanying text. The illustration and text are emotionally neutral but, as a perceived space, a toilet compartment is fraught with anxiety related to doing private things in public (Molotch 2010). And, as lived space, it is a place that diverse individuals use to fulfill their needs for personal hygiene and presentation of self. To the individual with a disability, the compartment design should support taking care of bodily needs independently, or with assistance if needed, without embarrassment and in privacy. This emotional content and the messiness of the lived experience is missing from the conception of space in the standard. It purports to be a solution that should satisfy all the needs of all people with disabilities, but its presentation does not communicate the perspectives of different people, so there is no way to evaluate whether it truly will accomplish that goal. For example, one user may need to empty a colostomy bag; another may be carrying a purse; a third may need some help to transfer; a fourth may need to change menstruation products. What accommodations are needed for each of these people? The standard conveys no information to address this question, and, neither do the primary reference books used in US architectural practice which, in general, simply copy or recreate, with some commentary about technical issues, the illustrations in the standards.

Scholars have commented on the neutered and abstracted images in standards like Figure 6.2 (Imrie 2003; Hamraie 2017). Some early accessibility standards had much richer illustrations of disability and lived experience. Standards can, for example, incorporate images of women and men, people of different ages, with different body types, hair, and clothing. The *Illustrated Handbook of the North Carolina Building Code* demonstrates what they could be like (Mace 1974). They can also include commentary that explained the purpose of different features and recommendations for exceeding the minimum standards to encourage better design. But building officials believe that illustrations and advisory material in regulatory documents cause confusion in interpretation. For example, an illustration of a woman in the compartment might imply that the dimensions shown did not apply to a men's restroom and vice versa. Thus, designers have much less information about lived experiences of people with disabilities than they could if the standards were perceived as an educational opportunity as well as a tool of regulation. They could consult other texts that provide additional information but those are hard to find, often expensive, and are not up to date.

Standards like these reflect a Euclidian notion of space that is "dissociated from the physical and social realities of lived experience" (Watkins 2005). Without that connection, it is a foregone conclusion that the minimum requirements in accessibility standards become the maximum provided since the designer has no way to know that improving on the minimum criteria could provide better access. In fact, many architects simply copy the illustrations into their drawings without thinking. They do not see the connection between these standards and the bodies of people with disabilities. They rely on their own experiences to imagine use of a space like a toilet compartment and, during their formative years as students, they are often actively discouraged from thinking about the engagement of people (of any type) with buildings because it disturbs the "purity" of a creative design (Imrie 2003).[2] Moreover, a major purpose of architectural illustrations is to persuade the teacher, the client, or the public to like the design. Thus, if illustrations of building inhabitants are included, the tendency is to make them conform to cultural paradigms of beautiful people (i.e., young and able bodied).

The space of standards development

The development of standards takes place in a contested but highly regulated space in which different interest groups work together to agree on norms. *ICC/ANSI A117.1 Accessible and Usable Buildings and Facilities* is referenced by local and state building codes as well as other government agencies that construct buildings. Its development is prescribed by the procedures of two standards organizations: the American National Standards Institute (ANSI) and the International Code Council (ICC). The ICC also promulgates the International Building Code (IBC), a "model" code adopted (sometimes with modifications) by most states and cities. While the technical criteria for accessible construction appears in the A117.1 Standard, the IBC includes "scoping criteria" that specify where and how many accessible features should be provided in each building type. Since the IBC references the ICC/ANSI A117.1 Standard, it is automatically adopted when the IBC is adopted, unless a state or municipality modifies the reference or substitute their own standards, which many have done. Both ICC/ANSI A117.1 and the IBC are revised every few years.

There are several federal disability rights laws that mandate accessibility, with responsibilities allocated to different agencies.[3] State and local disability rights laws address accessibility as well. Despite the attempts to coordinate standards, the numerous agencies with responsibilities for disability rights adopt standards at different times. Legacy standards may be in force in one place or through one agency while current standards are in force in another. This complexity reflects the political and legal system in the United States and the country's huge size. It has a significant bearing on the development of standards because the process of regulation is diffused across both space and time. For example, at the time of this writing, the current version of the A117.1 Standard was approved in 2017 but the current version of the ADA Standards was approved in 2010 (USDOJ 2010). The two have significant differences. Moreover, the IBC still references the 2009 version of the A117.1 Standard, not the current version, since the last revision of the IBC occurred before the 2017 standard was finalized.

Consensus standards like A117.1 are developed by committees of highly interested parties. Government standards are developed by agencies like the U.S. Access Board, which coordinates federal accessibility standards. They often create advisory committees to assist them. Most standards development processes have public review cycles through which any individual can comment and offer proposals that the committee or agency then reviews and addresses. Although ICC/ANSI A117.1 is called a "voluntary consensus standard," it becomes mandated when incorporated through government regulations. Control over its development and content lies with a committee of 50–60 people, many of whom serve only to protect very specific interests. The membership profile of standards committees plays a critically important role in the development of standards.

In the early development of accessibility standards, there was little direct input from people with disabilities. Even the advocacy and rehabilitation organizations on the A117 Committee were mostly represented by people without disabilities. This changed as citizens with disabilities became more active in policy initiatives. Table 6.1 illustrates changes in the membership of the A117 Committee by broad categories over its lifetime, which is now about 50 years. It shows that membership by government/regulatory agencies decreased; the number of advocacy organizations increased a bit; building

Table 6.1 Membership in the A117 Committee in 1971 and 2017

Member Categories	*1971*		*2017*	
Trade Associations	13	27%	15	29%
Professional Associations and Individuals	8	17%	18	35%
Advocacy Organizations	7	15%	10	19%
Government/Regulatory Agencies	13	27%	6	12%
Rehabilitation Institutions and Organizations	7	15%	3	6%
Totals	48	100%	52	100%

industry trade associations stayed about the same; and professional members increased substantially.

This table does not tell the whole story. At least nine of the professional members in 2017 were full time accessibility consultants, reflecting the increased demand for expert knowledge as accessibility laws were implemented. Further, by 2017, there were also at least nine members with disabilities, either visible or disclosed, and many more who had family members with disabilities (the number of members on the original committee with disabilities is unknown). The influence of professionals with disabilities is great because they tend to have a high level of engagement, deep technical knowledge, and moral authority. They often dominate discussion due to their knowledge of real-life issues. It is noteworthy that out of 52 members in 2017, eleven are women. Admittedly this is a low number but in 1971, only 4 of the 48 members were women. In the last cycle of revisions, three women professionals, all who have disabilities, frequently took leadership roles in the Committee's deliberations. Since only 20–30 members may vote on each proposal, it does not take many votes to swing a decision one way or another. Thus, if all of the members with disabilities support a position, and a few other members join them, the building industry members can be outvoted.

Despite the changes in membership, the space of standards development is still dominated by building industry trade associations and professionals because the form of the standards, the language used, and the process of development, reflects their conceptions about what standards should be like and how they are developed. Other members of the committee defer to their judgment on these matters. In addition to the abstract language and illustrations discussed above, the process for proposing and voting on changes follows long established rules that structure the spatial practices of standards development. To be actively engaged, members must become familiar with the details of the existing text, know the language of regulations, understand construction, and have the time and resources to attend long and frequent meetings. Trade associations invest more funding to ensure that their input is effective but some advocacy organizations are heavily involved as well.

The spatial practices of standards development restrict objectivity. Since each proposed change often affects one specific interest group, e.g., tactile signs, long-term care facilities, etc., a political process emerges in which members develop informal alliances to support each other's interests. Proposals to increase accessibility often face opposition by building industry and professional interests, often with vague and unsupported arguments about the cost impact. Further, industry and professional interests are continually proposing changes to make compliance easier but that also may reduce accessibility. Thus, disability advocates need to be vigilant to prevent backsliding. Empirical research is desirable for vetting proposals objectively, but the timing of balloting does not allow for new research prior to voting. Hundreds of proposals for revisions are submitted and they are not communicated to the Committee until a short time before discussion and voting on each proposal commences. Moreover, some needs for knowledge that emerge during the Committee deliberations require research that can take many years to conceive, fund, and publish. Thus, decisions are often made without the benefit of a reliable evidence base.

It is expensive, time consuming and uncomfortable to participate in the standards review process. Meetings are very long, spanning several days, and, up until the COVID-19 pandemic, required traveling to a meeting site. Over the last few cycles, the US Access Board hosted the A117 Committee meetings in their offices in Washington, DC. The site was conveniently located near accessible hotels and mass transit stations and the Board provided support for limited remote participation, real time captioning and ASL interpreters. This led to more direct participation by people with disabilities who were not committee members as "interested parties." During the COVID-19 pandemic, committee members learned how to participate in meetings remotely. This may overcome the barriers to attending in person and participation by people with disabilities could increase. This will also allow non-members to learn how to participate by observing the process. They cannot vote on proposals, but they can still speak and offer opinions.

Thus, over time, the participation of people with disabilities and their allies in the arcane process of standards development has increased significantly in the United States. Their involvement has broadened and deepened the understanding of accessibility by those engaged in conceiving the space of access. The availability of accessible communications technology now gives everyone an opportunity to participate from anyplace in the country, overcoming the barriers of spatial distance. The changes in the spatial practices of standards development increase the possibility for engagement by informed citizens. It could eventually lead to acceptance of different conceptions of standards that better capture lived experience. In contrast, increased access to participation also may lead to more influence by special interests, including a bias toward certain disabilities. In fact, historically, some disability advocacy groups have been more engaged than others. People with mental health conditions, the neuro-diverse, and those with cognitive impairments have had much less involvement and agency.

One persistent barrier to participation in the space of standards development is income and race. The ICC/ANSI A117 Committee members and interested parties attending meetings are almost exclusively white and middle class and, despite the increased participation of women, still predominantly male. This has a bearing on the priorities of committee members and interested parties. So, for example, a vast majority of middle-income Americans use private passenger cars for transportation. Thus, there is much more interest in standards related to parking than public transportation or design of public rights of ways. Moreover, the standards for dwelling units reflect middle class priorities and may not be addressing those of people who live in low-cost housing.

The space of policy

The United States established a foundation for accessible design in the 1970s that led to the construction of enough accessible facilities to increase social participation by people with disabilities, especially through access to public schools, universities, and government buildings. Parallel with this activity, new federal policies provided funding for education, independent living, health care, advocacy, and enforcement of laws. Although these policies have their gaps and limitations, there is enough support to help activists become engaged in the space of accessibility. As the scope of access regulations and activism expanded, new ideas for accessibility were developed at local levels, which were often incorporated into national standards. These ideas were often informed by the experiences of people with disabilities in their local communities.

This evolutionary process occurred over time as the lived space and perceived space of accessibility changed. For example, in the 1970s most schools in the United States were not accessible. In 1975, the Individuals with Disabilities Education Act (IDEA) was enacted, which required public school districts to provide free special education and related services that addressed their individual needs. Accessibility to schools led to participation in science classes. This, in turn led to activism by parents and faculty allies, and the recognition that laboratories, their equipment and furniture needed to be accessible. Once students with disabilities could obtain a good science education in high school they could move on to higher education and enter scientific careers. At each step, activists challenged ableist thinking in education and the scientific disciplines. Standards and regulations reflect this evolution. The A117.1 standard has grown from five pages of technical criteria to 160 pages and the scoping section of the IBC is 30 pages long. The ADA 2010 Accessibility Standards, which incorporate both scoping and technical criteria, are now over 252 pages long. The shift of emphasis from segregated education to mainstreaming reflects changes in the perceived space of access based on lived experience. This, in turn, led to changes in the space of conception … the standards themselves.

However, there are still unmet needs in the lived space of accessibility. One of the most serious is transportation service. In a national opinion survey designed to assess progress over the first 25 years of experience with the ADA, people with disabilities reported significant improvements in *physical access* to transportation but a serious problem with transportation to the work site (NCD 2007). The ADA and other disability rights laws cover design of stops, stations, and vehicles of public transportation agencies but they do not require municipalities to provide public transportation service or accessible routes (e.g., sidewalks) to transportation stops. If a sidewalk is present, it must be accessible, but many suburban and rural communities do not have sidewalks on all streets and older municipalities still are working on upgrading public rights of way. Although public transportation agencies are required to provide subsidized paratransit within their service area, it is notoriously unreliable and inconvenient (NCD 2007). The cost of paratransit service is growing even higher as the population ages, putting an enormous burden on transportation agencies, which are underfunded as it is.

Land use planning is another important barrier to participation in community life and underlies the transportation service gap. Since WWII, the predominant form of urban growth has included low density development, single use zoning, and high-speed highway systems. These spatial practices led to uncontrolled sprawl, created increased dependence on private vehicles, and reduced the viability of public transportation. People with disabilities in the United States are less likely to drive or have access to automobiles than those who do not have a disability (Brumbaugh 2018). Dependence on public transportation contributes to low levels of employment leading to a high rate of poverty (USBLS 2022). If community infrastructure does not support mobility, people with disabilities have difficulty participating in work and other aspects public life effectively, even if the places they want to go are accessible. This pattern of urban development not only is a factor in income inequality, but it also increases disability through inactivity and air pollution (Jackson and Kochtitzky 2001; Jackson 2003; Frumkin et al. 2004; Jackson and Sinclair 2012).

Housing policy is another spatial practice not adequately addressed at present. Since 1991, all new multifamily housing, including privately financed housing, must be accessible. But there is no federal law that requires accessibility to new single-family housing built with private financing, which is the predominant form of housing in the country. And, there is very little funding available to modify existing homes (Maisel et al. 2008). Another important housing issue is a health policy model that ties long term health care to institutional living. Although an important legal precedent, the "Olmsted Decision" (HHS 2022), ruled that people with disabilities are entitled to housing and care in the "least restrictive environment," health care regulations require certain types of care to be provided in licensed long-term care facilities. Further, there is a lack of policy to fund supported housing for people who have mental health conditions. Thus, many people remain homeless or institutionalized because they need health care that is not provided in community settings.

The current state of public transportation, land use planning, health care, and housing policy reflect American cultural beliefs and practices that transcend the discourse on disability. Writing in the mid-1980s, Robert Murphy, an eminent anthropologist with a disability, observed that a central theme in American culture is the ideal of a beautiful body – youthful, physically fit, well groomed, and well dressed. He also noted the trend, which has accelerated since he wrote, of a huge and growing gulf between the haves and the have-notes. People who do not fit the model of the beautiful body, including people with disabilities, people of color, homeless people, gender diverse individuals, and undocumented immigrants, are ignored, often invisible and even viewed as repulsive or met with hostility and violence. All these groups share a social identity as outsiders because they deviate from cultural norms. To overcome this identity, he argues, an individual with a disability must make an extra effort to establish status as an "autonomous, worthy individual." And, in doing so, they must "confront a physical environment built by people with whole bodies for people with whole bodies" (Murphy 1995).

In recent years, several threads of research have demonstrated that urban sprawl is literally killing Americans (Jackson 2003; Frumkin 2006; Jackson et al. 2013); the "freedom of the open road" does not extend to all (Sorin 2020); and living in low income neighborhoods has a negative long-term impact on physical and mental health, subjective wellbeing, and income (Ludwig et al. 2012; Chetty et al. 2016). Although Murphy didn't make the connection, single women, the LGBTQ+ population, low-income individuals, and people of color, also find themselves living in uncomfortable spaces – environments that were not conceived by them or for them. Increasing funding for public transportation, building more walkable (and wheelable communities), and increasing the construction of mixed-use neighborhoods and affordable housing can address the needs of many minority and underrepresented groups that have heretofore been ignored. Thus, the disability community has a lot to gain by building alliances with other movements focused on socially sustainable and healthy urban development.

The space of universal design

Universal design has not been adopted to the degree that the early proponents had hoped. This is surprising given the relevance of the topic. Worldwide, there is a growing interest in diversity and inclusion and an awareness that the aging of societies will require a deeper understanding of the disabled body. But Heylighen et al. note that there are multiple perceptions and many misconceptions about the concept, including that the beneficiaries are only people with disabilities. In a Belgian study, architects associated universal design with the top-down imposition of accessibility through legislation, restrictions on creative problem solving, a general increase in the burden of regulation, and a perception that there is no business case for universal design (Heylighen et al. 2017).

Given these perceptions, research and education on universal design, as advocated in the CRPD, are critical activities for advancing its goals.

Research is needed to demonstrate the value of universal design compared to minimal legal accessibility to convince all stakeholders, including the advocacy community, to adopt the new paradigm. But ultimately, the key to adoption is education. Young designers are not educated sufficiently on design for different bodies, or, in fact, design for difference in general. In the United States, all the professional design disciplines require curriculum content on social diversity and inclusion but only one, the interior design discipline, requires specific content on universal design. Adoption of the accessibility paradigm is an easy way out for professional schools since it does not demand a different approach to critical thinking and creative problem solving. There have been several efforts to advance universal design education in the United States and progress is being made (Hamraie 2017). A large majority of design educators in the United States report that that their school's curriculum addresses universal design, but the results may reflect conflation of the term with accessible design (Tauke et al. 2016). Nevertheless, even recognition of the term is a step in the right direction.

What should the space of universal design education be like? Teaching accessibility is not challenging from a technical perspective. The challenging part, where universal design comes in, is to address human performance issues beyond those covered in standards, rethink the scope of accessibility to include goals of public health and social participation, invent ways to engage the user perspective in the design process, and find aesthetic value from the study of diversity. Hamraie observed that the early conception of universal design by Mace foregrounded disability and offered a political stance in opposition to spatial practices conceived to serve the able-bodied population. Further articulations of the concept, starting in the late 80s, sought to make it attractive to a broader consumer public (Hamraie 2017). In her view, this depoliticized and neutralized the idea of design for disability as a critical practice. But appealing to a broader audience is not necessarily retrograde if a critical stance on spatial practices is still engaged. In fact, some educators around the world have been doing precisely that for years (Christophersen 2002; Steinfeld and Tauke 2002; Skavlid 2013; Clarkson and Coleman 2015). Unfortunately, it has not become mainstream.

Universal design offers a framework to interrogate normative spatial practices that produce and reproduce social exclusion. This includes attention to racial and income inequalities, ageism, health inequities, anti-immigration policies, inequality of women, and discrimination related to sexual orientation and gender identity. In particular, expanding the typical accessible design focus on mobility and sensory limitations to include public health increases the connections with other issues of exclusion. My colleagues and I recently taught universal design studio courses on housing for recent immigrants, rethinking the institution of prisons, design for homeless youth, and gay and lesbian history. All these studios critiqued spatial practices related to exclusion, including a focus on people with disabilities, and explored new practices that could foster inclusion.

Most importantly, they included a conscious effort to develop inclusive aesthetics. We find that this broader focus resonates with students strongly because it has a direct bearing on their own lives. Related efforts are underway in many other design schools around the world.

Tools are needed to position universal design within the broader framework of design for diversity. The definition of universal design incorporated in the CRPD is based on a definition developed almost 40 years ago and foregrounds function (Mace 1985). Through critical reflection on the limitations of that definition and a review of concepts that evolved globally over the years since, my colleague, Jordana Maisel and I developed an updated definition: "Universal design is a *process* that enables and empowers a diverse population by improving human performance, health and wellness, and social participation" (Steinfeld and Maisel 2012). This definition aligns universal design with social justice movements by centering the conception of space on shared aspirations of all people. It recognizes that the end users of physical environments must have agency in the space of conception to ensure that the production of space satisfies their needs.[4] And it acknowledges that reaching the goal of an accessible society requires constant effort and development. Viewed in this way, universal design becomes an ideological foundation for all design practice rather than a limited field of knowledge that can be taught in one course.

The accompanying "Goals of Universal Design" (Steinfeld and Maisel 2012), shown in Table 6.2, update the older conceptual framework, the "Principles of Universal Design" (Story 1998), by clarifying outcomes that were only implied,

Table 6.2 The Goals of Universal Design (IDEA Center 2012)

1	Body Fit	Accommodating a wide range of body sizes and abilities
2	Comfort	Keeping demands within desirable limits of body function and perception
3	Awareness	Ensuring that critical information for use is easily perceived
4	Understanding	Making methods of operation and use intuitive, clear, and unambiguous
5	Health and Wellness	Contributing to health promotion, avoidance of disease, and protection from hazards
6	Social Integration	Treating all groups with dignity and respect
7	Personalization	Incorporating opportunities for choice and the expression of individual preferences
8	Cultural Appropriateness	Respecting and reinforcing cultural values and the social and environmental context of any design project

and eliminating confusing and general terms. The goal of Wellness expands the scope of universal design to the prevention of illness and disability, an issue that is not only relevant to people who do not have a disability but also to advocates of public health and environmental justice. And the goal of Cultural Appropriateness is particularly important to clarify that the universal design is not about imposing universalized and standardized solutions to problems (Steinfeld and Tauke 2002; Heylighen et al. 2017). The goals provide a framework for developing standards that address health and wellness and social participation, and they offer direction for the development of policy in all domains of the built environment.

Conclusion

Space is produced in the physical world, but it also produced in the mind and through lived experiences. All three aspects of space interact with one another to produce our *known space*. Accessibility standards are conceived space that define norms for minimum levels of accessibility. They are produced through the spatial practices of standards development and applied through the spatial practices of regulation. Standards and regulations, however, are limited conceptions of inclusion since they are constrained by a negotiation process and reflect existing cultural beliefs. Universal design, on the other hand, incorporates the full set of aspirations of the CRPD. It expands on functional approaches to incorporate methods for improving social participation by supporting social integration, lessening stigma, and increasing autonomy and dignity. Implemented as a critical practice, universal design requires a constant effort to identify unmet needs, search for aesthetic directions, engage people with disabilities and other under-represented groups, and understand the role of physical and cultural context. If done well, it produces a different kind of space, free from the preconceptions of ableism, racism, sexism, and other exclusionary practices. In the process, the *space of inclusion* will redefine disability itself.

The CRPD conceives of a society in which all people with disabilities can experience equal opportunity, autonomy, fairness, and dignity – an admirable vision. The Convention delineates what parts of the environment should be accessible and many spatial practices that should be addressed, but apart from highlighting the need for standards, it does not offer guidance on the mechanism through which access can be achieved, and it downplays the role of universal design. The authors of the CRPD wisely avoided a top-down imposition of methods but this does little to prevent the adoption of approaches that might be ineffective or even counter-productive. As we can see from the case study of the United States, the space of accessibility standards is reductionist and limited, even though people with disabilities are engaged in its production. But the case study also demonstrates how the US cultural context led to specific practices that support a critical bootstrapping process to advance accessibility. Most interesting is that the limitations of the perceived space of standards led to the inspiration for universal design.

In other developed democracies access standards are simpler and leave more decisions to the judgment of professional designers and building owners. Some include background information from research to designers understand the lived experience of disability. A standard developed for international use, ISO 21542:2021, is a good example (ISO 2021). But reports from colleagues in other high-income countries suggest that their building regulatory systems lack the robust enforcement mechanisms for accessible design found in the United States which reflects our litigious culture. There are many other ways to ensure compliance, including good education for professionals, support for development of a strong advocacy community, empowerment of grass roots activism, and monitoring of building projects, especially those that are highly visible. All these accessibility practices require significant investment. So, an important first step in producing an accessible society is recognizing that there is a need to provide the resources for action beyond the relatively inexpensive activity of standards development.

Disability rights activists in the global south have the most to gain by rethinking the spatial practices of access. The models in use around the world are based on the Euro-American conception of disability (Dion 2006).[5] Whyte and Ingstad demonstrate, through comparative analysis of different cultures, how disability is perceived very differently across the globe (Whyte and Ingstad 1995). What constitutes a disability in one country may not be viewed as a disability in another. And human characteristics that are viewed as unrelated to disability in one culture may be central to the perception of disability in another. Similar differences exist in the conception and perception of the physical environment. For these reasons, the conceived spaces, related spatial practices, and the lived experience of accessibility and social inclusion can vary greatly from country to country and even within countries. It stands to reason, therefore, that Euro-American concepts of accessibility may not be effective in other locales. For example, in rural areas with few design professionals, no building officials, and limited access to industrialized construction technology, a highly technical standard may be impossible to enforce and thus be treated with disdain. In many countries that lack a history of accessible construction, concise standards would probably be more effective than complicated and detailed standards like ICC/ANSI A117.1 or even the ISO standard. The American experience illustrates that a continuous improvement approach to standards development can lead to an expanded scope over time as knowledge improves among professionals and advocates.

Without strong participation and advocacy by disability communities, the spatial practices of accessibility cannot evolve toward higher levels because there is no one with the lived experience to bring new issues to the table. Thus, a long-term commitment and investment is needed to support engagement of people with disabilities and their allies in the space of accessibility, including orientation and education about standards language, format, scope, and development processes as well as some basic understanding of design and construction. The use of accessible information technology can reduce the burden of participation and make it feasible to engage the disability community if adequate IT resources are available. But that alone is not sufficient since professionals control the space of conception.

Education of professionals is critical for changing spatial practices. An important educational goal is to help design students and professionals internalize the perspective of people with disabilities to create a different kind of perceived space. If design professionals learn about disability, engage with people who have disabilities, and learn how to accommodate their needs, it will lessen reliance on abstract and reductionist conceptions of disabled bodies. One way to do this is to recruit people with disabilities to start careers in the design professions and to become informed advocates for accessibility and universal design. Given the low income and low employment level of people with disabilities, financial support for such career development should be a high priority of government and educational institutions and can be perceived as an economic development activity for this population.

The broader project of universal design recognizes that disability is only a part of a person's identity. People with disabilities can be as diverse as anyone else. Disability is associated with other demographic variables such as age, income, and minority status. For example, in the United States, inequities in preventative health care and rehabilitation services leading to high rates of disability in low-income communities of color. Thus, education should expand the perceived space of accessibility beyond a purely functional approach to incorporate lessons on how design can support fairness, equality, autonomy, and dignity for all people who are often overlooked in the conception of space. This intersectional approach to design thinking is the basis for universal design. The hope is that it will be more effective in advancing social inclusion by addressing a much broader range of issues in architecture and planning than the narrow focus of accessibility standards.

Notes

1 In this chapter, I will refer to space as "perceived" since that is the term used by Levebvre and those who write about his ideas, but a better term might be space as understood. While our perceptual processes seek out information, our cognitive processes encode and store it for later use.
2 Imrie did his research two decades before this was written. Although this is probably still the norm in education, there is an increasing emphasis on depicting people using buildings in architectural renderings. But this does not necessarily indicate a better understanding of the body.
3 The details on federal laws and regulations in the United States can be found at https://www.ada.gov/cguide.htm.
4 The goals can be applied in the design of products and places and in the design of services, such as education, health care, and retailing, and even policies like laws and regulations for housing and transportation.
5 Although this document has universal design in its title, its content is a comparative analysis of accessibility standards. This is a good example of the confusion between the two different paradigms.

References

Brumbaugh, S. (2018). *Travel Patterns of American Adults with Disabilities*. Washington DC, Bureau of Transportation Statistics.

Chetty, R., N. Hendren and L. F. Katz (2016). "The effects of exposure to better neighborhoods on children: New evidence from the moving to opportunity experiment." *The American economic review* 106(4): 855–902.

Christophersen, J., Ed. (2002). *Universal Design: 17 Ways of Thinking and Teaching*. Oslo, Husbanken.

Clarkson, J. and R. Coleman (2015). "Special issue: Inclusive design." *Applied Ergonomics*46: 233–324.

Dion, B. (2006). *International Best Practices in Universal Design: A Global Review*. Canadian Human Rights Commission.

Frumkin, H. (2006). Cities, suburbs, and urban sprawl. *Cities and the Health of the Public*. N. Freudenberg, S. Galea and D. Vlahov. Vanderbilt University Press: 143–175.

Frumkin, H., L. Frank and R. J. Jackson (2004). *Urban Sprawl and Public Health: Designing, Planning, and Building for Healthy Communities*. Island Press.

Hamraie, A. (2017). *Building Access: Universal Design and the Politics of Disability*. Minneapolis, MN, University of Minnesota Press.

Heylighen, A., V. Van der Linden and I. Van Steenwinkel (2017). "Ten questions concerning inclusive design of the built environment." *Building and environment* 114: 507–517.

HHS (2022). "Serving people with disabilities in the most integrated setting: Community living and Olmstead." Retrieved 4-22-2022, from https://www.hhs.gov/civil-rights/for-individuals/special-topics/community-living-and-olmstead/index.html.

ICC/ANSI (2017). *ICC A117.1-2017. Accessible and Usable Buildings and Facilities*. Chicago, International Code Council.

Imrie, R. (2003). "Architects' conceptions of the human body." *Environment and Planning. D, Society & Space* 21(1): 47–65.

ISO (2021). *Building Construction – Accessibility and Usability of the Built Environment*. Geneva, Switzerland, International Organization for Standardization.

Jackson, R. (2003). "The impact of the built environment on health: An emerging field." *American Journal of Public Health* 93(9): 1382–1384.

Jackson, R., A. L. Dannenberg and H. Frumkin (2013). "Health and the built environment: 10 years after." *American Journal of Public Health* 103(9): 1542–1544.

Jackson, R. and S. Sinclair (2012). *Designing Healthy Communities*. San Francisco, Jossey-Bass.

Jackson, R. J. and C. Kochtitzky (2001). "Creating a healthy environment: The impact of the built environment on public health." *Sprawl Watch* 3(41): 2–19.

Lefebvre, H. (1991). *The Production of Space*. Oxford, UK, Blackwell Publishing.

Ludwig, J., G. J. Duncan, L. A. Gennetian, L. F. Katz, R. C. Kessler, J. R. Kling and L. Sanbonmatsu (2012). "Neighborhood effects on the long-term well-being of low-income adults." *Science* 337(6101): 1505–1510.

Mace, R. (1974). *Illustrated Handbook of the North Carolina Building Code*. Raleigh, NC, North Carolina Building Code Council.

Mace, R. (1985). *Universal Design: Barrier Free Environments for Everyone*. Los Angeles, CA, Designers West.

Maisel, J., E. Smith and E. Steinfeld (2008). *Increasing Home Access: Designing for Visitability*. Washington, DC, AARP.

Merrifield, A. (2006). *Henri Lefebvre: A Critical Introduction*. New York, NY, Routledge.
Molotch, H. (2010). Introduction: Learning from the Loo. Toilet. H. Molotch and L. Noren. New York, New York University Press: 1–20.
Murphy, R. (1995). Encounters: The body silent in America. *Disability and Culture*. S. R. A. I. Whyte. Berkeley, CA, University of California Press: 140–158.
NCD (2007). *The Impact of the Americans with Disabilities Act: Assessing the Progress Toward Achieving the Goals of the ADA*. Washington, DC, National Council on Disability.
Skavlid, S., H. P. Olsen, and A. K. Hugeto (2013). *Trends In Universal Design Oslo, Norwegian Directorate for Children*. Youth and Family Affairs.
Sorin, G. S. (2020). *Driving while Black: African American Travel and the Road to Civil Rights*. New York, NY, Liveright Publishing Corporation (a division of W.W. Norton & Company).
Steinfeld, E. (1986). *ANSI A117.1 a case study in the development of a research based building accessibility standard, The Cost of Not Knowing. Proceedings of the 17th Annual Conference of the Environmental Design Research Association*, Washington, DC, EDRA.
Steinfeld, E. and J. Maisel (2012). *Universal Design: Creating Inclusive Environments*. John Wiley & Sons.
Steinfeld, E. and B. Tauke (2002). Universal designing. *Teaching Universal Design - 17 Ways of Thinking and Teaching*. J. Christopherson and T. Ronnevig. Oslo, Norway, Norwegian State Housing Bank: 165–189.
Story, M. F. (1998). "Maximizing usability: The principles of universal design." *Assistive Technology* 10: 4–12.
Tauke, B., M. Basnak and S. Weidemann (2016). "Universal design in U.S. architectural education: Success and challenges." *Nordic Journal of Architectural Research*2: 139–162.
USBLS (2022). *Persons with a Disability: Labor Force Characteristics*, U.S. Department of Labor.
USDOJ (2010). *2010 ADA Standards for Accessible Design*. Washington, DC, Department of Justice.
Watkins, C. (2005). "Representations of space, spatial practices and spaces of representation: An application of Lefebvre's spatial triad." *Culture and organization* 11(3): 209–220.
Whyte, S. R. and B. Ingstad (1995). Disability and culture: An overview. *Disability and Culture*. S. R. A. I. Whyte. Berkeley CA, University of California Press: 3–32.
Williamson, B. (2019). *Accessible America a History of Disability and Design*. New York, NY, New York University Press.

7 Enabling equal citizenship

Responses from civil society

Ingunn Moser and Inger Marie Lid

Introduction

Norway ratified the UN Convention on the Rights of Persons with Disabilities (CRPD) in 2013, thus making the CRPD relevant and applicable to Norwegian public institutions and civil society. The CRPD sets out, among other things, the right to belong to a local community and to services which support the well-being of people with disabilities and allow them to flourish. The human rights perspective on welfare services and professional practice means that moral principles such as inherent dignity and equal status and values such as individual autonomy, privacy, self-determination, and full participation in society form the foundation for politics and service provision (Degener, 2016; Brennan et al., 2018).

The CRPD conceptualizes abilities and disabilities as relational, or interactional (UN, 2006; see also Chapter 1 in this volume). Ability as well as disability is seen not as static, but as the outcome of practices and processes in a given situation and context. This relational turn in the CRPD means that the individual is seen as a person with rights and duties rather than a patient and service user, in other words, a citizen, and citizenship is understood as the outcome of enabling circumstances and interactions.

The Nordic model in welfare research commonly refers to a welfare state where the government has assumed a large part of the responsibilities for citizens' rights, including rights to welfare, from the family, and where there is a fairly high level of public funding of welfare services related to health and social services (Sivesind & Saglie, 2017, p. 37). In many Western countries, including Scandinavian welfare states such as Norway, there is a welfare mix, which supports individuals by providing individual welfare services and personal assistance. Diaconal non-profit institutions are actors in the welfare mix. The term 'diaconal' refers in a Lutheran context to Christian social work. Diaconal and other non-profit institutions are generally referred to as representatives of civil society and the third sector, alongside the private and public sectors. The third sector represents 9% of welfare services in Norway. These organisations are long-term partners and non-profit organisations, delivering services on behalf of public authorities, but often also have other finances, due to their assets, private donations, and fundraising.

DOI: 10.4324/9781003052708-12

Civil society organisations, which have been drivers and pioneers of welfare in a Norwegian and Nordic context, are handling the transition from service orientation and welfare recipients to a human rights perspective and citizenship. With this chapter we wanted to add a civil society perspective to the present volume. We also wanted to raise awareness and contribute to a discussion among diaconal and other non-profit civil society actors on how faith- and value-based actors understand and seek to enable citizenship, focusing on principles and values such as equal status, self-determination, participation and inclusion in the community, for people with disabilities, as for all other groups without discrimination, through their activities and services.

The aim of this chapter is thus to explore, through a reflexive dialogue between institutional leaders, how three Norwegian diaconal, non-profit service providers who deliver welfare services to people with disabilities understand and support citizenship, and as such respond to and reflect the obligations and duties which follow from ratifying the CRPD. The organisations are Signo, Crux, and Diakonhjemmet.

In their recent article 'Being Number One is the Biggest Obstacle', Brennan et al. (2018) discuss implementation of the CRPD in Nordic welfare services. They assert that it is difficult to change well-developed welfare systems and that having the reputation of being a driving force and being number one in the provision of welfare services in itself may be a major obstacle to transforming the citizenship status of disabled people. Such welfare systems often develop strong professional interests and other system interests that have little space for flexibility and variation. They tend to maintain the imbalance of power and counteract reforms.

During the past few decades, service user participation has received stronger support in service provision through legislative changes in Norway (Ministry of Health and Care Services, 2019). The human rights turn goes further, as the objective for the services in a human rights context is to support people who need individual services provided in a way that they can live as an equal citizen and participate in society and the community. By exploring the practice of three diaconal organisations as described and reflected upon by the leaders, we discuss how citizenship can be enabled in practice and in welfare service.

This chapter draws on data acquired through an explorative group interview with three heads of diaconal organisations which provide health care and welfare services for people with different and often multiple and complex disabilities. In presenting and discussing five core topics from the dialogue in the group interview, we focus upon the following issues:

- The work of the welfare providers to create opportunities for citizenship and participation.
- The dynamics of segregation and inclusion.
- Framework conditions for services and their objectives and values: what is required to provide good services?

- The meaning of participation and the institutions' work in this area.
- The role and importance of diaconal non-profit organisations.

We argue that such organisations have the potential to develop services based on cooperation, recognising the service user as a citizen on equal footing with the service provider. However, it is necessary to be aware that the organisations have displayed dimensions of paternalism throughout their history, including in contemporary times.

The relational approach and justice

There has been a human right turn in the welfare services in Norway during the past 40 years, starting with reforms that led to a dismantling of large institutions and reconfiguring of care for people with disabilities in the 1980s (Tideman & Tøssebro, 2002). The institution was reconfigured as the big institutions were closed and practice shifted from institutional care to community care. Welfare service from that time on was provided in smaller environments, such as group homes and part time assistance. This reform was motivated by criticism of living conditions in the institutions and the paternalistic practices of institutional administrators who neglected the subjectivity of the residents. The reform of institutions called for person-centred services and thus more relational practices. However, the reform did not recognise service users as full citizens. Still there were paternalistic practices and little support for political and social participation for the residents.

At present, a relational understanding of ability and disability as described in the CRPD is integrated in Norwegian policy and research (UN, 2006; Bickenbach, 2012). A relational perspective on service provision means that capabilities, self-determination, autonomy, and citizenship emerge from relations and interaction with people, communities, and environments (Moser, 2016). If, for example, there is a focus on equal citizenship, this must inform the way services are provided. Up to now, people with disabilities in general and people with intellectual disabilities more specifically have been treated as persons with fewer rights and duties than their fellow citizens. Material, legal, political, cultural, and social change is needed for this to change.

Disability is identified as a lacuna in citizenship studies and should receive greater focus (Lister, 2007). Citizenship means more than nation state membership. More broadly it is understood as having social, cultural, material, and political dimensions. Citizenship must be facilitated, fostered, and realised in practices.

In general, the welfare society and welfare services in Norway developed in three phases: they started as civil society initiatives; transitioned to the institutionalisation of the welfare state; and now have shifted to a competitive-based welfare service approach (Selle 2016). Faith and value-based institutions, particularly in diaconia, were pioneers in the development of services and education long before the existence of similar public sector provision.

They eventually developed together with public actors and services, and many undertakings were integrated with or transferred to the public sector. Civil society actors thus played a key role in the development of what is currently known as the welfare state. After World War II, the welfare state provided a common framework where the state assumes overall responsibility for the human rights and welfare of all citizens, and for the common good in society, but with a variety of service providers. This evolving welfare state established a need for health and welfare professionals such as social educators and social workers.

The design and delivery of service provision is crucial for everyday citizenship for persons in need of services. Non-profit organisations which offer services to individuals can support social and political justice by providing the context for all citizens, including people with disabilities, to live a good life, experience wellbeing, and flourish on their own terms. In her capabilities approach, which is a theory of justice, the American philosopher Martha Nussbaum describes how a good life can be achieved for all people, including those with disabilities who require care and welfare services (Nussbaum, 2007, 2011). Important dimensions of life, such as belonging, health, and relations, are part of her approach. We find this productive in terms of understanding the meaning and objective of service provision. As a human rights approach, Nussbaum's perspective on justice is also relevant when discussing the concrete and everyday implications of human rights at the basic level in everyday practices in contemporary value-based organisations.

Methods

This chapter is based on a reflexive group interview with the leaders of three Norwegian diaconal institutions which offer services to people with different disabilities. The objective of the group interview was to explore how faith- and value-based civil society organisations understand and seek to enable citizenship, with a focus on principles and values such as equal opportunities, participation and inclusion in the community, in activities and services supporting people with disabilities.

Representativity was not the objective of the sample. We chose the three organisations to provide a carefully selected sample of civil society welfare providers with diaconal affiliation. The reason for this is that they are all key service providers, and as a group offer breadth and variation in organisation types, portfolios and target groups. These organisations also all have a history of paternalistic practices and discrimination of individual persons and groups. Therefore, it is interesting to facilitate and start a dialogue on human rights and citizenship in service provision with these actors.

The three organisations were Signo, Crux, and Diakonhjemmet. Historically, these foundations have been pioneers in their disciplines in terms of establishing services for vulnerable groups that have been isolated, excluded, and which have not been prioritised in policy, services, or higher education and research.

Crux focuses on vulnerable children and adolescents and provides services related to child welfare, mental health, and substance abuse. Signo provides activities and services for people with hearing impairments in combination with other disabilities and sensory impairments, often in a lifecycle perspective. Diakonhjemmet has an ecosystem of services, which includes a hospital, care services, education, and research. Throughout its history, it has specialised in health and care services for the elderly, people with mental health issues and other chronic conditions. For the purpose of this chapter, the focus is on old persons and persons with dementia, in a disability and citizenship perspective (Bartlett, 2019).

In the following text, we will draw on the dialogue material from this group interview, focusing on how the heads of the organisations articulate and reflect on their organisations' practices in light of the CRPD. The four participants in the dialogue were as follows:

Helmut Liessem (HL)	Crux
Hege Farnes Hildrum (HFH)	Signo
Ingunn Moser (IM)	Diakonhjemmet
Inger Marie Lid (IML)	VID Specialized University

This study applies a methodological approach which is based on the assumption that qualitative interviews generate data through exploratory and power sensitive conversations between differently positioned knowledge subjects, rather than distanced subject-object relations between the researcher and her informants (Haraway, 1991, 1994).

This chapter is placed in a section with institutional perspectives, and we have therefore chosen to start with a reflexive group interview with institutional leaders only. These initial dialogues and reflections can and should be followed up by additional and complementing studies of understandings, views and practices from other positions in and around the same institutions. They are however also interesting and important in and by themselves, because they spur reflection and further discussion and awareness raising on an institutional level on the roles of faith- and value-based civil society institutions in the turn to human rights and citizenship in welfare.

As for the differently positioned knowledge subjects in the dialogue in the group interview, they were four participants, two of them (Moser and Lid) facilitators and authors with academic affiliations and or backgrounds linked to disability studies, all of them institutional leaders or with former experience as institutional leaders. To build common ground for the group interview, the participants shared selected readings.

Lid took the facilitating role of the dialogue. The dialogue in the group interview was recorded, transcribed and translated to English. Approval was obtained from the participants. The data and the participants have not been anonymised.

As noted, the facilitators and authors have hybrid identities, combining a background in research with experience from the management of civil society organisations. Moser's academic background is in social studies of science and technology studies (STS) at the intersection with disability and gender studies. She heads Diakonhjemmet. Lid is a professor of disability studies and citizenship at VID Specialized University and has also former experience as head of a civil society organisation. VID Specialized University is a private, non-profit, independent, and civil society-based university, and the majority owner is Diakonhjemmet.

Based on the participants' respective experiences and perspectives as professional and engaged heads of diaconal institutions, issues were explored regarding how diaconal institutions understand enact and enable principles and values related to citizenship in concrete situations and in present day professional, regulatory, and financial contexts.

The dialogue in the group advanced the exploration of and reflection on principles and values in practice, on development of the knowledge base and of the professions, and on conditions of possibility in organisational practices, to a greater extent than regular individual interviews or also focus group interviews. Individual interviews as well as focus group interviews normally assign participants in interviews the position of object of analysis. The reflexive group interview, however, allowed all participants to take up positions as subjects and collaborators in knowledge production, and take part in reflection and analysis via a shared process of learning.

This is also reflected in the written form of this chapter, which is presented like a dialogue. In the dialogue, the distinctions between interviewers and interviewed informants are blurred into a shared, situated and exploratory conversation (Haraway, 1991, 1994). The articulation of organisational practices is integrated with reflection and analysis. However, Moser and Lid as facilitators have sole responsibility for the general framing and final discussion, and they are also the authors of this chapter.

The work of the welfare providers to create opportunities for citizenship and participation

The group dialogue began with an initial question for the group: how does your organisation work on the understanding and facilitation of service users' citizenship and the scope for participation?

Helmut Liessem (HL):

> I am taking a tentative step towards terminology I am not completely familiar with. Those we work with at Crux are people who have problems related to substance abuse, addiction, schizophrenia, and children in the child welfare system who carry a lot of pain. What prevents them from participating in society and having a voice?

It's about the mental and physical pain they feel. These persons do not have a form of communication that matches the context. They get it wrong, or the context gets it wrong. And that relationship is precisely what we are addressing.

It's a matter of helping and supporting in terms of figuring out who they are. If we ask, 'What do you want?', they often don't have an answer. We can easily say, 'We want you to join in. What do you want?' But they don't even know what the four words mean. So, we work on supporting and strengthening self-understanding and self-confidence. I think that that's part of the answer to what we are working with and how – giving our service users a voice.

Then there are more technical things, like hiring people who have experience as service users, and having co-determination, organised in the form of service user councils. And based on that focus, caring about their answer. But you need to respect the fact that it takes time to get an answer.

Inger Marie Lid (IML): I liked the example of how the understanding of the question is not a given. But could you be a bit clearer about how you work to support the process in terms of who I am, what I want, and what wanting something means?

HL: The approaches used by the different fields vary, but it's all about respect for the individual. I'm interested in heterotopic diaconia, meaning that the centre of the practice is the person outside the institution. The starting point is where you are and trying not to objectify, while remaining in the relationship with the subject. However, this isn't enough for some of the people we work with. Sometimes we need to objectify. For example, an important part of what we do is to add professional understanding and knowledge. This means that we offer psychoeducation.

Ingunn Moser (IM): This may be controversial, but it resonates with me. Sometimes you need to objectify to support subjectification, gaining or recovering status as a subject.

HL: Yes. A tendency to constantly ask, 'What do you want, what do you want, what do you want?' is something they also encounter with their general physician. GPs have expert knowledge, and they ask questions. But there's a limit to how many times you can ask, 'What do you want?' without adding knowledge and expertise to the decision to be made.

IM: We see something similar in care for the elderly and persons with dementia. The services must be adapted to the residents, not the other way around. The residents should also be able to participate in the activities in their home, on their own terms, and according to their own wishes. As long as they can and want to, they dust their own homes, are involved in preparing meals, help plant seeds that will become tomatoes or harvest potatoes in the garden. They can keep a pet cat in their room and receive visits from families and friends or go for walks in the local area. In order to learn who each person is and what they want, a document called 'My lifestory' is compiled. All carers involved with a person must familiarise themselves with this document. The process starts as soon as a new person moves in, and it involves the person, their next-of-kin, and employees' experiences with getting to know people who have difficulty verbally expressing who they are, have been and want to be. What is important to them. However, in this situation, it is mainly employees who acquire knowledge and competence through recognised programmes and methods – to be able to read and interpret signs and expressions of the individual's wishes, what constitutes quality of life and how to stimulate participation, all based on each person's capabilities.

IML: Is communication also a key condition for participation and citizenship in Signo's services?

Hege Farnes Hildrum (HFH): Yes. … our target groups at Signo, in accordance with the articles of association, only have one thing in common – some form of sensory impairment: being deaf, deafblind or having a hearing impairment. Apart from this, the level of disability varies greatly. Our services also vary greatly in terms of duration, level of communication difficulties and additional factors. At one end of the spectrum, we offer labour market initiatives for deaf adults who need help finding work. They don't stay with us for long. They usually find work, which is good. At the other end, we work with people who are born deafblind and who are so heavily dependent on adapted communication that individual accommodations are made for them. Signo is recently focusing more on universal design strategies together with individual accommodation. What Signo primarily does to contribute to citizenship is to include people in a community that they understand and that understands them. This is what I think is the most interesting aspect of Signo in these discussions, because the question of inclusion and segregation is practically turned on its head here. I think that hearing about this is really tough, and for me as a hearing person, it's quite difficult to understand when deaf people say, 'This is where I'm included. I'm actually segregated in society at large'. It is true that people have the right to an interpreter, and this is where we return to (individual) rights but try communicating via an interpreter for a whole day! It's exhausting. You get a bit lost in translation. That's why I think it's very important that we include people in a shared sign language community.

We teach sign language to professionals or teaching skills to persons whose first language is sign language.

The dynamics of segregation and inclusion

IM: I think Hege describes the conflict in these dynamics very well. First, how a certain form of limitation or segregation can be a prerequisite for inclusion. Second, that faith in being included in society at large in the same way is virtually utopic. It is possible to experience greater exclusion in society at large, even if one is included on one level, by law. Inclusion thus depends on limitation in a sense – being included in something. The next step is that inclusion also depends on certain political conditions. The example from Signo reminds us of this fact. For example, that the political conditions for an inclusive environment and services are partly related to the professional environment, professional standards, and language. We will never receive enough specialised competence and academic experts in every local community in society at large. To keep and develop a professional community, which in Signo's case means professional competence, competence in communication and being a communication community, the activities must be concentrated. The professional competence is both social and medical, depending on the service users' needs. In this case, this means in a type of institution, such as group homes. The question then is how the organisation works and what room there is to participate, influence, and be a citizen and subject.

This includes very important dilemmas related to framework conditions for these types of services and their objectives and values. What is required to provide good services, and what are the limitations associated with individual rights?

HFH: We are very clear about that: we run institutions. We run a nursing home in Bergen, and we run a rehabilitation ward at the Conrad

Svendsen centre, which is part of the specialist health service. Apart from that, all residents live in housing that they rent which is at their disposal.

HL: This is interesting. Because we see the same situation, or there are also parallels with us. After they finish their treatment with us, service users, drug addicts and persons who are mentally ill return and talk about how difficult it is to be in and participate in society at large. We accordingly established a number of centres around the country which were simply meant to be a place for people to go to after completing treatment with us. They can come here, spend time together and talk with each other, always with a view to moving on, but as a sort of decompression chamber so that they are able to move on. We started 8–9 centres like this around the country with groups for learning coping skills and fellowship. We still have them, in line with the users' wishes. The problem is the same: encountering a context and a society which aren't quite a good fit. It's difficult to be included in society at large.

HFH: But the main additional factor is that deaf people can't learn to hear, which is a key difference. This is something we discuss with our employees in connection with sign language training. That it's actually possible for hearing people to learn sign language but that deaf people can't learn to hear. It's as basic as that.

IML: This brings us to the heart of what is being discussed also in connection with the CRPD. When talking about equality, equal opportunities, inclusion, and involvement, it is easy to think that all people should venture out into the world. Some persons are then marginalised because they are the only deaf person in the group, class, confirmation preparation class, or local community. The only deaf child welfare recipient, or drug addict. To my mind, this dynamic between inclusion in wider society and having places where people can be at home and rest, among their own people and on the users' terms, touches on the concept of culture.

IM: As you've also emphasised, Inger Marie, the point isn't that everyone should master the same things. The criterion is not ability or normalcy, but human dignity and human rights. Citizenship in the sense of everyone having the right to use their abilities and capacity, develop and participate, on their own terms.

HHF: Isn't dignity a concept here as well? Our school in Andebu has 30 students, mainly people who are deaf and have disabilities or autism and those who are deafblind. It's a tiny school. What often happens is that going there is the first opportunity students have to make friends and develop a social circle. For the first time, they can participate in a community and feel at home there. We see that this is the first time that parents think, 'I can imagine my child living a full life here'. There is work, a social circle, opportunities for participation, and also a form of citizenship. It is of course possible to point out that this is only an option in Andebu and a few other places, but we are also limited by several practical, physical, financial, and other preconditions and constraints. There are 100 people in Norway who were born deafblind.

The meaning of participation

IML: Can we pause to think a bit about participation, service user participation and citizen participation? A lot has happened in this area in recent years, and it can be useful to differentiate between levels and types. After all, service user participation is primarily linked directly to services.

HFH: At Signo, we have tried to structure it. We have not yet established a central service user council, but we do have a service user ombud. This is probably linked to Signo's past and present organisation. The entities at Signo have been highly autonomous, and participation has been at a local and entity level. However, we are currently trying to standardise practice and make it more uniform.

IML: I remember a dilemma that arose in relation to participation at Signo. The head of the service user council at one location received insufficient support to do the job in terms of time and resources, while the staff said that they were afraid of influencing the service users. They felt that the service user council had to be completely independent and that if they took a hands-on approach, they might influence them. It is certainly an important dynamic. Many people need a lot of support to be able to exercise influence. And when you offer support, you always have the potential to influence the situation.

HHF: We have a new theme now that is similar. We have a project called 'I will vote'. There has been a collaboration with the Norwegian Federation of Organisations of Disabled People (FFO) to increase voter turnout among our residents. But people are also afraid of exerting influence here, but politics is, after all, all about influence. We are all influenced. So, there is a very interesting citizenship dimension. I think it's good to bring it up.

IM: Self-determination is, after all, relational. For everyone many things are regulated in education and in hospitals. We have service user representation and participation in clinics, the Clinical Ethics Committee, management and on the board. They have the right to attend and provide input and are very active.

In addition, work is being carried out on *shared decision-making*, i.e. where the service user/patient is involved in and participates in decisions about their own health and treatment.

In Diakonhjemmet Care, service user participation is organised at activity level, with service user councils and/or family councils, depending on the target group. And, as already described, a large emphasis is placed on the staff getting to know the person, so that they can interpret and understand how and what they communicate and provide person-centred care, with the aim of them being able to participate in and live an active life, on their own terms, throughout their life.

HL: At Crux, participation is systematically regulated on three levels. It starts with the individual level, where we want to ensure freedom of choice and opportunities to choose types of treatment or activities. Our organisations are not huge, compared to others, so we probably have fewer opportunities to choose from than large units. But we have been keen to ensure that the service users, young people, can choose activities based on their interests and wishes. At the next level, where we have boards locally, there are also service user representatives on the boards. These representatives have right to speak and to propose topics, but they have not a right to vote. In child welfare, we work with a service user organisation for children under the child welfare service, which conducts visits and gives advice to create change. It can be rather scary, but is also very rewarding, and is based on their experiences.

The last level is the institutional level, the foundation level. We are not quite on track with that yet. We are working on how we can make the board aware of what the service users are saying about what is important within the organisation. We still have some way to go, but we have started by establishing a service user council made up of so-called social consultants with [lived] experience, who give us advice on service development. Social consultants are employees but have previous experience as service users.

HFH: We are still facing the same dilemma, Inger Marie Lid, that you described in the history of Signo (Lid, 2019). We have a lot of service user representation on the board, including a number of representatives from various special interest organisations. But then there's the question: what about those with intellectual disabilities? But that group is so small, so no one takes complete ownership of it. We think that's a bit challenging.

IML: Perhaps this particularly applies to this group, that theirs is the quietest voice on the agenda?

H: Yes, the Norwegian Deaf Association is concerned about all deaf people. And our group of deafblind people is so small. And likewise, organisations for those with intellectual disabilities are concerned with everyone with an intellectual disability. Our groups of intellectual disabled, deaf and deafblind persons are so incredibly small.

HL: To be honest, I see some of the same dilemmas and dynamics in our boards, and the service users' interaction with our boards, that service users encounter in society in general. Where their voice is not necessarily heard. Not necessarily due to ill will, but because there are economists and lawyers, people with special expertise and people with broad-based competence. And then the service user representatives feel, 'What do I have to contribute here?' If the others have a mind to do so, they can just talk them down. If they disagree, they can just talk it down. How can we talk about it in boards and in these bodies? How can we find the space?

IM: One place and one way to thematise it is in the introduction to and training for board work. All board members are offered training and an introduction to board work with us, every time there have been elections for new board members. And then, as chairman, you have to seek it and make provisions for it, otherwise you won't be able to make your voice heard, as you say.

IML: In the public sector, we have training for elected politicians. I'm a member of Oslo's committee for persons with disabilities and we take part in the training for politicians. The issue of micro, meso and macro levels is interesting. Participation at the individual, organisational and institutional level. And the importance of structure here. If power and authority are unequally distributed, if, for example, someone has the right to attend a meeting and provide input, but not the right to make decisions, then you are in a weaker position.

IM: This is perhaps the point where we can go back a bit to where we started, and the fact that it is not a given and is not automatic that you know what you want and can choose. And that citizenship according to the CRPD is not based on ability and achievement. Is it a goal that everyone should learn to say what they want and what they don't want? It is also a very special type of subject position – to say what you want, yes and no, define your limits and choose. It is easy to imagine situations were communicating 'no' in particular and defining your limits can be important.

HFH: It is perhaps about the nature of the service to a large degree. At Signo, it's a lot about the latter, but that's because we work in a life-span perspective with many of our service users. Whereas if you have someone who only receives a short course of treatment, there is perhaps one important thing – to learn to cope with what comes afterwards.

IM: It may also be a question of where you are in your life. I was actually thinking about dementia, and cognitive challenges just now. People with dementia, can't learn sign language, anymore. So, we have to actually teach staff to read, hear, see, interpret and understand what someone wants and says in other ways, with non-verbal communication.

The role and importance of diaconia

IML: The CRPD includes guidelines on the entire welfare mix in Norway, of which you are a part today. But you all represent institutions with a long history, where the importance of participation, human rights, and involvement has increased over time. Does diaconia represent any resources of its own?

HFH: With us, the answer is probably 'yes and no'. We have asked, simply, because we have had a working group that has been preparing a document that describes what diaconia is for Signo. In this connection, we began by examining what diaconia is in Signo today. A kind of baseline. Many people come to us because of this distinctive character, i.e. the specialist environment in Signo, rather than the diaconal one. But we are in the middle of a process where we are trying to reformulate diaconia and turn it into a story that everyone can get behind. But I believe that diaconia is part of our established culture, which has been about how we relate to people, a culture that is still at work, even if not everything is articulated.

IM: Diaconia as a practice is not only what is carried out by people in specialist positions and functions, but everything which takes place within an organisational context defined as diaconal. However, this does not mean that diaconia is a practice, as opposed to theory, and knowledge and research based professional practice. Diaconia represents both its own professional and disciplinary resources and some faith- and value-based resources in the work in our activities, which together create an interpretive horizon for the organisation and its practice. Diaconia as Christian social practice therefore also represents a distinctive discipline and professionalism, which must be added, like the professional knowledge and disciplinarity, which we have talked about previously. However, it is also important to say that diaconia is also what surgeons, nurses and cleaners do. That they also actually carry out diaconial work, when they work with us and help us realise our aims in a specialised diaconal institution. Both the theory and practice of diaconia must constantly be developed, challenged, questioned, and renewed.

In my view, diaconia must be supported by both the culture and the structure of an organisation. It has to actually be incorporated into these. It cannot be taken for granted, it has to be nurtured and facilitated. We also have VID Specialized University in our midst with strong academic communities, and with dedicated study programmes, research, and knowledge development in diaconia. We also have a strategic diaconal council that advises senior management, we have a low-threshold forum for diaconia in practice and extra resources supporting service users' needs.

As head, I am responsible for making sure that this happens, not to police a specific definition, but to make sure that there is reflection and that it is an ongoing process. It is not defined once and for all, it is not given and cannot be taken for granted. Space must also be actively created here to enable that to happen. We must equip managers to be able to discuss it, to articulate, and to facilitate its existence.

HL: We are also working on this and putting together a core value statement. Diaconia drives what we do, but it depends on how it is interpreted and who you ask. When we ask people in our organisation what diaconia is, a variety of words and terms are suggested, such as care, benevolence, humanity, practical work, i.e. actions not words, equality, inclusion, seeing others, respect, and genuine care.

Concluding discussion: The relational dimension of diaconal practice

Above we have presented an extensive dialogue between leaders of diaconal non-profit institutions. When analysing the dialogue, the position of the participants emerges as interesting. The three participants in the dialogue discusses from the position as a *leader*. Thus, the service user perspective is seen through their perspective. This position comes with ambivalences. Two aspects are of specific interest here, first the understanding that it is important to uphold the service provider institution and second the leader's reflections on objectification. We will address both below.

There is a consensus among the participants that professional service provision is necessary for supporting citizenship for persons in need of assistance. This discussion section is written by the two authors of the chapter, who also took part in the dialogue, one as facilitator. The idea that professional service provision is needed to enable citizenship is contested in a critical disability perspective, based on a history of paternalistic practices (Pelka, 2012; Lid, 2019). However, as leaders of non-profit institutions, the participants have experienced that their services are needed and valued. Addressing the dilemmas in designing of the services, they argue for stronger structure supporting user representation at all administrative levels rather than dismantling the institutions with the professional knowledge held and administered by the institutions.

The other aspect of interest in the dialogue is the need of objectification of service users. It was argued by HL and supported by the others that it sometimes was necessary to objectify the service user in order to support developing a subject position and thus citizenship. The argument was anchored in the importance of supporting the person's process of becoming a subject. According to Nusbaum, support of individuals' ability to flourish is important and can be seen as a dimension of social justice (Nussbaum, 2007, 2011). When discussing a situational need for objectification, the leaders indicates that the diaconal practice build on an anthropology where the individual is seen as interdependent or dependent of others. Several feminist and disability care ethicists will support such an anthropology (Kittay, 1999; Pettersen, 2008).

The design and provision of health and welfare services are aspects of justice as everyday practice in communities and can be a factor supporting processes enabling citizenship status for service users. The context must however be an acknowledgement of the problems objectification of persons has led to and still can lead to, such as institutionalisation and misrecognition. One of the participants in the dialogue, HL, mentioned heterotopic diaconia, meaning that the centre of the social practice is the service user and not the institution itself (Wyller, 2009). Striving towards shifting focus towards enabling a good human life for the citizen is necessary for institutions providing welfare services today. It is however necessary to acknowledge the risk of having a stronger focus on the interest of the institution rather than on the best interest of the person.

Diaconal service provision to persons with disabilities relates to users and local and national government. As stated in the introduction, a characteristic of the Norwegian welfare state is that the government assumes overall responsibility for the common good in society and for the human rights and welfare of citizens, but also works through civil society service providers. This means that the state is contracting, and funding care and services provided by, for example, diaconal institutions. As explained earlier, this is common practice in Norway. However, it comes with a price, as the organisation works in the dynamics between supporting individual needs and adjusting to the funding and other regulations offered by the authorities. The gap between the two: individual needs and funding offered, impacts on service user participation and citizenship at the societal level. The services in the Nordic welfare states in general, and more specifically in Norway, are not at the level epitomised in the CRPD (Brennan et al., 2018).

This framework condition impacts on the scope to act. If we understand justice as relevant to people's everyday lives, in line with Nussbaum's capabilities approach, access to resources is a topic of interest for theories of justice, along with dimensions such as health, relations and participation in everyday life. Diaconal civil society organisations will then on the one hand advance justice and the good life for persons in vulnerable life situations, and on the other hand, work loyally towards state and national regulations. This can make justice a challenging topic and can also hamper the recognition of persons with disabilities as equal citizens. We need constantly to ask ourselves what justice means for us, what role justice plays in the design of services, how our institutions can support and promote justice, what roles we as diaconal institutions can and must play, and what competence is required.

As the dialogue with heads of institutions suggests, diaconal organisations have a clear relational and contextual understanding of ability as well as disability, and how this relational conceptualisation of ability as well as citizenship needs to shape design of and approaches in services and activities. The focus is on the service user as person and subject, on enabling, supporting and empowering the person to live a good life, and to find out what a good life implies for them, including health, relations, and participation. This includes but is not restricted to individual rights and choices. The focus is on how both person- and subjecthood and the good life must be supported in a context of everyday life and practices, and rests on an inclusive communicative community which for many necessarily also implies a professional community and professional services. The professional and institutional context may thus also represent the conditions of possibility of an inclusive environment and of equal participation and citizenship.

In this situation, diaconia represents both disciplinary and professional resources and faith- and value-based non-profit resources for the institutional culture and for the design and approaches of service provision. But diaconia is not given and cannot be taken for granted, and needs to be added, cultivated, and challenged, as any disciplinary knowledge and research tradition, and any knowledge-based practice, in an organisational and societal context. Diaconia as rights- as well as faith- and value-based, diaconia as contextual and as focusing on supporting and empowering the person and citizen, develops in exchange with the granting authorities and with society at large. Therefore, diaconal organisations can never simply assume the role of service providers. Diaconal organisations also need to nurture the role of value-conscious organisations guarding and or advocating for human rights and for the moral values and principles in welfare provision. And, accordingly, also the role of pioneers, constantly improving and developing activities and services, in close collaboration and coproduction with service users, to remedy needs that are not acknowledged, met and given priority in the welfare state.

What is recognised among the leaders is that the organisations also need expertise in human rights. The CRPD sets out the individual's right to language, such as sign language and alternative supplementary communication. Organisations can remind the granting authorities of this right, and by doing so help to strengthen the rights of service users. Most local and county authorities do not have specialist expertise in human rights. This can be part of the expert's role and highlight civil society's response to the human rights turn in service provision.

There is a possible conflict in goals when the organisations are both supporting individual service users' rights and aim at providing services tailored for individual choice on the one side and working in accordance with political regulations on the other side. Often such conflict remains without good solutions. By standing in the dynamics between the individual and the institutional the third sector has the possibility to focus on the rights of the individual person.

References

Bartlett, R., Nedlund, A-C., & Clarke, C. L. (2019). *Everyday Citizenship and People with Dementia*. Dunedin Academic Press.

Bickenbach, J. (2012). *Ethics, Law, and Policy*. Los Angeles: SAGE.

Brennan, C., Traustadóttir, R., Rice, J., & Anderberg, P. (2018). Being Number One Is the Biggest Obstacle: Implementing the UN Convention on the Rights of Persons with Disabilities within Nordic welfare services. *Nordisk välfärdsforskning*, *3*(1), 18–32. doi:10.18261/issn.2464-4161-2018-01-03

Degener, T. (2016). Disability in a human rights context. *Laws*, 5, 3510.3390/laws 5030035.

Haraway, D. (1991). Situated Knowledges: The Science Question in Feminism and the Privilege of Partial Perspective. In *Simians, Cyborgs and Women: The Reinvention of Nature* (pp. 183–201). London: Free Association Books.

Haraway, D. (1994). A Game of Cat's Cradle: Science Studies, Feminist Theory, Cultural Studies. *Configurations*, *1* (1994), 59–71.

Kittay, E. F. (1999). *Love's Labor. Essays on Women, Equality, and Dependency*. New York: Routledge.

Lid, I. M. (2019). From Institutionalisation to Citizenship: Lessons Learned from Studying Diaconal Practice in a Norwegian Context. *Diaconia*, *10*(1), 51–66. doi:10.13109/diac.2019.10.1.51

Lister, R. (2007). Inclusive Citizenship: Realizing the Potential. *Citizenship studies*, *11*(1), 49–61. doi:10.1080/13621020601099856

Ministry of Health and Care Services (2019). Pasient-og brukerrettighetsloven (Lawon pasients and users rights). https://lovdata.no/dokument/NL/lov/1999-07-02-63

Moser, I. (2016). *Sociotechnical Practices and Difference: On the Interferences Between Disability, Gender and Class* (pp. 405–426). Antwerp, Belgium: Garant.

Nussbaum, M. C. (2007). *Frontiers of Justice: Disability, Nationality, Species Membership*. Cambridge, Mass: Belknap Press of Harvard University Press.

Nussbaum, M. C. (2011). *Creating Capabilities. The Human Development Approach*. Cambridge, MA: The Belknap Press of Harvard University Press.

Pelka, F. (2012). *What We Have Done: An Oral History of the Disability Rights Movement*. Amherst: University of Massachusetts Press.

Pettersen, T. (2008). *Comprehending Care: Problems and Possibilities in the Ethics of Care*. Lanham, Md.: Lexington Books.

Selle, P. (2016). Frivillighetens marginalisering [The Marginalisation of Voluntarism]. *Tidsskrift for velferdsforskning [Journal of Welfare Research]*, 19(1), 76–89.

Sivesind, K.H. & Saglie, J. (eds.) (2017). *Promoting Active Citizenship. Markets and Choice in Scandinavian Welfare*. Cambridge: Palgrave Macmillan.

Tideman, M., & Tøssebro, J. (2002). A Comparison of Living Conditions for Intellectually Disabled People in Norway and Sweden: Present Situation and Changes Following the National Reforms in the 1990's. *Scandinavian Journal of Disability Research*, 4(1), 23–42. doi:10.1080/15017410209510781

Wyller, T. (2009). The Heterotopic Citizen?: Some Aspects for a "Science in the Making". In *Heterotopic Citizen: New Research on Religious Work for the Disadvantaged* (Vol. 1, pp. S. 8–17). Göttingen: Vandenhoeck & Ruprecht.

Interlude 3
Global Disability Summit

How to realize "nothing without us"

Gagan Chhabra

Introduction

This interlude is broadly divided into three sections. The first section accentuates the background that led to the genesis of the Global Disability Summit (GDS). The second section provides historical perspectives from the two GDSs held thus far. The third section provides insights from the Civil Society Forum (CSF), which was an integral element of the GDS 2022. This interlude is based on personal reflections of the author and does not represent the view of the organization Atlas Alliance.

Background

Annually since 2006, individuals and organizations from around the world have gathered at the United Nations Conference of State Parties to discuss the implementation of the landmark Convention on the Rights of Persons with Disabilities (CRPD). This convention has been a watershed moment for the disability rights movement, as article 32 of the CRPD calls for greater international cooperation. Over the course of the last decade and a half, persons with disabilities and their representative organizations have leaned on the human rights framework of the CRPD, to combat disabling barriers and create enabling societies. The disability rights movement has rallied behind the slogan, "nothing about us without us," and has stressed the significance of representation across local, national, regional, and international fora. Globally, disabled people and their organizations have jointly created avenues to share knowledge, lived perspectives, and best practices that will promote their full and effective participation in society.

The theme of disability rights has largely been situated on the periphery of international development and humanitarian work. After the adoption of the Sustainable Development Goals (SDGs) in 2015, there was a greater impetus to center disability rights and promote the realization of disability justice within the international development sector. The GDS can be viewed as a concerted effort to put disability in development more firmly on the international agenda.

DOI: 10.4324/9781003052708-13

The GDS, historical perspective

The GDS is an international conference on disability in development, arranged by the International Disability Alliance (IDA) and two host countries, approximately every 3 years. At the GDS state representatives, civil society, and other stakeholders pledge commitments to ensure disability inclusive international development, and humanitarian aid, as well as to strengthen local and national policies that aim to fulfill the human rights of persons with disabilities.

On July 24, 2018, the UK Department for International Development (DFID) and the IDA hosted the first GDS in London in collaboration with the Government of Kenya. The aim was to promote the realization of the rights, freedoms, dignity, and inclusion of all persons with disabilities and strengthen disability inclusion in international development work. In the spirit of "nothing about us without us," a CSF was organized prior to the GDS 2018. This forum witnessed broad participation of representatives from organizations of persons with disability, multilateral agencies, and mainstream organizations.

During this historic GDS, 171 national governments, multilateral agencies, donors, foundations, private sector, and civil society organizations made 968 individual commitments. These commitments encompassed four themes associated with the GDS such as ensuring dignity and respect for all, inclusive education, routes to economic empowerment, and harnessing technology and innovation. The commitments also covered cross-cutting themes such as women and girls with disabilities, conflict and humanitarian contexts, and disability-inclusive data disaggregation. Over 320 organizations and governments signed a collective action plan, the *Charter for Change*. This visionary, collective plan was grounded in the human rights framework and centered the theme of disability inclusion within the international development agenda. Of the commitments made at the GDS 2018, 25% are completed, while most of the commitments, 62%, are reported to be on-track to completion.

In February 2022, IDA, the Government of Norway, and the Government of Ghana hosted the second GDS. The Atlas Alliance, the largest umbrella organization of persons with disabilities in Norway, collaborated and assisted the organizations in the first ever digital GDS. The GDS 2022 was an online 2-day summit in February 2022. It was preceded by both a CSF and a Youth Summit (GDS Youth). More than 11,700 individuals registered for the 4 days of GDS, including 3,029 participants for the GDS Youth, 1,463 participants for the CSF, and 7,112 participants for the high-level GDS meetings.

The GDS 2022 was able to solicit more than 1,400 individual commitments by national governments, multilateral donors, civil society organizations, and others, under five thematic areas including, meaningful engagement of organizations of persons with disabilities (OPDs), inclusive education, inclusive health, inclusive livelihoods, and inclusive humanitarian action. At the GDS 2022, it was announced that the next summit, which will convene in 2025, will be hosted by the Government of Jordan and the Government of Germany, in collaboration with IDA.

Both the GDSs have encouraged national governments, multilateral agencies, and donors to commit to disability-inclusive change. These summits have offered a significant opportunity to undertake disability rights advocacy, at the grassroots level as well as at the upper echelons. Persons with disabilities and their representative organizations can, and should, use the momentum created by the GDS and lobby with their respective national governments to implement the UN CRPD. GDS has not only provided human rights advocacy fora for persons with disabilities and their representative organizations has also opened new avenues to ensure that disability-inclusive national policies could be formulated, and disability-inclusive budgets could be created, which in turn positively influences the trajectory within the international development domain.

The CSF 2022

Background

Under the rubric of the GDS 2022, the Atlas Alliance and IDA organized a CSF. The forum was organized digitally on February 15, 2022, with the view to amplify the voices of persons with disabilities, accentuate the issues pertinent for the disability rights movement, and assess the realization of the SDGs and the principles of the UN CRPD.

The CSF 2022 involved an eclectic and engaging group of speakers from around the globe, ranging from Norway to New Zealand, Ghana to Greece, Uganda to the United States, Denmark to the United Kingdom, and Ireland to Mexico. The forum had a global audience with 1,463 participants registering for the event. The international audience entailed participants from OPDs, mainstream organizations, national governments, multilateral agencies, and humanitarian organizations. In the spirit of "nothing about us without us," the forum was hosted by Gagan Chhabra who is a blind project manager for inclusion at the Atlas Alliance.

Nothing without us

One of the core themes that stood out from the opening session of the CSF was the shift in the focus within the disability rights movement. In 1998, James I. Charlton wrote the book, *Nothing About Us Without Us: Disability Oppression and Empowerment.* This has been a popular banner under which the global disability rights movement has been mobilized to demand for better representation, increased inclusion, and equal human rights. Mr. Yannis Vardakastanis, serving as president of the IDA, talked about focusing on *Nothing Without Us.* If we want to create inclusive communities, resilient societies, and a sustainable world, we must appreciate the fact that disability is a part of the human condition, and it is a universal phenomenon. We have to include persons with disabilities while designing all policies, creating all programs, and building all projects. All funding in the domain of international development work and humanitarian action should be disability inclusive. In addition, persons with disabilities must be part of all the conversations, undertake joint decision-making, and monitor all the international development work if we want to realize the Sustainability Development Goals and fulfill the 2030 agenda of "Leaving no one behind." This priority on including persons with disabilities in all development work was also echoed by other speakers in the opening session who participated in the CSF.

Creating a strong social movement

One of the crucial themes which emerged in the first session of the CSF was to highlight the fact that disability is a part of human diversity, and we should strive to create a broad-based social movement together. There are avenues that overlap between the disability rights movement on the one hand, and the gender movement, climate justice movement, and racial equity movement on the other. We should strive to have a broad tent wherein individuals from diverse age groups, genders, nationalities, racial and socioeconomic backgrounds can come together and advocate for human rights for persons with disabilities and advocate for disability justice. It is time to integrate persons with disabilities and their agenda across all different social movements, which ought to be built up from the grassroots.

Paddling together in the same canoe

One of the significant themes addressed during the second session of the CSF was that we live in an interconnected world. The COVID-19 pandemic has demonstrated that no one is safe until everyone is safe. Martine Abel-Williamson, the president of the World Blind Union, shared the New Zealand indigenous peoples' wisdom that "we all are paddling in the same canoe together." Therefore, it is crucial to build systems, structures, and societies that are fully inclusive for all individuals irrespective of their ability status. The COVID-19 pandemic has revealed the fault lines wherein persons with disabilities were often excluded from labor markets, marginalized in healthcare systems, and frequently forgotten in the process of agenda setting. As we begin to emerge out of the pandemic, we have a unique opportunity to reshape societies and reimagine futures that operate from a disability rights and disability justice perspective, and do not merely work to "include" disabled people in an ableist society. Disability justice need not be a sole responsibility of persons with disabilities and their representative organizations. It is a collective responsibility for all of us as we sail together from the turbulent COVID times to a more inclusive future.

In essence, the CSF 2022 offered an excellent opportunity to highlight the priorities for the disability rights movement, which facilitated in setting the agenda and undertaking discussions in the high-level meetings of the GDS. The core themes of the CSF 2022 opened novel pathways to ensure that the voices of persons with disabilities and their representative organizations are heard and registered and created avenues where disability justice and international development work can be a reality.

8 Universal human rights and universal design for people with disabilities

Challenges and lessons from Sub-Saharan Africa

Korydon Smith

Introduction

As countries across Europe were mired in war, Franklin D. Roosevelt, the 32nd president of the United States, delivered his annual State of the Union Address on January 6, 1941. Later known as his "Four Freedoms Speech," Roosevelt laid out a rationale for why America, in an isolationist posture until then, had an obligation to intervene: protecting freedom of speech, freedom of worship, freedom from want, and freedom from fear. Despite many advances since WWII, these freedoms remain unmet in many countries, particularly for people from various disability groups living in low-income settings.

Human rights have always varied from place to place. Disability rights are no different. Moreover, the divergence widens at each scale—from international agreements, to national policies, to funding, to local implementation. As such, the global strive toward equality in education, healthcare, employment, housing, and other areas—not to mention basic access to food, water, and sanitation—remains uneven. Though imperfect in all contexts, the way that disability rights policies are enacted, implemented, and enforced vary significantly between Western high-income countries and the Global South. Economics is a major driver of difference, but other factors also impact disability rights and lived experiences. In places like the Great Lakes Region of central and eastern Africa, factors include ecological and climatic challenges; relatively weak political systems, institutions, and enforcement mechanisms; constraints in materials, technologies, and supply chains; and limited capacity in both the labor force and design professions.

At the same time, there are positive lessons to be gained from countries such as Rwanda, Uganda, the Democratic Republic of the Congo (DRC), and Zimbabwe. While human rights organizations often disparage many African, Latin American, and South- and Southeast Asian countries for their disability rights policies, cultural views, and building practices, that narrative conceals an array of exemplary programs and projects, from which all countries might learn. Rather than taking a paternalistic view or adopting a deficit model, the aim of this chapter is to seek out and understand the "wisdom" of the Global South.[1]

DOI: 10.4324/9781003052708-14

This chapter, therefore, provides four brief case studies, each illustrating unique approaches to striving toward Roosevelt's four freedoms and other human rights.

A brief international comparison

Before discussing the cases, a brief international comparison is useful to provide a broad look at the challenges that both high- and low-and-middle-income countries face. Even comparing a small sample, Colombia, Uganda, and the United States illustrates a breadth of issues.

Like the African contexts discussed later, Colombia has a complex, decades-long history of internal conflict. As a result, violence-related injuries, such as those caused by landmines and psychological trauma are common among the military, police, and civilians alike. Legislation and culture-change efforts have focused on improving lives and reintegrating survivors and victims of conflict in society, particularly the education and employment sectors.[2] Colombia was a member of the GRULAC (Group of Latin America and Caribbean Countries) that sponsored the UN Convention on the Rights of Persons with Disabilities (CRPD). In addition to ratifying the CRPD in 2011, Colombia has disability rights legislation that both precedes and follows the CRPD. Compared to other low- and middle-income countries (LMICs), architectural design codes are fairly robust in Colombia. However, building design and construction are inconsistent, particularly between urban and rural areas, and code enforcement is limited.

In Uganda, 94% of children with disabilities do not complete primary schooling. While stigma, family expectations, teacher preparedness, and other social factors contribute to this problem, the built environment is also a major challenge. Long travel distances, coupled with minimal transportation infrastructure, are one hindrance. The design of schools, especially inaccessible and unsafe restroom facilities, are equally problematic—a hidden threat to education equality for girls as well. Yet, the work of organizations such as WaterAid provide an international model for integrating disability-centered practices into a wide array of efforts, such as access to clean water and improving education equality.

The United States, by contrast, has major national legislation (notably the Americans with Disabilities Act of 1990), evidence-based building codes (e.g., the Americans with Disabilities Act Standards for Accessible Design), a comparatively high level of training among building professionals, and strict code enforcement backed by litigation. Of course, this does not ensure that all buildings provide equal access for people with disabilities, nor does it protect against discrimination by organizations or individuals; but the United States, Australia, Japan, and many European nations are often considered the leaders, if not innovators, in inclusive and universal design. Despite all these apparent efforts toward human rights, the United States, as of 2021, was the only country in the Western Hemisphere (other than the Pacific archipelago of Tonga) not to have ratified the CRPD. Of the UN's nine fundamental human rights treaties, "the United States has ratified only three."[3]

The purpose of these three examples is not a deep, analytical comparison. It simply serves as an entrée to broader principles. These three nations, as well as others, face different challenges to human rights, yet, they also have unexpected similarities. Colombia, a South American country of more than 50 million people with a history of internal conflict, is a global leader in disability rights legislation, but, like other nations, needs additional training of architects, engineers, builders, and code officials. While robust policies and building codes exist, many buildings remain inaccessible to people with disabilities due to what ultimately gets designed and built.

Uganda, an impoverished African country of less than 50 million, like Colombia, needs increased expertise and capacity in the building sector, but Uganda also needs educational programs to increase societal commitment to disability rights. Without complementary progress in the built environment and the social environment, major initiatives like education equality and health equity cannot be achieved. The United States, a global leader in multiple categories of human development, demonstrates the reality of uneven progress. The United States has made significant progress in both disability rights legislation and the quality of the built environment, but lacks cohesion in its stated human rights values and in its commitment to protecting the rights of its citizens equally across racial, ethnic, gender, and class divides. Similar to Uganda, the uneven approach across various goals and populations—e.g., equal pay for women, quality housing for people in poverty, healthcare for older adults, or equal education for children with disabilities—can impede progress for all groups. This is particularly the case when issues overlap or characteristics intersect. In Rwanda, for example, rural women with disabilities have a literacy rate of 28%, about one-third the rate of the broader population.[4] The US' inconsistent adoption of UN treaties sends a perilous and implicit message to other countries: that human rights are choices, not universal.

The examples also demonstrate the complexity of developing and implementing strategies for improving disability rights. Breakdowns can occur at any number of levels (Figure 8.1), from cultural differences in the definition of disability, to the inability to ratify international treaties, to a lack of code enforcement in the construction of buildings. These breakdowns may be persistent or may change over time.

The grand, global ambition of universal human rights

On March 30, 2007, the United Nations Convention on the Rights of Persons with Disabilities (CRPD) opened for signature and yielded the highest number of signatories of any Convention in UN history. This signaled a strong global interest in advancing educational, social, and economic equality for people with disabilities. As the first comprehensive human rights treaty of the 21st century, the CRPD sprung from decades of work by member states as well as international non-governmental organizations (INGOs), and built on the efforts of the World Health Organization to collect and report data, including the

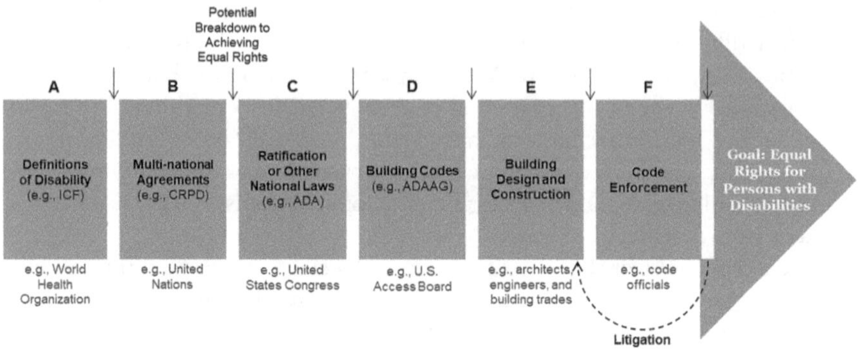

Figure 8.1 Potential breakdowns in achieving equal rights for persons with disabilities. The translations that occur at each phase (A–F) present challenges, as the actors who oversee each element are different, e.g., the United Nations (B) or code officials (F). Litigation is one of the last tools to overcome earlier breakdowns and remediate the built environment, but it is not available or effective in all contexts.

Source: © 2022, Korydon Smith.

development of the International Classification of Functioning, Disability, and Health (ICF). But, like other Conventions, CRPD ratification (or accession), i.e., formalizing the Convention in each signatory's national laws, has been protracted and varied. As previously stated, ratification is but one of several phases where achieving the overarching purpose—"to promote, protect and ensure the full and equal enjoyment of all human rights and fundamental freedoms by all persons with disabilities"—can break down.

While the ICF sought to provide a common understanding of disability, we must understand disability not as an objective fact, a condition of the body, but as a cultural construct. Through this, we uncover high variability in the definitions and perceptions of disability. Not unlike language, food, or music, outside of one's own cultural context, some constructs seem perplexing, idiosyncratic, even humorous. In Mali and other countries, for example, having small buttocks, regardless of gender, is seen as a disability.[5] This does not align with a medically oriented view of disability, but, if this "impairment" impedes social advancement—e.g., marriage, thereby negatively impacting economic, educational, or other attainment—it "functions" as a disability.

Likewise, in other contexts, congenital disabilities may be viewed differently than age-related disabilities or compared to disabilities from sudden injuries. Sometimes disability is intertwined with religious beliefs. Various disabilities may be viewed negatively, positively, or somewhere in between in different contexts, as shown in Figure 8.2. This might range from "stigma," e.g., how menstruation is viewed in parts of rural Nepal, to "heroism," e.g., the portrayal of disability in some children's books. An analogy may be drawn to the spectrum

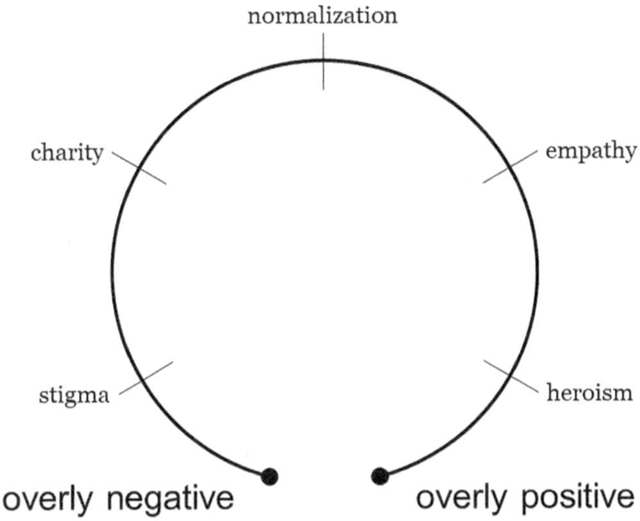

Figure 8.2 Conceptual diagram of cultural attitudes toward disability. Normalization is a middle ground, whereby the treatment of people with disabilities is consistent with cultural norms and behaviors in the broader population; right and left of this center are increasingly divergent and harmful attitudes toward disability.

Source: © 2022, Korydon Smith.

of political views—liberal, moderate, and conservative—where the far right and far left are not represented on a line as opposites, but bent together to illustrate their similarities.[6] The "normalization" and integration of disability in society is a goal in many contexts. In any case, a culturally nuanced view of disability is important, as it contributes to the ways that both nations adopt (or resist) articles of human rights and building professionals include (or exclude) people in the built environment.

In short, achieving universal human rights is not likely to occur through a universal approach.

The corollary: the design and construction of the built environment is also contextual. As such, we see that many contemporary approaches to universal design integrate context as a critical factor. Each place has a set of social, economic, technological, environmental, and legal factors that impact the processes and outcomes of everything from roads to schools, houses to public spaces, businesses to civic buildings. Gender norms, the availability of financing, conventional construction materials, topography, building traditions, and other factors influence where and how things are built. In turn, the responses to these factors either improve or encumber access for people with sensory, cognitive, mobility, and other disabilities. To deepen this discussion on the importance of context, four cases from the Great Lakes Region of Africa are discussed.

Four Cases from the Great Lakes Region of Africa

Case 1: Access to infrastructure and decision making: Kigali master plan, Rwanda

The term "accessibility" has various meanings, both related to and outside the frame of disability. Wheelchair accessibility at building entrances, to restrooms, or in public transportation is a relatively narrow, but common, application of the term. Accessibility, as access to power and decision making is a different, but complementary notion. The two concepts—one physical, related to freedom of movement, and one non-physical, associated with sovereignty and autonomy—are reciprocally linked. Diminished access to one can impede access to the other. One example is voting rights, where both policies (who can vote and how people vote) and design (the spaces and technologies used for voting) can significantly affect people with disabilities. Another example is urban planning, infrastructure, and development.

Kigali, the capital city of Rwanda, is a rapidly growing urban center of around one million residents. Like many other African cities, several factors are driving population growth: rural-to-urban migration, relatively high birth rates, and improved healthcare and increased lifespan. In addition, since the 1994 genocide, Rwanda has been one of the most stable and safe countries in the region, contributing to immigration from nearby countries, along with the return of Rwandan refugees. Rwanda is already the most densely populated country in Africa, with the Netherlands as its closest European proxy, and also has one of the fastest growing rural populations in the world. With national policies and investments to support international commerce, the expressed goal for Rwanda, especially Kigali, is to become the international economic hub for eastern Africa.

However, the majority of Kigali's residents live in informal, hillside settlements. More broadly, much of Rwanda's land and property transactions are untitled, stemming from both a traditional land-tenure system and the disruptions from past conflicts. In informal settlements around the world, it is common for residents not to participate in elections (because they do not hold land), and even more may have little input regarding neighborhood planning decisions. Expropriation (forced relocation) can also be common, as has occurred in various locations in Kigali (Figure 8.3).

Rwanda did not begin a formal land titling process until 2008. As such, the confluence of rapid population growth, untitled land, and traditional building practices have resulted in improvisational urbanism that lacks the infrastructure—water, sanitation, roads, public spaces, civic buildings, and societal institutions—needed to support the safety, wellbeing, and prosperity of dense neighborhoods. Accessibility is also not well addressed in steep, urban settlements that often rely on improvised footpaths, which are narrow, uneven, slippery in the rain, and unnavigable to most people using walking aids or wheeled mobility devices.

Figure 8.3 Informal settlement in Kigali. Self-built hillside settlements are common throughout Kigali, but present health and safety challenges to residents and are particularly difficult for people with disabilities to navigate. Residents also have little control over planning decisions that directly affect them.

Source: © 2017, Korydon Smith.

The systematic gathering of disability statistics is also relatively recent, and appears to underestimate the prevalence of disability, particularly regarding the wide array of injuries sustained during the genocide. Nevertheless, a number of recent national policies have aimed to advance disability rights and improve outcomes. In many policies, disability safeguards are allied with supports for survivors and victims of conflict, women, children, and people living in poverty. These laws and institutions build upon Rwanda's constitution and amendments, which declare protections against discrimination in and convey supports for education, employment, healthcare, and other sectors. Recent legislation and programs also draw on "Rwandan values of mutual respect, support, and belief in home grown solutions."[7]

This approach has enabled a number of seemingly disparate policies to produce positive outcomes. These include, but are not limited to, laws on gender equality, investments in Internet infrastructure, shoring up the healthcare system, ongoing post-genocide reconciliation efforts, and a continuation of land titling efforts. The combination of efforts has had a powerful impact on social, economic, and health outcomes across populations, including women and girls, rural and urban populations, conflict victims, and people with disabilities.

Inclusive of the above policies, there has been a particular emphasis through the Kigali master plan to improve roads, water and sanitation, stormwater management, housing, and access to public spaces. While participatory planning is not the norm, individual projects can not only provide long-term benefits to neighborhoods but can also facilitate the hiring of neighborhood residents in design, construction, and maintenance—providing residents with direct economic benefits, a path for input, and a sense of ownership. This might address immediate needs for improving the accessibility of roads, sidewalks, and walking paths; upgrading the design of public water points, public restrooms, and residential bathrooms; and meeting the need for assistive technologies.

At a higher level, Rwanda's National Council of Persons with Disabilities (NCPD) facilitated stakeholder meetings that led to the 2021 National Policy on Persons with Disabilities. A key aim of the policy was to ensure stronger coordination across sectors, organizations, and initiatives. The policy, therefore, established a requirement for ten ministries and a number of other influential organizations to identify a disability liaison to work with the NCPD. Rwandan-grown strategies, further leveraged here or in other contexts, could provide people with disabilities deeper influence on problem solving and on planning, design, and construction decisions. Led by MASS Design Group, two exemplary cases are Butaro Hospital (2011), in rural Rwanda, and Umubano School (2011), in Kigali. The construction of both projects provided direct economic benefits to locals; and the design of the building clusters and sites paid specific attention to ensuring contiguous accessibility for people using wheeled mobility devices.

Key considerations from this case for future human rights and development work:

1. How people with disabilities and other marginalized populations might have direct economic benefits from involvement in development projects, such as in data-collection, planning, community organizing, and construction jobs.
2. How to proactively include people with disabilities and other marginalized populations in making decisions about the location and design of water points, sanitation, public spaces, schools, health clinics, and other critical neighborhood infrastructures.
3. How to ensure voting and other rights of marginalized populations particularly during transitional times, such as migration, land-tenure disputes, and other factors that might be intertwined with human rights.
4. How to interweave a set of complementary policies and actions—even incongruent, on first glance—toward deeper and wider benefits to multiple marginalized groups.

Case 2: Access to housing, education, and civic rights: Bidi Bidi Refugee Settlement, Uganda

With armed conflicts in Syria, Venezuela, Ukraine, Afghanistan, South Sudan, Myanmar, and elsewhere, the world is amidst the largest humanitarian refugee crisis since World War II. Global media coverage has illustrated the challenges that both refugees and host countries face. Reporting has highlighted the harrowing journeys of refugees, their plight in refugee camps, and the policies and security concerns of pass-through and destination countries. However, there has been less attention paid to proactive, effective, non-camp resettlement strategies, such as those seen in northern Uganda. Despite the policies of the United Nations High Commissioner on Refugees (UNHCR), the international agency charged with protecting the rights and wellbeing of refugees, which privilege repatriation and integrative resettlement, camps remain a prevalent strategy.

Uganda is an outlier. By contrast to many regions of the world, Uganda does not utilize refugee camps, but provides planned, durable settlements integrated with resident populations. In fact, UNHCR considers Uganda to have "one of the most favorable refugee protection environments in the world, providing refugees with freedom of movement, the right to work, and access to social services including primary and secondary education through a generous asylum policy."[8]

The significance here is that disability rates tend to be higher in refugee contexts due to violence, injury, malnutrition, and other factors, which is why the *UNHCR Emergency Handbook* includes added focus on disability. In addition, the UNHCR now emphasizes an inclusive, rights-based approach to disability in conflict settings, including recommendations for the "universal design" of facilities and programs.[9] Conflict, forced migration, and resettlement are immensely complex topics. This case, therefore, narrows into a few key lessons of resettlement practices in Uganda, focusing specifically on the Danish Refugee Council's work to provide housing.

In recent history, Uganda has hosted refugees fleeing violence and other insecurities from Rwanda, Burundi, the DRC, and other LMICs. By the end of 2016, Uganda hosted more than one million refugees from South Sudan alone. South Sudan, the world's newest country, has experienced international and domestic conflicts since its secession from the Republic of Sudan in 2011. Fighting, which began in July 2016, forced hundreds of thousands of people to flee to Kenya, Sudan, and other regions within South Sudan, but primarily to Uganda. Between the months of August and November 2016, an average of 5,193 South Sudanese refugees crossed into Uganda each day.[10] During a similar timeframe, refugee settlements in various districts saw an influx of nearly 1,000 refugees per day, making places like Bidi Bidi the largest refugee settlement in the world, with around 250,000 residents[11] (Figure 8.4).

Figure 8.4 Bidi Bidi Refugee Settlement. Home to approximately 250,000 refugees from South Sudan, the Bidi Bidi settlement comprises traditional home construction, built primarily by refugees themselves, pit latrines, food plots, and walking paths and roads, as well as water points, health clinics, and schools. The image shows the reception (arrival) zone, with self-built storefronts and homes, and solar panels for electricity.

Source: Frenciscobcn, "Bidi Bidi Reception Centre Zone 1," August 29, 2020, CC BY-SA 4.0.

The lessons of this case truly begin with land acquisition. The Danish Refugee Council negotiates with local Ugandan elders and leaders to identify and secure land agreements. Ugandan refugee settlements are built on land borrowed from the local population, and settlements are planned to provide resources—e.g., roads, water wells, health clinics, and schools—to both native inhabitants and immigrants. The local population, therefore, has a stake in each development. By purposely involving host communities and refugees in site-planning, design, and resource-allocation decisions, settlements have, broadly speaking, maintained a peaceful coexistence.

Upon arrival in a settlement area, the Danish Refugee Council and other agencies provide refugees with a tent, sleeping mats, blankets, kitchen sets, water cans, and emergency supplies. They also provide toolkits and technical assistance for homebuilding and the digging of latrines. This approach aims to support refugees' abilities to build for themselves, with two benefits. First, given the higher numbers of refugees over a short time, housing construction needs to keep pace and be done within the resources available. The Danish Refugee Council's estimated budget for housing is $800 per dwelling. The self-built (or assisted) approach stretches available human and material resources. Second, the practice ensures the building of culturally meaningful places. Refugees frequently seek out natural materials for dwelling construction, including mud, brick, wood, and thatch, common to homebuilding practices in South Sudan. Some families with greater resources will purchase more durable materials, such as iron sheets for roofing, also common to the region. The Danish Refugee Council plans the layout of housing settlements, including the necessary infrastructure and agricultural lands to support them. They appear as durable, not temporary, settlements; however, because of the materials used (for the most part), homes can be demolished and returned to the earth, minimizing environmental impacts and keeping land agreements intact.

In addition, the Danish Refugee Council and other organizations provide durable shelters for individuals or families with specific needs, such as the elderly, unaccompanied minors, and persons with disabilities. These are typically located in less steep areas and closer to community-based services. Nevertheless, this sometimes results in segregated enclaves of people with disabilities; in addition, other physical, cultural, and structural barriers remain for individuals with disabilities, such as integrated schooling for young children with disabilities who do not speak the local language. As 72% of people with disabilities in northern Uganda "live in chronic poverty," advancing education equality for children and adults with disabilities is critical to opening up economic opportunities.[12] So what are the barriers and paths to education, employment, and economic equality?

Coupled with the Danish Refugee Council's facilitation of housing, Ugandan policies provide freedom of movement and access to healthcare, education, and employment for all refugees, highly unique compared to other refugee contexts. Settlement planning supports these rights by integrating health clinics and schools into each settlement. These policies, however, would benefit by a stronger emphasis and integration of accessibility policies. With policies and space planning synergies, a third factor adds value: refugee organizations aim to leverage the skills and training of refugees, not only toward housing construction but also to provide professional services, such as mental health care, legal advice, and dental care, as well as other services, like hair cutting, to the immigrant and host communities.

Nevertheless, barriers remain. Only about half of teachers have training in special education or inclusive education for children with physical, sensory, psychosocial, or intellectual disabilities. Education for parents and caregivers is also needed. Not all schools are universally designed or accessible, though this is improving, and learning materials are rarely available in alternative formats.[13] Resource and capacity limitations are clearly a problem, but, a second, often-overlooked problem is one of data and information. High-income countries are often data rich, even to a point of information overload. By contrast, low-resource contexts, particularly in times of crisis management, are often focused on and structured to solve problems, while remaining under-resourced and under-capacitated to gather important quantitative and qualitative data. Government and non-government organizations in Uganda have been filling this gap in recent years—capturing everything from comprehensive statistics on demographics, health outcomes, and other key metrics to the individual experiences and daily lives of refugees. UNHCR and its partners are using this information to target social and physical interventions that can advance education equality. Priority interventions are discussed in coordination and delivered in thematic monthly UNHCR reports that highlight data-informed strategies and action items.[14]

Key considerations from this case for future human rights and development work:

1. How to meet urgent and sizeable humanitarian needs, such as healthcare, of diverse populations in an integrative, cross-sectoral manner.
2. How to leverage national policies that promote civil rights, such as freedom of movement and access to employment, and augment them with culturally/locally viable practices, such as securing land for housing and civic infrastructure.
3. How to provide layered supports, such as various forms of housing assistance, for moderate-, high-, and critical-need populations.
4. How to fill the knowledge gap in order to make more informed and targeted decisions that maximize resources toward major priorities, such as inclusive education for children with disabilities.

Case 3: Access to mental health services and social participation: Friendship Bench, Zimbabwe

Zimbabwe is illustrative of post-colonial challenges in Africa. Political power, land rights, economic policies and benefits, access to education and healthcare, and other issues have been contentious, at times boiling into violence and breaches in human rights. Race, specifically conflicts between descendants of white colonists and indigenous populations, and ethnicity have often been at the center of the strife; and torture, rape, and other brutalities have been used to exert power. As a result, psychological trauma is extensive and interventions are needed.

Mental illness, cognitive impairments, and intellectual disabilities are commonly stigmatized in both high- and low-income countries.[15] Western approaches to mental health, however, may not be culturally accepted; and expertise in such methods may not be present. There is a paucity of resources dedicated to mental health by comparison to the need; fewer physicians are trained or specialize in mental health and neuro-therapeutics; there are less psychologists, clinical social workers, and counselors with advanced training and licensure on par with Western standards; and there are fewer researchers, administrators, and professionals with expertise in diagnostic tools and program assessment. These scarcities in human resources are even more apparent for people with comorbidities, such as those with physical, psychological, and social "wounds."[16]

By contrast, community health workers in many African, Asian, and Latin American contexts—particularly rural areas—provide a variety of services. This may include prenatal care, assistance with childbirth, child health care, adult health care, well checks, emergency medical response, mental health care, and referrals to more advanced health services. Training of such frontline workers may be in formal educational institutions, by INGOs, through hands-on work or apprenticeship, or some combination of these. Community health workers often are also members of the communities they serve (Figure 8.5).

Utilizing the local norms of healthcare delivery, international partners, and ultimately an INGO, developed the Friendship Bench in 2006 to address the mental health crisis in Zimbabwe. In 2016, they received international funding for a randomized controlled trial, which proved its efficacy. Friendship Bench organizers train community health workers, often female elders (grandmothers), in fundamental concepts of screening, therapy, and referral, along with how to open conversations with individual community members. A modest spatial intervention complements this training, whereby a small bench is placed near health clinics, schools, and other common, yet discreet, "safe" spaces. This helps to make the first session, or conversation, more informal, or normalized. Sitting with someone on a bench, particularly while waiting for a bus or waiting in line at a health clinic, is common; sitting on the bench may be organic or may occur by referral from a friend, relative, or past recipient of services. The Friendship Bench uses this piece of normal, daily life as an entry point for services, which may otherwise be stigmatized.

Figure 8.5 Friendship Bench. The program uses a small physical intervention, a bench for two, coupled with training for female elders to deliver much needed mental health services in a non-stigmatizing manner.

Source: Costa Juta, "Friendship Bench Grandmother and Client Having a Problem-solving Therapy Session on the Friendship Bench in Harare, Zimbabwe," October 21, 2022, CC BY-SA 4.0.

Counselors integrate a basic mental-health assessment into these first conversations. From there, they determine what, if any, next steps are needed. Supplementary, deeper sessions may be recommended. In addition, organizers facilitate group sessions, where trusted community members who have experienced trauma and who have benefited from therapeutic services engage in listening and problem-solving sessions. Again, multiple layers and types of services are available depending on individual needs, including referrals to other providers. Moreover, to further normalize the effort, the team organizes a variety of group workshops on gardening, crocheting, and other activities. The organization also includes researchers and individuals trained in assessment in order to evaluate outcomes and continually improve the program.

Scalability of interventions and programs is a central consideration among international development funders and implementers. The Friendship Bench is exceptional in this regard. The concept requires nominal investment for physical infrastructure, enabling the bulk of resources to be directed toward training and programming. Six countries in the Global South have now implemented the Friendship Bench practices, and a number of Western contexts, such as college campuses, are now using similar strategies to ease the entry into mental-health supports.[17]

Key considerations from this case for future human rights and development work:

1 How to leverage existing cultural norms, spatial behaviors, and health structures to provide services that are impactful, culturally resonant, and within resource constraints.
2 How to merge Western expertise in research methods, best practices, and program assessment with local wisdom and experiences.
3 How to provide interventions that are easily scaled and deployed—economically, spatially, and in human resources and training—along with a constellation of supports that meet the variety of individual needs.

Case 4: Access to employment and peace: Idjwi Center for Coffee, Leadership, and Peace, DRC

The DRC is among the largest and most resource-rich countries in Africa, spanning from the Atlantic Ocean inland to the Great Lakes Region. It is also home to one of the longest-standing conflicts in the world, much of which has been concentrated in the east, along with deeply entrenched poverty. Unstable national and local institutions have impeded efforts to improve gender equality, health outcomes, education equality, and safety, among others. Landmines and undetonated ordnance exist in many rural, predominantly agricultural areas, leading to severe injuries to children and farmers, and the subsequent need for medical care, prostheses and assistance technologies, economic supports, family and community education, and paths to other employment. The Idjwi Center for Coffee, Leadership, and Peace—a collaboration between the Polus Center for Social and Economic Development, CPNCK (cooperative), and others—is the final case in this chapter. It is a novel approach to workforce development for people negatively impacted by conflict. The driving ambition of the Idjwi Center and its leaders was to augment other peacebuilding and economic efforts by increasing access to the coffee value chain for survivors and victims of conflict, people with disabilities, and women.

The path to peace, in the DRC and elsewhere, is complex. It is often protracted and multifaceted, including external mediation, internal reconciliation talks, targeted social and educational programs, and the construction of symbolic places and customs for healing. Providing economic opportunities is also critical, as many combatants join or are recruited not for reasons of vengeance but for pragmatic, economic motivations.

This region of ongoing violence is, paradoxically, awe-inspiring with natural beauty. Idjwi, the second-largest inland island in Africa, located in the eastern DRC, is a lush, sloping landscape in the center of Lake Kivu. In addition to exotic timber and other resources, the island hosts a rising specialty coffee industry. Bean quality is improving, productivity is increasing, and the weather has remained stable despite global climate change, which has negatively affected many other coffee-growing regions of the world. The island has also been a peaceful haven amidst decades of conflict in the region, partially due to its difficult access across the lake.

Like other commodities in Africa, coffee has offered economic opportunities for producers, brokers, retailers, and other members of the value chain. Coffee farmers, however, often see the least economic benefits and are often the most negatively impacted by price volatility. The added significance here is that the majority of cooperative members (farmers) in the region are women. There is a saying among "fair-trade" companies that the coffee industry exists, quite literally, "on the backs of women," who may carry large sacks of coffee cherries miles over difficult terrain to processing facilities. Gaining access to other jobs in the coffee value chain has numerous benefits. First, occupations such as cupping, i.e., taste-testing and evaluating coffee, are more lucrative, less prone to price instability, and more revered. Employment in these areas can advance social standing in the community and provide economic stability to both individuals and families. Second, these jobs rely less on physical strength and stamina than production jobs. Not only does cupping pay more, it also is less taxing on the body. Workers may be able to have a longer-running career, and, if redesigned, many of these jobs can be done by people with a variety of disabilities. Third, adding know-how and capacity at the quality-control phase benefits both the people in those positions and farmers. Knowing how to assess and improve the quality of beans can enable producers and their co-op leaders to gain access to the specialty coffee market, improving the marketability and price of harvests (Figure 8.6).

Nevertheless, becoming a cupper requires specialized training in a specialized facility. No such facility, prior to the Idjwi Center, existed on the island; and the closest mainland facility did not meet international standards, nor was it accessible to people with disabilities. While the coffee industry was the primary focus, the center has a long-range vision of offering training programs for other sectors, such as energy or healthcare. This offers the triple benefit of opening even more economic opportunities, providing added income to the coffee cooperative, and filling critical needs on Idjwi island.

The design of the building, therefore, emphasized five fundamental principles:

1 Quality: ensuring facility design commensurate with producing high-grade specialty coffees. The building was designed according to international standards for cupping labs.
2 Flexibility: designing for multiple functions and change over time. The building includes both specialized spaces for cupping and interior and exterior flex spaces for other forms of training, small-group and community meetings, and social events.

Figure 8.6 Idjwi Center for Coffee, Leadership, and Peace. The architectural rendering shows an accessible ground level with entry area, offices, and classrooms, with an accessible lower-level courtyard, constructed using local materials.

Source: © 2020, Korydon Smith and Stephanie Cramer.

3 Affordability: efficiently utilizing local materials, knowledge, and builders. The building is made primarily of brick and timber sourced from the island.
4 Inclusivity: improving access for everyone, including landmine survivors, victims of conflict, women, and people with disabilities. The entry and main level of the building are wheelchair accessible, as are the restrooms; and other elements, such as daylighting and doors, emphasize universal design.
5 Inspiration: constructing facilities beyond conventions, with the capacity to enhance the mind, body, and spirit. The project includes an integrated, multi-purpose courtyard, a moving view of Lake Kivu and the mainland, and user-controlled natural ventilation and lighting.

More than a cupping lab, the center serves as a training hub for the region, with a future ambition of leadership in peace building. While practical in its origins and funding, i.e., supporting training in the coffee industry, the project illustrates how larger, more complex goals can be integrated in localized interventions.

Key considerations from this case for future human rights and development work:

1. How to connect local needs, such as workforce development, to national priorities, such as peace building.
2. How to expand simple objectives, such as constructing a cupping lab, to include other unrelated activities, such as training for the energy sector, that benefit more community members.
3. How to integrate design for disability into building practices and standards that have not yet incorporated accessibility or universal design, ultimately benefiting both people with disabilities, e.g., through employment, and the industry, e.g., through market image and product quality.

Conclusion

It appears that some of the challenges and pathways discussed above are squarely in the domain of public policy, others are in service and program design, and others are the domain of the building sector. The case could be made, however, that, for the building sector to succeed, legislation is essential. For instance, increasing capacity among architects, builders, and inspectors in rural Colombia requires dedicated funding at the national level. Likewise, in Uganda, a multi-pronged strategy is likely needed to advance education equality. Such an approach might include a comprehensive policy that integrates (a) social education programs, such as for family members and school teachers, to combat stigma, with (b) funding for school renovations, and (c) specialized training for the construction trades on designing for children with disabilities.

In complement, the emphasis on spatial and construction practices that focus on inclusion is not simply about meeting a functional goal. Ensuring accessibility for purposes of eating, bathing, and other activities of daily living is, of course, critical. But the higher ambition of the CRPD and universal design is community integration—socially, economically, and politically. It is through universal design, in both physical and virtual settings, that people with disabilities have access to self- and group-advocacy, i.e., access to the people and systems that can improve equity in education, healthcare, employment, transportation, housing, recreation, etc. at the macro, meso, and micro levels.[18] For example, without safe and accessible roads a person who lives in an informal settlement and uses a walking aid cannot attend and participate in a public meeting to discuss plans for a new community health clinic.

In the march toward universal rights for people with disabilities across the globe, context matters. It is nearly impossible to legislate culture change top-down.

Thus, a place-based approach may be a valuable policy strategy because it focuses action on community needs and priorities. While many individual policies can be shared among nations, it is the unique "constellation" of policies—designed for each cultural, climatic, economic, and environmental context—that can overcome intractable discrimination. The same strategy may also be valuable for the design of social programs, approaches to urban planning, and health interventions.

The cases above subvert the preconception that the Global South can learn from the Western World and demonstrate how lessons from the Global South can inform international efforts to create an accessible world. Taken together, the cases illustrate many challenges—entrenched poverty, engrained discrimination, and decades-long conflicts, that significantly surpass the challenges of Western nations. They also demonstrate innovative and creative solutions to what seems intractable that emerged from unique contexts. Of course, they are not without limitations or flaws. But the circuitous path toward universal human rights may become more visible by journeying, unexpectedly, through places where the struggle for human rights and disability inclusion are most challenging. Through these lesser-known projects in Rwanda, Uganda, Zimbabwe, and the DRC, a more inclusive future can be most easily visualized.

Notes

1 See, for example, Basil Davidson, *The African Genius: An Introduction to African Cultural and Social History* (Boston: Little, Brown, 1969), who discusses the history, culture, and ordering systems of Africa not from a colonial or paternalistic perspective but from a view that values "native genius."

2 Approximately half of survivors in Colombia and elsewhere are children. The term "survivor" is used in reference to people who have directly experienced physical or psychological injuries; "victim" refers to the indirect effects of those injuries on others, such as family members of survivors.

3 The United States has struggled to ratify a number of UN treaties. One set of challenges have been philosophical, while other challenges have been structural or legal. As exemplified in UN treaties related to healthcare, there can also be a mix of these obstacles. As the United States relies on a privatized healthcare system, the UN value in health as a fundamental human right is philosophically incongruous with US policy as currently practiced. The UN's emphasis on universal, state-sponsored healthcare is incongruent with US laws and political beliefs. Moreover, ratification of UN treaties, including those related to health, requires the political will of the US Congress to pass legislation. Often, bills do not even make it to "the floor" for a vote. Regarding challenges to ratifying the UNCRPD, see Arlene Kanter, "Let's Try Again: Why the United States Should Ratify the United Nations Convention on the Rights of People with Disabilities," *Touro Law Review*, *35* (2019): 301.

4 Gertie Steukers, "New Policy on Inclusion of Persons with Disabilities is an Opportunity for All of Us," United Nations Development Programme, Rwanda, 2022.

5 Iryna Babik and Elena S. Garder, "Factors Affecting the Perception of Disability: A Developmental Perspective," *Frontiers in Psychology*, *12* (2021); and Fatima Halatine and Gunvor Berge, "Perceptions of Disabilities among the Kel Tamasheq of Northern Mali," in *Disability in a Cross-Cultural Perspective*, F.J. Brunn and B. Ingstad, eds. (Cambridge, MA: Blackwell Science, 1990), 49–58.

6 For the purposes of this chapter, the figure focuses primarily on the more moderate cultural views of disability. It does not include the most extreme views of disability that can result in death, imprisonment, or forced isolation/segregation.
7 Rwanda Ministry of Local Government, "National Policy of Persons with Disabilities and Four Years Strategic Plan (2021-2024)," May 2021.
8 Paula Hidalgo-Sanchis, "Using Big Data and Machine Learning to Respond to the Refugee Crisis in Uganda," UN Global Pulse, March 5, 2018.
9 UNHCR, "Working with Persons with Disabilities in Forced Displacement," 2019, https://www.unhcr.org/4ec3c81c9.pdf.
10 UNHCR, Operational Data Portal: South Sudan Situation, 2017, https://data.unhcr.org/en/situations/southsudan.
11 UNHCR, Operational Data Portal: South Sudan Situation, Adjumani, 2017, https://data.unhcr.org/en/situations/southsudan/location/1925.
12 Ryan Duly, "Access to Humanitarian Services by Persons with Disabilities in Imvepi Settlement Arua District, West Nile Region of Uganda: Barriers and Facilitators Assessment Report," Humanity and Inclusion, August 2018.
13 Innovative Education and Research Consultancy Firm, "Final Special Needs Assessment Report: Needs Assessment on Children with Special Needs in Bidi Bidi and Omugo Refugee Settlements," N.D.
14 See, for example, UNHCR, "UNHCR Uganda Monthly Update: Protection – Education," September 2019.
15 For more on global mental health care, see Rembis in this volume.
16 Wolfensberger outlines 18 physical, psychological, and social wounds. See Wolf Wolfensberger, "The Systematic Stripping of Valued Roles from People," *The SRV Journal*, 6(2), 15–18; Wolf Wolfensberger, *A Brief Introduction to Social Role Valorization: A High-order Concept for Addressing the Plight of Societally Devalued People, and for Structuring Human Services*, 3rd ed. (Syracuse, NY: Syracuse University Training Institute for Human Service Planning, Leadership & Change Agentry, 1998).
17 See, for example, Thomas Insel, *Healing: Our Path from Mental Illness to Mental Health* (New York: Penguin Press, 2022).
18 For further information on universal design at these three scales, see Lid in this volume.

Postscript

Dialogue between Rosemarie Garland-Thomson and Inger Marie Lid

Rosemarie Garland-Thomson and Inger Marie Lid

From the editors: This conversation between Rosemarie Garland-Thomson (RGT) and Inger Marie Lid (IML), two leaders in disability studies in their respective countries, took place on September 18, 2022 in Oslo, Norway. We present it here because it captures many of the important themes emerging in disability studies and reflected in the diverse contributions to this book. As such, it provides a postscript.

The conversation begins with Garland-Thomson and Lid explaining how they came to disability studies. This serves as both an introductory preface and a vivid reminder that disability is a fluid and contingent identity and an embodied experience, which can be characterized by pain. At the same time, disability holds tremendous potential to build a shared sense of community, belonging, and purpose. For many people, "becoming disabled" is not represented in a discrete moment or as a physical fact; it is a process of politicization. The continual and changing act of experiencing the world and the people in it through a disabled body raises one's consciousness.

RGT: I was born disabled. Like so many people born with disability, I was born into a family who were at the time non-disabled, [and] had no idea about what disability as we know it might be, and so my disability was never recognized as such, and because I didn't have medical treatment, and didn't have any access [to] or associations with anyone else with disability, I didn't understand myself as being a person with a disability until the feminist movement taught me about what it meant to be a woman, and I read Simone de Beauvoir, who said you are not born a woman, you must become a woman, and I realized then that I could become disabled and needed to do that in order to do my work of studying disability culture and the kinds of things that I knew how to do from literary and cultural studies, and that is analyze the way that identity and representation make meaning, so I became disabled at that time, by identifying as disabled, entering into community with other disabled people, like you my beloved friend, Inger Marie.

IML: So, for me, there was also no conception of disability. I wasn't born disabled. My first encounter with disability was when I got scoliosis, and

DOI: 10.4324/9781003052708-15

that was a condition that my parents and the doctor wanted to be treated. And it was through a meeting with the hospital in Oslo – we lived in Stavanger. The act of correction at the hospital, the act of changing my body as it was, and altering it to a more correct body and that was a medical understanding and also a medical experience, but also a very physical experience in order to correct the incorrect body. I was hung from my neck, to stretch out, and [was] told to wear a Boston corset to straighten out what was unstraight. So, thinking back, the disability experience in that was the experience of being wrong and something more than; someone [who] had to be altered. The reason for that was double; it was for some understanding of health reason[s] but also a normalcy reason. And as a member of the welfare state, this experience had social consequences, for example in school, I needed to have a different kind of chair and desk from the rest of the pupils, and I could not lift objects. So I had to have two sets of text books and so on, but also the embodied experience of pain, of course because the corset was inflexible and tight, and a kind of being different, sort of a combination of a body and a shelter, the soft body and the shelter but pain was the most present experience through those years. So, I think that the term disability, which was absent, was something I sought for in a way, and at the same time, the ideal was to act as if it was nothing. To hide and act as if it was nothing. But it was not until I as a scholar started to work on my PhD thesis, and at this time I was 40 and had had other medical conditions, I got multiple sclerosis when I was a student, and other things, so it wasn't until I started to read disability studies, and among this your challenging and comprehensive work, Rosemarie that I found the concept I sought for, it became available as a reference of understanding. So, I think I have been related to disability studies perspectives without having the concept and then recognized it later on.

RGT: It is interesting that the stories we are telling were there. It supports the truth of life that we need to have words in order not to just understand ourselves but in order to live intentionally. The words, when they are not available for us, make it difficult and even impossible for us to make decisions and structure life, the sense of self without the words, but also the other things we are saying is that we need a community or a set of relations because of course words are to be exchanged with one another in order to establish a sense of self in the world and to be an agent. Both of us needed these words and these understandings, and the experience of being. Your words are exactly right, being corrected and especially being corrected by people and institutions and authorities, our parents, doctors, teachers; we learn to be disabled and that means that we learn in some way that there is something wrong with us. But along with that, if we also had the opportunity to make community and to learn about civil and human rights and that understanding of disability and other identity groups, that gives us a story to put up against the really destructive history of being corrected.

IML: Disability can be actual, it can be physical, it can be embodied, but it can also be in literature, and in other words and this is one reason why it is important to write and be part of a public discourse because by doing that we do not establish the language but we try the language and the concepts, by using it, and by that we can open up a space for also talking more about what is a good life and what is important to be part of sharing a good life. The act of correcting a person is an act of altering what is not as expected closer to what is expected, never really close, just closer. And that is very different from the condition and for example asking what one needs in order to live a good life, and for me the pain came with the treatment, I didn't have the pain before and probably would not have had it if it wasn't for the treatment. So in fact it is also shared experience with others because the correcting is in itself painful and can be in opposition to sharing a good life.

From the editors: In this section, Garland-Thomson and Lid begin by discussing the complex relationship between disability studies and disabled people and medicine. They then move into a conversation about what constitutes "a good life" and what types of supports they and other disabled people might need to live that life. Lid calls this creating a "culture of access."

RGT: We tell a similar story; corrections can be a violation. But I do think there are other people whose correction was welcome because of the nature of their disability. So, in order to establish relationships with medical treatment, I think we have to be careful to have a way of establishing ourselves as the directors of our own medical treatment, to understand ourselves as having the capacity to make our own decisions on medical treatment, which is very difficult for children as they don't have that capacity. And I was shocked by you saying no to a medical treatment because I don't think I ever said no. I think one of the things that disability studies can do is give people the sense of agency that they can manage, and they have the right and the obligation to manage their own relationship with medical science and medical treatment.

IML: I think the discussion related to medical treatments is one of the complexities and sometimes contradictions in disabilities studies, the technologies and the different contexts and different experiences and different needs, and this is why I think it is important to enter into a dialogue, [to] try to find out what is a good life for you, what is supporting for you, [to] try to find out how to come closer to that. And then there is of course the dilemma [of] living in a society where normalcy is valued, so we need to talk about diversity to acknowledge that it is possible to live a good human life from various positions and with various conditions. The problem with not sharing experiences with disability, especially in human relations, is that you build a cage that is difficult to leave. So, for the intimate relations and those relations that are important, I think it is difficult to hide such experiences. And of course, hiding disability status also means that it will not be possible for you to use your experience – in dialogues with others. But for more distant relationships, I do not think that everybody needs to know. To your story about being the agent of your life, you decide what to share and with whom. As we grow older, more people experience loss, illness, cancer, accidents; I feel it more necessary now to share my story as a door opening to others' stories, so it is less an option not to share. And the risk of being discriminated at work or when applying for a job is also less threatening today as a professor than when I was younger and in more vulnerable positions. This is also something we need to talk about in a realistic way. If you risk being discriminated against you are not obliged to say something about health or disability. I think it is necessary to acknowledge the value hierarchies of the society you live in and take care of yourself and what you need, and not make yourself more vulnerable than necessary.

RGT: I think that many people with disabilities who are afraid in the way we are talking about can be served well by education and public conversation about the UNCRPD; we in the United States don't have that but we have the ADA, and that kind of legal scaffold can support a life that feels as if it is collapsing. When, for example, someone says I can't do this job anymore, I am so afraid, that if they find out, that I will lose my job. I have found that it is important to say, and if that happens, here is the name of a law firm that you can go to, and that lawyer can write a letter to your school, etc. And even if they don't ever end up doing that, I think it is helpful for them to understand that this scaffold of legal support exists, that it is there for them, if, what they imagine as the worst thing that can happen, happens.

IML: And here is perhaps a difference between the Norwegian and the US context, law is less used like that in Scandinavian countries, and so, I know a person now, who has got a chronic condition, and this person is afraid of sharing it, not because of the risk to get fired, that doesn't happen very often, but there is a risk not to be promoted, not to have interesting tasks to do at work.

Scaffolding, I like that word; we need to use "scaffolding," to use that word, building a community of awareness at the different work places where we know of the UNCRPD; know of the need to be supported, so you can support and create what I like to call a culture of access where we can live with those experiences we have, and that culture of access is partly architectural and partly social, so barriers are to a large degree social. For myself, I do not look disabled, so people talk about disability differently to me than they would if I had a visible disability. And that is problematic, so a culture of access also has to do with how we talk, and this is also why disability studies is important for creating that awareness in everyday socio-cultural practices.

From the editors: In this third brief section, Garland-Thomson and Lid discuss what it means to "learn to be disabled."

RGT: I like to say that people need to learn to be disabled, that is what I have suggested. Therefore, what people need to learn, what they need to know, are four things. They need to know their history, meaning they need to know the history of disability as a concept and the history of their culture and society that emphasizes disability and people with disability they need to know that history. They also need to know their culture and their art. When someone studies music, they need to know that Beethoven was deaf. When they study literature, poetry, they need to know that Milton was blind. They need to know that disability as an experience and as an idea, even though that was not the word used, disability is throughout all cultural periods and products, that it has always been there in human communities. They also need to know more specifically what I call their rights. People with disabilities in at least the rich countries have become a protected group of people endowed with rights and obligations. And last, they need to know their technology. Because technologies are being developed as interfaces between our bodies and our ways of being in the world and the demands of the world, and we need to know how the technologies are and how to use them and that they are available to us. So that we can be included in the expectations that the social and cultural and political order has for us.

IML: Learning to be disabled is also a kind of self-affirmation, a work of self-affirmation that is sociocultural and individual.

From the editors: In the final section of the conversation, Lid and Garland-Thomson contemplate the future of disability studies and disability rights and activism. They focus on "diversity" and "inclusion," as practice and lived experience, and as an aspirational goal.

IML: Now, when summing up the talk I think we should focus on the future, what is on the horizon of disability studies. Focus on the rights of people with disabilities and equal status, but at the same time we need to recognize that there is a risk of austerity, that there will be increased neglect partly for economic reasons and partly because of bio-technological reasons.

IML: We have been talking about disability theory. How can you think of the application of theory in practice and envision the future?

RGT: I feel quite positive about the adoption in the business sector of the concept of "diversity and inclusion," over the last years, as I am seeing it in the United States, what is understood as diversity and inclusion. I think it is an important opportunity to institutionalize disability awareness and knowledge because disability is structurally apart from diversity as diversity is defined in government. Often it is not clearly understood how it operates, but I think there is a certain freshness, a certain curiosity coming from institutions – that is, corporations, schools, hospitals, institutional structures – that are mandated now to have diversity and inclusion programs. These institutions now have groups that are interest groups in their companies. The institutionalization of the principle of diversity inclusion is a legal mandate, that I find very fruitful, and in part disability studies and other identity studies in school have laid the groundwork for this in other business and in NGOs. What I see, at least in the United States is an interest in at least structurally having included these groups that brings disability awareness forward as a part of disability equity and inclusion. Is that happening in EU and in other countries that have approved the treaty, what are you finding?

IML: In Scandinavia, disability history as part of history is still rather neglected. Disability awareness is only in its beginning. This partly has to do with the structure of the welfare state, few persons with disabilities are in paid work. There are several architectural, pedagogical, technological, and attitudinal barriers in higher education also, so fewer people with disability have access to higher education, and also persons with disability have higher risk for dropping out of higher education prior to graduation. So, I think it is necessary to work in the context of the welfare state in Scandinavia to establish disability awareness. What I think of as promising is the activist work represented by the disability rights organizations youth section.

For example, for my generation (born 1965), disability has been a low esteemed identity, whereas now, the young persons' organizations, for example in mental health, use the term disability, and I think the UNCRPD has been important for that. If there is a change, I think the Convention will be one reason why that happens, so the convention's potential for learning what disability means both at the individual and the structural level is promising.

Editors' Conclusion: The conversation in this Interlude is ostensibly about the lives of two individuals. But, at another level it is about the status of disability in the world today. Reading below the surface uncovers themes that run through the other contributions to this book. Elucidating these themes can provide insight into the nature of disability and what the future might bring.

One theme is the construction of identity as a social act. The life experiences of people with disabilities are extremely varied. And each individual constructs their identity differently. Some people born with what others might describe as disability may never view it as a defining aspect of their lives, and others may come to realize that they have a disability only after many years. The construction of identity takes place within a social context of family and social networks, education systems, institutions and subcultures, and the norms of a society. For example, in this conversation, RGT relates how her family did not have any concept of disability. Thus, her identity developed without influence from the medical establishment or the subculture of disability. She eventually chose to be disabled, a political act, informed by her exposure to the feminist movement, and an act that gave her a community.

A second prominent theme is the experience of agency or lack thereof. IML recounts how her medical treatment taught her to be disabled and, through her exposure to disability studies she learned how to reflect on the treatment she received, question its effectiveness, and recognize that what the medical establishment views as a "correction" can be a harm. Throughout the book, we encounter other examples of agency but also examples of people whose agency is constrained or who seem to lack the means to gain it. Thus, it is an obligation of all of us to recognize the power relationships inherent in systems of care and to create a means for people who are vulnerable not only to gain protection but also to respect the right of individuals to make decisions about their own lives.

A third theme is the experience of being different. Any personal characteristic, be it a physical or mental ability, unusual aspect of appearance, or quirk of behavior can lead to lesser status in the view of others. The features of difference that hold salience in the construction of status vary from culture to culture, within subcultures or specific social contexts. For example, the corset that IML was required to wear and the posture it produced marked her as different. But, that same corset might, in the world of high fashion or at a different time in history, be viewed in the opposite way. The attribution of diminished or stigmatized status reflects on the individual who or on structural forces that can take different stances toward it. RGT and IML note that intentionally joining a community provides a context through which that social identity can be transformed into pride through sharing a history with others, redefining the group's social identity, sharing life's lessons, and learning how to become an agent for oneself and one's community. There are also broader lessons learned by gaining insight and empathy into other modes of being in the world, which include race, gender, and class.

A fourth theme addressed in this conversation and in the book is the importance of public education for building awareness. The two commentators view the UNCRPD as a scaffolding for creating a culture of access. In effect, it defines the scope of policies needed to achieve that goal but, as they and other contributors to this book explain, that scope could be more expansive. And the implementation of such a culture depends on changing attitudes and practices, not just passing laws and writing regulations. Full citizenship for people with disabilities requires an ongoing effort. Just as individuals learn to become disabled, a culture must learn to become accessible. That journey never ends. Public education, especially on the history of disability, the opportunities provided by disability rights legislation, and the technologies for mediating the relationship of people with disabilities and their world are critical to achieving that goal.

The conversation between a US American and a Norwegian disability scholar about the future is particularly interesting because it illustrates the importance of social context for advancing disability rights and the role of disability studies in achieving those rights. Rosemarie Garland-Thomson, an American, sees the "diversity and inclusion" initiative in the business sector, in response to legislation, as an opportunity to change attitudes and practices toward disability. In American culture, the business sector certainly has an outsized impact on many aspects of life, and thus, it is a hopeful sign to see major businesses embrace diversity. The implication for disability scholars and researchers is to gather evidence to prove that disability inclusion can benefit business. Inger Marie Lid, on the other hand, focuses on the role of government. She reflects on the unintended consequences of the "welfare state" as practiced in Norway. While the state provides strong support for living with a disability, this can reduce the necessity to obtain a higher education or be employed. There are fewer demands on the education and work sector to institutionalize accessibility, which contributes to the devaluation of disability and disabled people. This suggests that an important agenda for disability studies might be to understand the dynamics of welfare state practices toward disability and learn how such practices can increase motivation to pursue higher education and reduce disincentives for entering the work force. It also suggests that scholars and activists must continue to question the appropriation and commodification of "diversity" and "inclusion" under capitalist systems. The path ahead may differ substantially even in two highly developed regions. Each culture has its own opportunities and its own barriers to full citizenship. Understanding those differences and directing energies to the key issues in each society is an important challenge for scholars and researchers.

That the conversation featured in this postscript took place between two white, elite, well-educated, cis-women living in wealthy countries speaks to the need for continued work in disability justice and social justice more broadly. Too often, queer, trans, poor, non-English-speaking people, people of color, and people living in the global South are left out of conversations about disability theory and disability activism and politics. The situation is changing; disability activism and disability studies have become increasingly global in recent decades, aided in no small way by advances in technology that make virtual meetings and collaborations possible. But much work remains to be done. As the contributions to this book show, exciting possibilities emerge when diverse people come together to share ideas and culture. Forging a broad coalition of disability activists and scholars, and their allies, is the most powerful way to create a culture of access.

Index

Note: *Italicized* and **bold** page numbers refer to figures and tables. Page numbers followed by "n" refer to notes.